INNOVATIONS
IN
PSYCHOTHERAPY

Adelphi University
Postdoctoral Program in Psychotherapy
Conference Series

INNOVATIONS
in
PSYCHOTHERAPY

Compiled and Edited by

GEORGE D. GOLDMAN, Ph.D.

*Clinical Professor of Psychology, Supervisor of Psychotherapy
and Director, Postdoctoral Psychotherapy Center
Institute of Advanced Psychological Studies
Adelphi University
Private Practice
New York, New York*

and

DONALD S. MILMAN, Ph.D.

*Professor of Psychology and Co-Director, Postdoctoral Program
in Psychotherapy, Institute of Advanced Psychological Studies
Adelphi University
Consultant, Mill Neck Manor Lutheran School for the Deaf
Private Practice
East Norwich, New York*

CHARLES C THOMAS • **PUBLISHER**
Springfield • *Illinois* • *U.S.A.*

Published and Distributed Throughout the World by
CHARLES C THOMAS • PUBLISHER
BANNERSTONE HOUSE
301-327 East Lawrence Avenue, Springfield, Illinois, U.S.A.
NATCHEZ PLANTATION HOUSE
735 North Atlantic Boulevard, Fort Lauderdale, Florida, U.S.A.

© *1972, by* CHARLES C THOMAS • PUBLISHER

ISBN 0-398-02295-X

Library of Congress Catalog Card Number 79-172456

With THOMAS BOOKS *careful attention is given to all details of
manufacturing and design. It is the Publisher's desire to present books
that are satisfactory as to their physical qualities and artistic possibilities and appropriate for their particular use.* THOMAS BOOKS *will
be true to those laws of quality that assure a good name and good will.*

Printed in the United States of America
N-1

CONTRIBUTORS

SABERT BASESCU, PH.D.: *Adjunct Associate Professor of Psychology, Graduate School of Arts and Sciences, New York University; Clinical Professor of Psychology, Adelphi University; Associate Editor, Review of Existential Psychology and Psychiatry.*

LEOPOLD CALIGOR, PH.D.: *Faculty and Supervisor of Psychotherapy, William Alanson White Institute of Psychiatry, Psychoanalysis and Psychology; Co-Director, Supervisor of Psychotherapy, and member of Research Coordinating Committee, Union Therapy Project, William Alanson White Institute of Psychiatry, Psychoanalysis and Psychology; Clinical Professor and Supervisor of Psychotherapy, Postdoctoral Program in Psychotherapy, Institute of Advanced Psychological Studies, Adelphi University.*

MAGDA DENES-RADOMISLI, PH.D.: *Associate Clinical Professor of Psychology and Supervisor, Postdoctoral Program in Psychotherapy, Institute of Advanced Psychological Studies, Adelphi University; Supervisor, New York Institute for Gestalt Therapy.*

ALBERT ELLIS, PH.D.: *Executive Director, Institute for Rational Living; Director of Clinical Services, Institute for Advanced Study in Rational Psychotherapy.*

GEORGE D. GOLDMAN, PH.D.: *Clinical Professor of Psychology, Supervisor of Psychotherapy, and Director, Postdoctoral Psychotherapy Center, Institute of Advanced Psychological Studies, Adelphi University.*

ALAN GREY, PH.D.: *Clinical Psychology Faculty, Fordham University; Psychotherapy Supervisor, Research Committee of the Low Cost Clinic, William Alanson White Institute of Psychiatry, Psychoanalysis and Psychology; Peace Corps.*

v

PETER HOGAN, M.D.: *Private practice; formerly Associate Professor of Psychiatry, Institute of Health, Education and Welfare, Adelphi University, 1959-1961; Medical Director, Mental Health Center, Adelphi University, 1959-1961; Psychiatric Consultant to Psychological Foundation and Services, Columbia University Teachers College, 1964-1966.*

ASYA L. KADIS: *Now deceased; formerly Director, Group Therapy Clinic, Co-Director, Family Therapy Training Program Postgraduate Center for Mental Health; Fellow, American Group Psychotherapy Association; Past President, Eastern Group Psychotherapy Society.*

SEYMOUR R. KAPLAN, M.D.: *Associate Professor of Psychiatry, Albert Einstein College of Medicine; Head, Social and Community Psychiatry, Department of Psychiatry, Montefiore Hospital and Medical Center.*

ERNEST KRAMER, PH.D.: *Chairman of Clinical Psychology Training, University of South Florida, Tampa, Florida; Editor, Psychotherapy Bulletin.*

ALEXANDER LOWEN, M.D.: *Executive Director, Institute of Bioenergetic Analysis.*

MICHAEL MERBAUM, PH.D.: *Associate Professor of Psychology, Adelphi University; Consultant, Nassau Center for Emotionally Disturbed Children, Inc.; Supervisor in Psychotherapy, Psychological Services, State University of New York at Stony Brook.*

DONALD S. MILMAN, PH.D.: *Professor of Psychology, Adelphi University; Co-Director, Postdoctoral Program in Psychotherapy, Institute of Advanced Psychological Studies, Adelphi University; Consultant, Mill Neck Manor Lutheran School for the Deaf.*

DALE H. ORTMEYER, PH.D.: *Faculty, Supervisor of Psychotherapy, and member of Research Coordinating Committee of Union Therapy Project, William Alanson White Institute of Psychiatry, Psychoanalysis and Psychology; Faculty and Super-*

visor of Psychotherapy, Postdoctoral Program in Psychotherapy, Institute of Advanced Psychological Studies, Adelphi University; Associate Clinical Professor, Psychological Services, Adelphi University.

BERNARD F. RIESS, PH.D.: *Director of Research, Senior Supervising Psychotherapist, Postgraduate Center for Mental Health; Faculty, Postdoctoral Program in Psychotherapy, Institute of Advanced Psychological Studies, Adelphi University.*

EMANUEL K. SCHWARTZ, PH.D.: *Dean and Director of Training, Postgraduate Center for Mental Health; Adjunct Professor of Psychology, Graduate School of Arts and Sciences, New York University; Clinical Professor, Postdoctoral Program in Psychotherapy, Institute of Advanced Psychological Studies, Adelphi University.*

LEONARD SMALL, PH.D.: *Chief Consulting Psychologist, Altro Health and Rehabilitation Services; Adjunct Associate Professor of Psychology, Graduate School of Arts and Sciences, New York University; Chairman, Board of Trustees, Psychological Service Center, New York Society of Clinical Psychologists.*

DAVID J. VAIL, M.D.: *Now deceased; formerly Director, Division of Medical Services, Minnesota Department of Public Welfare; Clinical Professor of Psychiatry and Neurology, University of Minnestoa; Past Member, Board of Directors, National Association of State Mental Health Program Directors; Fellow, American Psychiatric Association.*

CARL A. WHITAKER, M.D.: *Professor of Psychiatry, University of Wisconsin, College of Medicine.*

BENJAMIN WOLSTEIN, PH.D.: *Clinical Professor of Psychology, Postdoctoral Program in Psychotherapy, Institute of Advanced Psychological Studies, Adelphi University; Faculty, William Alanson White Institute for Psychiatry, Psychoanalysis and Psychology; Lecturer, New School for Social Research.*

To Our Parents

INTRODUCTION

IT IS QUITE EVIDENT from the literature of psychotherapy that a wide variety of techniques and approaches exist. Some of these techniques are very directly associated with and have developed from a particular theoretical frame of reference; others, although associated with a theory, seem not to be completely logical outgrowths of that theory. Then, of course, there are isolated technical developments without any apparent theoretical underpinnings. In addition to noting this therapeutic diversity we were also struck by the apparent isolation from each other of disparate technical innovations and theoretical models of psychotherapy. We found it difficult to reconcile the scientific curiosity and creativity of many of the pioneers in psychiatry and psychoanalysis with their seeming unwillingness to share or experiment with developments from others. In this introduction we will try to present some ideas and hypotheses related to the question, why therapeutic diversity? The book itself is an attempt to bring together divergent points of view, with the hope that this effort will result in making different theoretical and technical approaches more available for utilization in psychotherapeutic practice.

In this context it is important to try to determine if there is a basic model of psychotherapeutic practice and, if so, of what this foundation consists. There is little doubt that much of what psychotherapists consider standard practice is derived from Freud and psychoanalysis. Many of the usual things that we do in practice, as the timing of sessions, the method of developing the therapeutic relationship, the relative inactivity and inaccessibility of the therapist, the use of interpretations, and so forth, come directly from Freud and his early co-workers. Despite the common roots there are also differences in technique between what is considered psychoanaylsis and psychoanalytic psychotherapy. Moreover, even in what is considered basic to psychoanalysis itself there are disagreements among many of the proponents of analysis. For example, Freud indicates as essential to psychoanalytic treatment the basic characteristics of transference and resistance, while for Eissler the *sine qua non* of technique is interpretation. And diverging a little to other psychoanalytic schools would bring in further "irreducible minimums" of psychoanalytic practice.

Eissler's 1958 article is a milestone in the development of psychoanalytic technique. In it he outlines those aspects of technique that make an approach psychoanalytic. Furthermore, in terms of the development of deviations from analytic technique, Eissler developed the idea that parameters of treatment may be introduced in dealing with different psychological conditions. Because of Eissler's stature within analytic circles, his article provided an impetus for more flexible approaches within the orthodox milieu. He was, however, just as adamant about the need to return to the basic psychoanalytic structure of interpretation and the elimination of the introduced parameter as soon as possible. The criticism leveled at psychoanalysis that it is too rigidly mired in the past might also be raised against Eissler, particularly since he indicated that parameters are necessary in the treatment of all groups except the conversion hysterias, and at the same time seems so committed to the basic model. Thus although we owe much to Freud and to Eissler for the development of current practices in psychotherapy, there is also more than a grain of truth to the idea that psychoanalytic orthodoxy has limited innovation and experimentation.

Another impediment to initiation of new techniques and the willingness to experiment with techniques developed by others is the confounding of theories of personality development with theories of psychotherapeutic intervention. For some clinicians the two are inextricably interwoven and the validity of one presupposes and includes the truth of the other. For others theory and technique may have little or no relationship to each other. At least it is theoretically possible that the course of one's personality development and the existing dynamic interplay of forces might have little to do with how one changes present personality structure.

Thus it may be that the existential analysis of the cultural influence of science on mankind is correct in assuming that this has led to detachment and mechanization, yet incorrect about the need for more "being" on the part of the therapist. Or conversely the existentialist's stress on the effectiveness of "being" might be accurate, and inaccurate in its view of the genetic factors that cause man to be the way he is or even the reasons why "being" on the part of the therapist might be effective. As a further example, even though many behavior modifiers believe their techniques are thoroughly embedded in and directly derived from learning theory, it would be possible to use these techniques with a Freudian psychoanalytic conception of personality development or some other theoretical notion of personality development as well. This type of commitment to a particular philosophical position regarding the status of man frequently prevents a realistic perception of how a technique might readily be adapted and used by a therapist with a different persuasion and may even blind a therapist to a fuller understanding of the technique he employs.

The question of efficacy of therapy is directly relevant to the issue of the further improvement in our therapeutic armamentarium. Research has been equivocal in indicating the effectiveness of psychotherapy, and the experts in evaluating outcome studies are as divided in their assessment of the research as are the studies from which they draw their conclusions. The multiple variables that are involved in the therapeutic process, including such obvious factors as the therapist's and patient's personalities, differences in technique, problems of measurement, and criteria of improvement, all make assessment of validity a complicated task with uncertain and conflicting findings a likely result.

One logical conclusion, and this may not be patently obvious, is that certain psychotherapeutic approaches work most effectively with certain categories of patients because of the patient's character structure. An obviously oversimplified case could be made for the effectiveness with hysterical patients of psychoanalytic approaches residing in the techniques which focus on the intellectual and rational—those aspects of personality most limited in hysterics. A parallel explanation could be offered for the ef-

fectiveness of the conditioning or behavioral modification approaches in phobic or anxiety cases. Continuing along an oversimplified continuum, the nondirective therapist who emphasizes
the reflection of feelings to the patient may be using an effective
tool to deal with the overintellectualized college student—the frequent target of nondirective research. And we may also be seeing
in the existential use of interaction and encounter an attempt to
deal with a fairly frequent problem of detachment and alienation
found in many of our obsessional and schizoid patients.

Extending this latter notion to the wave of popularity of mar-
athons and sensitivity groups, we may be witnessing an interaction
of technique with the needs of the patients. Some individuals
may be trying to find that therapeutic environment which will
enable them to be less cut off from their fellow man. However,
because a patient sees a technique as fulfilling his personal needs
does not by itself demonstrate that this technique will meet his
developmental needs. Marathon and encounter approaches may
be useful in eroding too rigid and encrusted defenses but may not
resolve the problem of unrelatedness central to a lifelong schizoid
or schizophrenic adjustment. The moments of closeness and human interaction generated in a marathon group may fleetingly
alleviate the hunger for human contact but, like the food addict,
he may have to return again and again to try to quell an appetite
that cannot be satiated in real life unless he develops a new schema
of human relatedness.

In this very much oversimplified conceptualization of the interaction of technique with patient personality is a design that
suggests the need for flexibility in the therapist but may also be
part and parcel of the problems of technique as well. The possibility exists that the use of an approach can and often is a result
of countertransferential problems. Therefore, Freud's inhibition
of his exhibitionists trends may have led to his use of the couch
to avoid being stared at. Another therapist's acting out of his ex-
hibitionistic needs might lead to such techniques as groups, face-
to-face therapy, or psychodrama. Needs for relatedness on the part
of the therapist as well as the patient can be utilized in the service
of the patient or the therapist with resultant emphasis on inter-

action and extended time sessions. It is not always clear how much of the technique derives from the therapist's needs or how much is realistic inventiveness serving patient's needs in these evolving nuances of therapy.

In any discussion of changes and new directions in a psychological area, the effect of culture is a mandatory topic. However, cultural evolution and the related idea of cultural relativism are such extensive topics that we cannot do them justice here; we will only indicate with the broadest possible strokes some questions of cultural change that may have some relevance to the topic of psychotherapeutic innovation and change.

The recurrent question that arises in any consideration of cultural impact is, Has cultural change produced a difference in the type of neurosis we are now seeing? It is readily apparent that the attitudes toward sexual behavior and the resultant repression that Freud encountered in the early 1900's is no longer extant and that emerging trends and attitudes in this sphere are evolving in the direction of even greater freedom. Permissiveness in regard to all forms of behavior seems also to be increasing. Anyone who conceptualizes human behavior as being dictated to a great extent by culture would of necessity expect these new interpersonal attitudes to have a major impact on the structure and content of present-day personality. It is also apparent that many of these trends were set in motion by the discoveries of Freud and his contemporaries and that shifts in technique might be necessary to meet and deal with these new demands and the present human dilemma.

It has been frequently stated that the threats of the atom bomb, the population explosion, and ecological difficulties make the immediacy of the present much more relevant than the future. In addition, the complex interaction of these threats to human survival with the dehumanization produced by massive industrialization may have generated or precipitated problems more related to neutralization of aggression than sexuality. Hence we may be facing a whole new generation of neurosis, different in drive and substance from the sex-anchored difficulties of the early part of this century, which may require an entire rethinking of our concepts of psychogenetics and the treatment of these new problems.

Moving from the broadest cultural designs to more specific and limited ideas we can perceive a vast shift in orientation toward psychoanalysis and psychotherapy today. Whereas Freud was challenged and harrassed at every step of his scientific development, the status of mental health professionals within the community presently is considerably different. Psychology, as a professional choice, is number one among high school students presently, in contrast with a ranking of over four hundred just twenty years ago. The Adelphi University doctoral program in clinical psychology annually receives over four hundred applications for twelve places. Psychology, psychiatry, and social work have their place in the professional sun today; there is no longer a struggle for existence.

This change in attitude towards the profession is accompanied by the obvious growing acceptance of psychotherapy. The dissolution of the stigma associated with mental health problems could also account for the different patient population making themselves available in our consulting rooms. It may also supply the security necessary to experiment with newer techniques. We no longer have to defend the past or adhere to a model or technique that carries with it status value. The strength of the developments in the professions of psychology and social work may also shift them away from allegiances to the older gods developed in the environs of psychiatry. It does not, of course, obviate a devotion to newer gods and structures that can be just as rigid and stultifying as past structures. However, there is no longer a single truth nor a single right way that is generally accepted.

Concomitant with the development of professional security and status are the myriad demands made upon the professions. In the past, psychotherapeutic practice and aspects growing directly from it, such as writing and research, were the main concerns of the leaders in the field. Today the extraprofessional demands are so extensive on those theoreticians who provide direction for the field that their involvement in practice frequently is quite different from that of the early pioneers, with their almost ivory-tower existence.

These are the basic, broad characterizations of some of those features which might produce or encourage therapeutic diversity. There are many more explanations for the emerging divergent trends. This book is an attempt to bring together some of the major influences at work in the therapeutic community. We hope it will encourage experimentation with different approaches, both theoretical and technical. And most optimistically we hope that it enlivens and enlarges our psychotherapeutic arsenal.

The chapters in this book do not follow the order of presentation of the original conference on which this volume is based but are organized to make for greater clarity and cohesion for the reader. The book goes from the theoretical to the applied, from the base line of those who write from a psychoanalytic frame of reference to one where the authors are nonpsychoanalytic.

Following this general format, the book begins with Dr. Benjamin Wolstein's presentation on psychoanalytic innovations in technique. This is followed by Dr. Leonard Small's discussion of the handling of crises, using an analytic theoretical base.

While the above two papers are in terms of individual treatment, the next group covers group methods and techniques, with the authors having an analytic base. These are Dr. Emanuel K. Schwartz, paper on group therapy, the late Asya L. Kadis' presentation on family therapy, and Dr. Carl A. Whitaker's discussion of multiple therapy.

The next group of papers are by people who have moved from the analytic model to create for themselves techniques and theories that are underlying them that are variations of the analytic model. These chapters are those by Dr. Sabert Basescu on his existential approach to treatment, Dr. Magda Denes-Radomisli on Gestalt therapy, Dr. Alexander Lowen on his variation of Reichian techniques, the bioenergetic approach, the Drs. Grey, Ortmeyer, and Caligor on their variations of Sullivanian techniques with blue-collar workers, and finally, Dr. Albert Ellis on his approach to rational therapy techniques.

The next section of the book has to do with innovations in techniques that do not have an analytic base and includes Dr. Michael Merbaum's discussion of behavior therapy approaches to psychotherapy, Dr. Ernest Kramer's paper on hypnotic techniques of psychotherapy, and Dr. Peter Hogan's description of videotape usage in therapy.

The last three presentations in our book have to do with therapy in special settings. These include Dr. David J. Vail's description of milieu therapy, Dr. Bernard F. Riess' paper on techniques in industrial practice, and lastly, Dr. Seymour R. Kaplan's offering on therapeutic techniques with the disadvantaged.

G.D.G.
D.S.M.

ACKNOWLEDGMENTS

The editors would like to thank the Sanford M. and Nancy E. Epstein Foundation for their contribution, which helped support the conference on which this book is based.

We would also like to give our thanks and appreciation to Enid Clott and Kathryn Crescimanni, our secretaries, for all their help with the conference, this book, and for making our lives at Adelphi much simpler and pleasanter by their efficiency, effectiveness, graciousness, and charm in doing their jobs. In addition, for her excellent editorial assistance and effective manuscript typing, our thanks to Grace Dey Vinciguerra.

G.D.G.
D.S.M.

During the time which elapsed between the conference and publication of our book, the field of psychology lost Asya L. Kadis, a warm, outgoing, and lovable woman. We wish to take this opportunity to remember her for all the wonderful things she was and did for our field and for her many patients.

Subsequently, the field of psychiatry also lost an important leader due to the untimely death of Dr. David J. Vail. Dr. Vail contributed significantly to the literature of psychiatry and was one of their outstanding leaders in administering mental health services. We will miss him professionally and most profoundly feel his death as a personal loss.

CONTENTS

INNOVATIONS
IN
PSYCHOTHERAPY

**Publications from the Postdoctoral
Program Conference Series**

Modern Woman: Her Psychology and Sexuality—George D. Goldman
and Donald S. Milman

Psychoanalytic Contributions to Community Psychology—Donald S.
Milman and George D. Goldman

Innovations in Psychotherapy—George D. Goldman and Donald S.
Milman

The Neurosis of Our Time: Acting Out—Donald S. Milman and
George D. Goldman

D<small>R.</small> B<small>ENJAMIN</small> W<small>OLSTEIN'S</small> paper is a unique and original exposition of psychoanalytic theory and technique from its histori-
cal antecedents through the present status and ending with a
personal commitment in psychoanalytic technique that encompasses his view of the emerging trend towards transactional or shar-
ed-experience psychoanalysis. His succinct review of developments focuses initially on the transformation that psychoanalysis
has undergone from an id-oriented theory and practice to the
more recent inclusion and emphasis on the interpersonal or
social influences in the psychogenesis of man's difficulties. For
him, even though psychoanalysis is in transition, there is a sufficiently agreed-upon structure and foundation to withstand considerable innovation and change. And for himself also he sees
changes in technique and theory in the wind, but the present
order will easily incorporate the newer perspectives. The present
status of this area of psychological knowledge is brought into
clear perspective by Dr. Wolstein's concise detailing of the major
streams coursing through psychoanalytic history. His historical
review is particularly useful in elucidating the differences that
emerged primarily on philosophical and metapsychological
grounds.

His foundation for an exposition of the newer developments in
psychoanalysis are laid in a detailing of the major aspects that
characterize Dr. Wolstein's psychoanalytic inquiry. At the risk of
oversimplifying a very complex and profound assessment of current consensus, he cites the individual and unique values and
conditions that the therapist and patient face. Adjustment is no
longer to a stable and concrete set of values nor to culture that is
evolving in a consistent fashion; thus, individuals need to be
assisted to discussions about themselves and to participation in a
world of systems and values that is constantly in flux and unique

for each individual. And so we are led to the challenges that face each patient and therapist, and which would have confronted us more strongly without Dr. Wolstein's brilliant analysis.

G.D.G.
D.S.M.

Chapter 1

THE PSYCHOANALYTIC STUDY OF SHARED EXPERIENCE

BENJAMIN WOLSTEIN

PSYCHOANALYSTS are working toward a new structure of inquiry and experience of therapy that differs from those of the biological and sociological models and toward refinement and restatement of the basic outlines of psychoanalytic knowledge. Of all psychological therapies undergoing change today, psychoanalysis is probably in greatest ferment and is probably changing in the most fundamental ways. To see why this is so, consider the distinction of new knowledge from new technical applications, for it is very useful in reviewing innovations in any psychological therapy. Transference and countertransference, resistance and counter-resistance, anxiety and counteranxiety, and their coordinated inquiry are, for example, innovations in psychoanalytic knowledge, while their intensive study in biological, sociological, and psychological models of therapy or in psychoanalysis of individuals, groups, families, and mass movements are special technical applications.

Anyone can distinguish knowledge from technique in accordance with his chosen perspective on the philosophy of science or psychology, in general, or psychoanalysis, in particular. I do not discuss that here, nor do I discuss the difference between new knowledge and new applications of old, nor the notion of genuine novelty in knowledge or technique—I leave such fundamental questions to philosophers of science. All I mean to indicate is the practically self-evident proposition that a body of knowledge is not, literally, a set of techniques and that innovations in one are neither identified nor worked out in the same ways as innovations in the other.

To illustrate this, take the difference between behaviorism

as a program of theory and research, for example, and varieties of behavior therapy designed to apply that program—adding new techniques of behavior modification rather than new basic knowledge of behavior. Consider further that it is possible to apply a technique without knowing its rationale or know a rationale without applying its technique. In the internal development of any science, therefore, it is possible to develop new knowledge without extending technique or to develop new technique without extending knowledge.

MODELS OF PSYCHOANALYTIC THERAPY

There no longer is and probably never again will be only one model of psychoanalytic therapy. The biology of id impulse is no longer an either/or proposition—if, really, it was ever that—and perspectives and procedures are no longer excluded from the structure of psychoanalysis on the ground, simply, that they are not consistent with it. This has been true at least since Reich, A. Freud, Hartmann, and Sullivan, among others, made their contributions to the sociology of ego-interpersonal relation. For after character analysis, ego psychology, and interpersonal relation, it is fair to say that the biological model is in partial eclipse, to be used in conjunction with the sociological model. Since the recent reconstruction of psychoanalysis as therapeutic inquiry into the individual and shared experience of its coparticipants, it is now also fair to say that the biological and sociological models are both in partial eclipse, to be used in conjunction with the psychological model.

Furthermore, the distinction of knowledge from technique serves to contrast these three models and indicate how each one developed in response to its predecessors, because they all significantly expand psychoanalytic knowledge. Overemphasizing biology of adjustment, however, id therapy does not illuminate inquiry into unconscious experience without question. The arguments over libido and instinct theories are old and tired, and I shall not again review them here. The ego-interpersonal modification of this therapy, overemphasizing sociology of adaptation, also does not illuminate inquiry into unconscious experience without question. The arguments over ego defense and interpersonal securities are getting old and tired, too, and I shall not review them here either. Instead, I shall contrast the two with the psychological model now being increasingly practiced.

Psychoanalysis of shared experience reflects deep and thorough-going changes in the structure of psychoanalytic knowledge. There no longer is any single dominant perspective from which to view the conduct of psychoanalytic inquiry, any single dominant interpretation within which to understand general human experience of specific psychological problems, nor any single dominant model according to which psychoanalysis stands or falls as structure of inquiry and experience of therapy. All this is now so well worked into leading principles that it is not about to be reversed in the immediate or proximate future. Not that psychoanalysts oppose interpretive metapsychology as such but rather that they oppose it as the foundation of psychoanalytic structure. And not that psychoanalysts seek to reveal a deep and pervasive secret philosophy of human experience in the contemporary scene but rather that their major and distinct concern today is a special type of inquiry under special conditions in accordance with special terms for the special outcome of transforming unconscious into conscious experience.

It has always been true, of course, that psychoanalysts could choose among many metapsychologies. At no time does Freud's instinctual dialectics ever dominate this field to the actual exclusion of all others. Besides his perspective, recall Adler's struggle for power, Jung's collective unconscious, Rank's absolute will, and so on, and how each once new and self-sufficient perspective entails its own new and self-sufficient procedure. However, it is rather curious about this early period that innovations at any level —empirical, systematic, interpretive—usually lead to the formation of new and exclusive schools. Each innovator then seems compelled to take a separate yet dogmatic view of the same orderly field of psychological inquiry. In this way, psychoanalysis itself is very soon a series of parallel closed systems whose adherents— Freudian, Adlerian, Jungian, Rankian, and so on—rarely end up probing their differences with one another. Interpretive metapsychology comes first, empirical and systematic inquiry second. One is Freudian, Adlerian, Jungian, Rankian, and so on, first; psychoanalytic therapist, second—but not any more.

The present situation exhibits indelible signs of change. Most obvious is that, with unnoticed but increasing frequency, psychoanalysts tend to refer to themselves simply as psychoanalysts and, only if asked, then identify their perspectives on metapsychology. Even though there always was more than one perspective in which to make interpretations, they could not always demarcate empirical and systematic orders to precede the interpretive order (as they now can) in the general structure of psychoanalysis.

This is the historical point. Since the empirical and systematic orders of present inquiry precede its interpretive order both logically and therapeutically, psychoanalysts no longer identify themselves by metapsychology because it no longer identifies their inquiry. Instead of having to split into an increasing number of psychoanalytic schools, they rely on the fundamental unity of its underlying structure. Innovators in metapsychology, on the other hand, no longer have to recreate the whole field of psychoanalysis in the image of their own terminologies. They do not have to recapitulate it as a special version of their separate system or do it over as the framework for their innovations. It is clear that the structure of psychoanalysis is now firm and well enough established to make room for new interpretive perspectives without being seriously dislocated at its empirical and systematic foundations. Observations, definitions, postulates, and theory demarcating it from other structures of psychological inquiry are no longer displaced or even shaken by new metapsychology. (See Table 1-I.)

The recent rise and large turnover of existentialist perspectives illustrate this point well. They were first existentialist psychology and psychotherapy, then daseinanalysis and psychoanalysis, and now existentialist philosophies or dimensions of psychoanalysis and psychotherapy. In response to various existentialisms imported from Europe over the last twenty years, it proved necessary to learn the hard difference between process or pattern and its interpretation. Since the middle 1960's, existentialisms have

TABLE 1-I
SYMBOLS OF REPRESENTATION

Orders of Psychoanalytic Inquiry				
Empirical		Systematic		Interpretive
Observation	*Definition*	*Postulation*	*Theory*	*Metapsychology*
(1)	(2)	(3)	(4)	(5)
transference	transference	genesis	unconscious experience	Freudian
t_n	*t*	G	*U*	$[M_1]$
resistance	resistance	function		Adlerian
r_n	*r*	F		$[M_2]$
anxiety	anxiety	structure		Jungian
a_n	*a*	S		$[M_3]$
counter-anxiety	counter-anxiety	dynamism		Rankian
ca_n	*ca*	D		$[M_4]$
counter-resistance	counter-resistance	immediacy		•
cr_n	*cr*	I		•
counter-transference	counter-transference	reflection		•
ct_n	*ct*	R		$[M_n]$

been used as philosophies, not as whole systems, of psychotherapy. That is to say, one can practice any type of therapy—short-term, hypnotic, supportive, nondirective, as well as psychoanalytic—and still be or not be existentialist in metapsychology. It is now possible to agree or disagree about issues of psychoanalytic inquiry and at the same time agree or disagree about issues in metapsychology. But it is no longer possible to make a straight-line relation of terms, conditions, and procedures of inquiry to beliefs, values, and ideals of metapsychology. In other words, a particular psychoanalyst may adopt existentialist or biological or sociological or psychological or other metapsychology and still pursue psychoanalytic inquiry.

Pluralism and diversity were not always so clearly established in psychoanalysis as they are today. When Freud, Adler, Jung, Rank, and other early innovators first produced new perspectives for interpreting psychological disturbance, they declared them separate and independent. After segregating their groups and organizations, they engaged in ad hominem argument and, of course, public psychoanalysis of their opposition. To defend their own systems, they criticized others as limited and incomplete— even short-sighted and wrong-headed—or simply dismissed them as unpsychoanalytic and untherapeutic. Adlerians rejected Jungians; both rejected Rankians; Freudians rejected them all. If it was not their type of therapy, it was not psychoanalysis.

In our current view of their self-enclosing acrimony and bitterness, it is not difficult to understand the reason why. It is, clearly, that their differences are essentially ideological and speculative— mostly philosophical and literally metapsychological. Here again, recall that Freud roots psychological problems in conflicts between instinct and culture, Adler in struggles for power, Jung in archetypal manifestations of collective unconscious, Rank in failures of absolute will. As though such wide varieties of perspective do not express their intense singularity, they compound it by giving their versions special names in the hope of gaining full possession of the new field. One calls it psychoanalysis; another, individual psychology; another, analytical psychology; another, will therapy. But in their innovative work, it is interesting to note, their different systems all hang from different perspectives on metapsychology instead of being supported from the empirical and systematic side.

They do it this way in order to put their differences front and center since they so sharply disagree about interpreting what ails the suffering patient and what he has to make conscious in order to heal and become whole anew. They could not agree on the significant experiences and interpretations of psychoanalytic therapy, and around such disagreements they separately systematize whole approaches to the field. But no matter what else they are, it is now clear, they are psychoanalysts by virtue of their common objective to become aware of some unconscious processes or patterns during effective therapeutic inquiry.

STRUCTURE OF PSYCHOANALYTIC INQUIRY

The situation is changing, and (as already noted) the signs are clear and distinct. Consider the recent and radical interest in psychoanalytic structure. It is, I believe, a first attempt to get at the root structure of psychoanalysis—not merely at beliefs, values, and ideals about which psychoanalysts may agree or disagree among themselves and with patients, but mainly at the relation of their metapsychologies to psychological processes and patterns observed, defined, transformed, and explained. While the new approaches to this root structure vary in detail, they all attempt to define, consolidate, and extend the foundations of psychoanalysis. For even though any interpretive metapsychology is in some sense relevant to every psychological inquiry regardless of where and when it is constructed and applied, no interpretation can displace the results of empirical and systematic inquiry. As distinct from metapsychology, psychoanalysis now focuses on intensive inquiry into processes and patterns specifically covered by the theory of unconscious experience. Apart from this inquiry, interpretive metapsychology is no longer related to psychoanalytic structure.

This change is further accompanied by deeper changes in the psychological orientation of psychoanalysis. It may now be safely assumed, for example, that transference, resistance, and anxiety as well as countertransference, counterresistance, and counteranxiety indicate that, first, these observations, when defined, also point up regular features of human experience in general; second, any psychoanalytic inquiry presupposes their statement as universally human; and third, since human beings manifest them differently in various cultures under whatever metapsychology, whatever else being human does or could mean, it certainly requires the capacity to manifest them. Unlike these critical observations, however, various postulates or points of view are simply adopted by the standard that, at present, they best guide transformation of defined observations and explanation of defined and transformed observations by the theory of unconscious experience—the basic and enduring theoretical construct of all psychoanalytic inquiry.

Consider briefly that these four orders of observation, definition, postulation, and theory are the hard psychological core of psychoanalytic structure. Add to these the fifth order of metapsychology, embracing all established and evolving perspectives that abide by certain standards of intelligibility, principles of logic, and rules of procedure. Even a moment's glance, then, at this structured relation of observation through theory to metapsychology would suggest that no single system of beliefs, values, and ideals is the single key to psychoanalytic experience. Psychoanalysts instead base their work on a structure of inquiry that results in special experience that, in turn, differentiates it from other psychotherapies. Since constituents of these five orders recur in every psychoanalytic inquiry well done, whatever else the psychotherapeutic experience involves, it is psychoanalytic to the extent that it involves these constituents of structured inquiry.

The significant thing about this structure of inquiry, as already noted, is its unreserved openness to wide varieties of experience of therapy. Its terms make it possible for psychoanalysts and patients holding the most diverse perspectives to work together in mutual respect. The reason for this may be found in the structure; namely, in the basic distinction of observation through theory from metapsychology that, within structured inquiry itself, supports efforts to demarcate empirical from systematic and both, in turn, from interpretive aspects of psychoanalytic judgment. Note that unconscious experience is a theoretical construct that explains, while metapsychology is a perspective on beliefs, values, and ideals that interprets. The difference between explanation and interpretation, of course, is basic; it marks the claim of psychoanalysis to scientific discipline. This difference enables psychoanalysts and patients who disagree about beliefs, values, and ideals to cooperate in exploring unconscious experience and remain objective about their disagreements. Agreeing or not about metapsychology, that is, they can still observe, define, transform, and explain psychological processes and patterns without, at the same time, interpreting them in the same way or with the same level of confidence.

This difference has two other important consequences for the shape of psychoanalysis to come. It makes possible, first, the vision of a more harmonious community of psychoanalysts, who may disagree about metapsychology and still cooperate in advancing the empirical and systematic structure of their inquiries; second, it is the basis for opening the structure to a new pluralism in metapsychology, whose importance is becoming more apparent with patients in transition from biological and sociological to psychologically diverse metaphors of experience. For the progressive development of models of therapy from biology of id impulse and sociology of ego-interpersonal relation to psychology of shared experience also reflects these changing beliefs, values, and ideals.

PERSPECTIVES ON METAPSYCHOLOGY

It is in this way, above all, that psychoanalysis since World War II has responded to the democratic ethos of humanistic and scientific philosophies. Recent extensive practice of psychoanalytic therapy with patients raised in American frontier traditions, the best-educated generation of the most affluent society in history, has made even authoritarian-minded psychoanalysts develop new respect for the integrity of each particular patient's psyche. Moreover, of the younger generation of psychoanalysts trained during this same period, some also find it necessary to break through the rigidly oversimplified interpretive schemes of the biological and sociological models. These psychoanalysts, not unlike these patients, inherit and also try to live the same beliefs of humanism, values of science, and ideals of democracy.

If all this is now so, the id or ego-interpersonal psychoanalyst may ask, Then why does this patient seek psychoanalytic experience? Self-knowledge. He seeks more and better knowledge of his available psychic resources outside awareness in relation to those within—for making choices, clarifying judgments, and sharpening decisions. The more a patient knows about his affective and cognitive resources, the more significance he may actually realize. With it, he can change his life—added to mere change, he becomes self-directing; to mere behavior, he acts toward ends-in-view; to mere communication, he commits himself; to mere relatedness, he is involved. No matter the perferred terms, there is a genuine difference between natural change and self-direction, behavior and action, communication and commitment, relatedness and involvement. Considering the first and second terms of this series, that difference comes down to the essential power of significance to transform beliefs, values, and ideals.

In the present era of rapid change that indefinitely extends the range of possible future experience, what psychoanalyst thinks he can still tell his patient what to feel, how to think, why to act? Especially since he faces the very same personal choices and decisions among beliefs experienced, values known, and ideals enacted. If consulted, would he, for example, attempt to psychoanalyze President Johnson or President Nixon? Governor Wallace or General LeMay? Dr. Spock or Rap Brown? As therapist of psychological suffering, every psychoanalyst would at least make the effort, if no one else were available, to practice his psychoanalytic inquiry with any person in serious trouble—no matter who he is, where he lives, what he believes.

But this is not the point. It is, rather, that patients no longer suffer simply from frustrated id needs according to the biological model, or from failed adaptations according to the sociological model. While patients now seem to make it in bed, at work, and in society at large, they still have to make other far more radically personal choices and decisions that require genuine individuality. Such issues are at least two generations away from biological adjustment and at least one generation away from problems of social and ego-interpersonal security. Psychoanalysts since Freud and Sullivan no longer question their therapeutic ability to deal with intimacies of the Oedipus complex or the interpersonal scene of family romance. For it is no longer clear, with the traditional family coming apart, that all the family therapists who could be trained in the next one hundred years would be able to return it to its prior state.

Other sources and manifestations of social and cultural change are, of course, to be found outside the family structure as well. Although definition of their basic patterns and movements is not directly within my field of inquiry, it is difficult to continue psychoanalyzing from day to day and to act as though it were still the 1890's or even the 1930's. A list of some of these sources and manifestations of social and cultural change includes instantaneous communication, computer technology and atomic energy, outer-space flying and inner-space tripping, bisexuality and trans-sexuality, rising black and female aspirations, communal pads and sociological families, individualized clothes and fantasy costumes, rock and soul rhythms, mysticisms east and west, astrology and the occult, hippie living and digger commerce, sing-ins and love-ins and be-ins.

At the risk of being called square, I may have some serious reservations about aspects of this new culture; however, I would also have to be clinically unaware and inert to act as though it is not really happening. It may be argued that these changes are not yet crystallized into anything distinct and developed enough to be called a new culture, but there is no doubt that something new is here—a new mood made up of new perception, new thought, new action—which, if it continues to derive its meaning from the spontaneous here and now, the casual and experimental, the unexplored and unique, may well require a more decisive break with the dominant id and ego-interpersonal satisfactions and securities than so far suggested. Without fundamental changes in psychoanalytic therapy, those engaged in this new generation of culture will probably have to forego the psychological inquiry governed by psychoanalytic structure. They will have to go elsewhere because these new beginnings mark a decisive break with the nineteenth century pursuits of historicism, reductionism, materialism, authoritarianism, and that one-sided rationalism deriving more from reflective than immediate experience.

A still more important change for psychoanalysis of shared experience—therefore reserved for special attention—is new interest in both individuality and participation. Exploration of the psychology of shared experience, among other things, requires a genuine sense of individuality worlds apart from Freud's id ego and Sullivan's interpersonal self. The reason why such astute clinicians take these perspectives on the personal uniqueness of human psyche is to be found in the history and sociology of human sciences since Darwin's (1859) *Origin of Species.* Elsewhere I discussed some aspects of Darwin's influence on psychoanalysis and other sciences of man,[2] for this influence raises serious questions about the basic methodology of all human sciences: Does it always simply follow the lead of natural sciences —such as, in this case, biology—or may it modify and extend that lead, or even branch out and build its own?

The best way to account for this unexpected agreement of two such different psychoanalysts as Freud and Sullivan is that both follow the lead of natural sciences. In spite of their different perspectives, the one's id ego and the other's interpersonal self have no sense of personal uniqueness about them. Though intended for use in psychological therapy (since both terms approach the psyche from points external to it in its outside environment) they are, curiously enough, psychologically impoverished notions. Thin, flat, dry, they unexpectedly resemble one another; ego is so objectified, self so depersonalized as to gloss over its most important feature—individuality, uniqueness, or, literally, sense of self-possession. Their common denominator, I propose, derives from assumptions about human psyche and its exploration in depth that relate id therapy to biological and ego-interpersonal therapy to social Darwinism—assumptions about evolution and development shared by other great nineteenth century thinkers such as Hegel, Marx, Spencer, and Huxley.

At the present time, however, the patient is not presenting problems for therapy, as a matter of course, solely within established confines of either the biological or the sociological model. Id and ego-interpersonal psychoanalysts use procedures and seek goals that presuppose established patterns of biological, social, and ego-interpersonal behavior to which the patient tries but cannot adjust and adapt—as though these changes do not affect psychoanalysis of the human psyche. The working inquiry in their experiential fields of therapy, therefore, requires his irrational dependency on the person of his id psychoanalyst as father image or his ego-interpersonal psychoanalyst as professional expert and moral guide who, working it all through, then points the way to promised adjustment and adaptation to the expectable environment. But if, after id needs are satisfied and ego-interpersonal defenses secured, the patient still feels miserable, how may this therapeutic inquiry proceed? Since future alternatives in his ego-interpersonal environment are already becoming more diverse, less explicit, and hardly expectable, how can this therapeutic inquiry even work?

In a word, it also changes. In their common effort the patient does not ordinarily want or need his psychoanalyst to point out what he has to do, get him to understand why, and then show him how to go about it. With established patterns of biological, social, and ego-interpersonal behavior in such flux, moreover, the range of his possible future extends indeterminately outward and indefinitely inward. As one result of this, he does not easily surrender direction of his life; nor, of course, does he easily share his own responsibility for it.

Today, psychoanalytic study of shared experience requires genuine individuality whose function is participation—genuine participation whose function is individuality. Because the id ego is too passive and the interpersonal self too detached, because a new kind of patient whose sense of self does not fit this passive or detached mood is seeking psychoanalysis with increasing frequency, because social and cultural changes are not yet over—for these reasons, at least, it is necessary to keep the structure of psychoanalysis pluralistic at the order of metapsychology. For these reasons, as well, it is possible to keep psychoanalytic therapy available to patients whose metapsychologies are still in the process of being formed. These, in short, are some reasons why some psychoanalysts are now working with a new structure of inquiry toward a new experience of therapy.

The psychological model is one effort in this direction. In shared study of shared experience, inquiry may focus more on the psychological and less on the metapsychological; psychoanalytic structure reflects this. Therapy may focus more on the exploratory and less on the didactic; psychoanalytic experience reflects this. Therapeutic inquiry may focus more on observation and inference and less on interpretation and speculation; to reflect this, the psychoanalytic emphasis moves away from contents of beliefs, values, and ideals over to relations of conscious and unconscious experience. For this distinction of exploratory psychology from didactic metapsychology, recall the earlier discussion of the difference between explanation and interpretation. As a result the psychological model exists to put these changes into effect. The psychoanalytic experience it makes possible is more intensive and difficult because it is more immediate and personal; however, its psychological outcome is also more reliable and enduring because it is more participated and individuated. Sought from the point of view of this rapidly and uniquely changing historical situation, this experience of therapy is subject to further change and search and, of course, to further ingoing participation and outgoing individuality.

A Personal Note

In order to undertake this study of shared experience, a psychoanalyst has to know who he is and what he stands for. He may know what he believes in metapsychology without having to push it or apologize for it and, since he happens to hold that particular perspective instead of another, simply bring it into his experiential fields of therapy. He may, of course, do so without either becoming partisan about his own or turning a deaf ear to another his patient holds but—I would hope, from my own point of view—remaining faithful to beliefs in humanism, values of science, and ideals of democracy. Beyond who he thinks he is and what he believes he stands for, however, what he is is there psychologically in the field of therapy, open and visible to his co-participant in psychoanalytic inquiry. Aware of the psychological challenge from unconscious experience, his own as well as his patient's, he enters into every psychoanalytic inquiry both encouraging his patient and preparing himself to study anything, anywhere, any how or why. Afterwards, with awareness expanded to the limits of that shared experience, the patient may then also know who he is and what he stands for.

Whether in the biological or sociological model, it always takes solid conviction to practice psychoanalytic therapy. In the third and current psychological model, it takes at least a similar measure of conviction. Even a brief glance at the wide gaps separating these major metapsychologies—from biology to sociology to psychology—would indicate this. There are no irrefutable arguments in favor of any one above the other two; about each, at present, there are many unanswerable questions. So long as arguments cannot be refuted and questions remain unanswered, these three models will continue to coexist. Even a brief look at the study of human psyche in all three soon makes it clear that no special biological impulses determine it, no special social and ego-interpersonal patterns condition it, and no special moral doctrines liberate it. From a strictly psychological point of view, nothing arbitrary or conventional ever attains privileged or transcendent status in ongoing, intensive psychoanalytic inquiry— which, finally, submits to the authority of human reason and syntactic intelligence alone.

Putting it on a personal basis, I find great openness in the psychological model. I like the raw, tender, and unprotected directness of this therapeutic experience. I seek a free sense of my psyche, experiencing my patient's sense of his so that we may both participate our affective and cognitive individualities in the shared psychoanalytic inquiry—usually curious in the searching, sometimes pleased with the finding, usually changing and moving about, sometimes stopping at points of review in which we sense the further, still uncharted inner spaces of the human psyche waiting to be explored. This psychoanalytic study of shared experience encompasses efforts at their exploration in this field of inquiry.

REFERENCES

1. Wolstein, B.: *Theory of Psychoanalytic Therapy.* New York, Grune & Stratton, 1967, p. 157.
2. Wolstein, B.: *Human Psyche in Psychoanalyses.* Springfield, Thomas, 1971, Chap. 5.

$\mathbf{A}$N ESSENTIAL step in dealing with an issue is detailing the aspects of the problem with which you are concerned. Dr. Leonard Small begins with a thorough review of the concept of crisis both from a definitional aspect and a full delineation of those elements that comprise the dynamics of crisis. His scholarly assessment brings into sharp focus the continuum from emergency conditions through traumatic states to the more usual, long-term adjustment problems. Thus perception of the problem focuses on the interaction of individual dynamics with the environmental factors that influenced their genesis, both in the present and in the past. An important aspect of Dr. Small's theoretical approach is his emphasis on psychoanalytic theory as a basis for his understanding of the totality of the situation that creates crisis in an individual. And very important to his theoretical formulations are contributions from the area of ego psychology, with particular emphasis on some of the formulations of Small and Bellak.

Additionally he makes it abundantly clear that the theory he utilizes is not the only one available and that theoretical understanding is separate from, although an integral part of, the treatment process. For him the technique of therapy, therefore, is not necessarily psychoanalytic, although modifications and adaptations from psychoanalysis can be and are applied when appropriate. He considers that flexibility of approach in the technique of therapy is of the essence, and the therapist should and must adapt appropriate techniques from any available source. This is not to imply that Dr. Small's presentation is general and all-encompassing. On the contrary he clearly and concisely details the technical and theoretical structure that he considers fundamental to successful intervention in crises.

G.D.G.
D.S.M.

Chapter 2

CRISIS THERAPY: THEORY AND METHOD

LEONARD SMALL

CRISES ARE as ubiquitous as sex in the lives of human beings and as varied in their manifestations. Discussion of crisis therapy suffers from this prevalence and diversity as well as from the ambiguity of language that they generate. Such ambiguity is not uncommon in psychotherapeutic theory and practice. For example, with similar ambiguity we often speak about, write about, theorize about, and profess that we deal with personality manifestations we call ego functions, their strengths and their weaknesses.

Just what is a crisis? Is it the same as or different from an emergency? Webster offers three definitions:

1. The first is borrowed from medicine—"that change in a disease which indicates whether the result is to be recovery or death."

2. "The decisive moment, a turning point."

3. "A crucial time, specifically the culminating point of a period of business prosperity following which a period of liquidation ensues."

The Comprehensive Dictionary of Psychological and Psychoanalytic Terms defines crisis as a turning point. An emergency is defined by *Webster's* as an unforeseen combination of circumstances which calls for immediate action. Now to the views of workers in the field.

Greenblatt[11] defined an emergency succinctly as any "case that has to be seen right away." Cohn[4] was both more specific and descriptive. He defined an acute emergency situation as "a manifestation of sudden decompensation of homeostasis or an impending actual summation of dynamic factors in an otherwise nonemergency condition."

21

The view that the emotional crisis may be a social phenomenon rather than an individual, personal one is advanced by
Miller.[17] He often finds that the requirement for help comes from
outside the person in trouble rather than from the person himself,
as if the individual's crisis is primarily disruptive to his social
environment. From the individual's point of view, Miller sees the
emergency as a condition in a person who expects or experiences
catastrophic panic and seeks help for it. Such a person develops a
sudden and rapid disorganization in his capacity to control his
behavior. The suicidal emergency is, of course, a primary example
of this kind of situation.

Suddenness of onset is frequently found in the definitions of
both crises and emergencies. Garetz[10] defines an emergency as a
condition that is sudden and unexpected, a situation that requires
immediate attention in order to avoid or prevent deleterious
effects. He states that there must be an existing treatment that
can be expected to prevent these effects for the situation properly
to be classified as an emergency. (One would then suspect that a
situation for which there is no treatment would be defined as a
catastrophe.)

Coleman and Errera[5] observe the absence of fundamental
agreement in the literature as to what constitutes a crisis or
emergency. They cite Miller's definition of rapid disorganization
in capacity to control behavior or carry out activities, but they
note that this definition omits the subjective distress that induces
many people to present themselves for help. They have observed
crises arising in persons who have been experiencing manipulation and rejection by family members or in people unable to
reach those on whom they might otherwise depend. They find
that the sociological concept of alienation runs parallel to the
depersonalization or derealization which is often associated with
changes (such as death or birth) in the families of persons
especially vulnerable to stress.

Still another view is that the crisis or emergency is a rather
commonplace aspect of human life and experience. Goshen[12] sees
crises as human emergencies that are as complicated as homosexual panic or as commonplace as a child's nightmare. He finds
that human emergencies have three basic causes:

1. *Danger,* the real sense of which a person may or may not be aware. The danger may be to the person or others, and the danger may also be to the person's biological or social existence.

2. *Fear,* which is based on the idea of danger.

3. *Anger* against the causes of the danger and fear of the consequences of one's anger.

He identifies mixtures of these as the bases for the various complexities of depression and paranoia.

Forer[9] observes that the very nature of life processes from birth to death assures that for everyone there will be both sudden and gradual crises. In his formulation, crises are both inevitable and a prerequisite to growth. He distinguishes between disasters and psychological crises, observing that it is erroneous to attribute a crisis solely to an event. He observes that individual thresholds for critical experiences vary, that "one man's crisis is another man's thrill."

Disasters do not necessarily give rise to psychological crises; they may, according to Forer, often be curative in that they enable the individual to externalize the sources of his difficulty, thereby reducing both guilt and feelings of inadequacy. In the *social crisis* there is often a sense of community and of family that provides strength and enables individuals to endure situations that, were they alone, would be catastrophic.

In the *developmental crisis* (there are many of these; for example, the repeated discovery that we are separate—separate from mother, parents, family, and friends) there is always a task of mastery. In the mastery of various and successive developmental crises the individual supposedly acquires through discovery new and different ways of coping with needs and challenges. In a normal sense the developmental crisis brings new techniques of mastery, new interests, new ways of relating, and through these the modification, change, or acquisition of character traits. Failures in these early developmental crises set the stage for psychological destruction later in life, even in response to relatively innocuous stimuli, primarily because the energies of the individual are wrapped up in sheer preservation. For these individuals a modest degree of stimulation may produce a disastrous crisis. For those who have learned to respond to developmental crises with adaptive behavior, subsequent crises may provide an opportunity for change and growth in significant ways, permitting the utilization of new experiences and new information in new ways.

Forer presents a continuum of crisis, ranging from the kind of developmental experience that is the corollary of any creative effort to one that is so intense and so disruptive as to threaten the integrity of the personality. It appears possible to establish some general categories that apply universally to the definitions of an emotional crisis that requires rapid intervention, the crisis that is at the extreme of disruptive possibility: (1) the onset is sudden, (2) it is accompanied by the sense of a threat of disorganization, and (3) there is a loss of or diminishing capacity to control.

The developmental crisis that Forer describes is often the basis for an individual's entry into psychotherapy, a decision that has not too much urgency about it, but permits thought, deliberation as to time, and even shopping among therapists. The crisis that is an emergency in nature is found in situations of acutely disruptive emotional pain, in severely destructive circumstances, and in situations which actively endanger the life of the patient or others. Between these two points are a variety of situations which may lead to major psychological problems and which justify intervention on an emergency basis. Bellak and I[3] note that the biological processes of birth, marriage, death and injury, family situations of children in trouble, parents in disagreement, financial problems, and others pervade the existence of all human beings. The psychotherapist can no more refuse to treat these problems with brief psychotherapy than the physician can refuse to stop arterial hemorrhage because the patient needs a prolonged course of vitamin treatment.

The dictionary definitions are a good fit. There are crises in which the question of life and death is implicit. There are others which represent a decisive moment and turning point from which further growth and development may proceed. There are crises which simply must be resolved if living merely as before is to go on.

THE APPLICABILITY OF THE
THEORY OF TRAUMATIC NEUROSES

The many definitions of crisis in the literature roughly parallel the general theory of traumatic neuroses. Fenichel[7] defines the traumatic situation as one in which there is an increase in stimulation to an unmanageable intensity; those conditions which are closest to this kind of phenomenon are the ones more likely to benefit from "external efforts to help the person's autonomous and spontaneous efforts to re-establish equilibrium." He thus distinguishes the traumatic effect from other types of neurotic phenomena in which internal tension has accumulated because of decreased discharge as a result of previous blocking experiences. These conditions require a dissolution of defenses; therefore, they are not likely to respond as readily to brief therapeutic interventions. Fenichel describes seemingly contradictory efforts at spontaneous recovery in the traumatic neuroses: (1) efforts to get distance, rest, as if to store energy for the recuperative effort at mastery and control, and (2) efforts to discharge tension, evidenced in restlessness and other motor behavior, spells and emotionality, repetitive dreams and other symptomatic behavior.

Fenichel comments that the nonneurotic, the so-called normal individual, encounters conditions of acute upheaval in which the precipitating circumstances would be comparable with trauma. The person in relative stability may encounter circumstances that disrupt his equilibrium: the loss of a loved person, an episode damaging to self-esteem, alterations in living arrangements or circumstances. Any of these may require acceptance of a new and painful reality and the warding off of tendencies to repression, dependency, passivity, or preoccupation with fantasy. If the person encountering such precipitating circumstances has latent conflicts of a defensive nature, a true neurosis may emerge. Fenichel's conclusion is that both the normal person and the latently conflicted one may be helped by similar means to reestablish equilibrium: (1) rest, with permission given for limited regression, dependency, and compensatory wish fulfillment, coupled with (2) discharge techniques that, through verbalization, clarify the reality task required to reach stability and enable ventilation of irrational reactions.

Kardiner,[14] from his study of war-produced traumatic neurosis, arrives at a somewhat different theoretical view of traumatic conditions and consequently of treatment. He conceptualizes the traumatic neurosis as an abrupt disruption of or injury to *adaptation,* with failure of the organism to make the required abrupt change in adaptation. The traumatic neurosis itself is the new adaptation, which consists of the symptomatology. The major feature of the traumatic neurosis is an inhibitory process. The inhibition may be complete, as in paralysis, or partial, as is most often presented in people seeking the help of crisis-service facilities. Kardiner acknowledges Freud's contributions to the theory of traumatic neurosis—that when the normal defense against stimuli is broken, efforts (the symptoms) are made to master the overwhelming stimuli. He argues that instinct theory does not illuminate those activities that constitute techniques of adaptation to external environment.

These techniques are learned, they are heterogeneous, they are complex *action syndromes.* They develop in relationship with experience, and because of incomplete myelination at birth the process is not completed for three or four years. The infant, born with zero capacity for adaptation to the external world, develops action syndromes through all of the developmental tasks with which we are familiar: sucking, swallowing, seeing, standing, walking, talking, and so forth. The quality of developmental influences will determine inhibition or promotion of action syndromes, as in the character and timing of weaning or in parental reactions to masturbation, among others. Thus, it is the *effective ego executive functions*—those that coordinate perceptual processes and are involved in adaptation—that are affected adversely by the traumatic situation and that must be strengthened in the treatment. Treatment that facilitates the acquisition of mastery, the restabilization of action syndromes, when swiftly applied, can prevent the hardening or perpetuation of inadequate ego states.

TECHNIQUE IN CRISIS INTERVENTION

Techniques emerge and develop as an amalgam of theory and experience. Thus in a survey of crisis techniques one finds that they seek to resolve conflict, to provide emotional distance, and to strengthen coping mechanisms.

We must examine techniques in a context. They exist in relationship to a setting and to the individuals who participate in that setting. It should be clear at the outset that the context of "timelessness" which characterizes much of long-term psychotherapy is not applicable in crisis intervention. The crisis context is one of urgency. Within that urgency, the therapist must practice a form of dualism: on the one hand, comprehending, participating in, and experiencing the urgency; on the other, maintaining the degree of distance that permits his cognitive functions to operate.

Next I shall present some general aspects of crisis treatment. Sometimes I will enunciate a specific technique, more often an approach toward aspects of the emotional crisis.

A Model for the Crisis Intervention

Various models are available for the conduct of emergency psychotherapy. Grinker[18] has written about this, as have Baker,[1] Levy,[13] Wolberg,[23] and Wolk,[24] among others. Bellak and I[3] have proposed a specific six-step model for the general progress of most brief psychotherapies. In this model, the first step is the identification of the presenting problem. This initiates and stresses the establishment of a precise set of formulations and conceptual expectations which the history will either confirm, modify, or negate.

In the second step, a history secures data to illuminate the personal experiences of the patient and permit a diagnostic formulation—not, as we shall see, the same as a diagnosis. The exigencies are such that most of the first session may be devoted to the taking of a detailed history of the personality. The very briefness of the process requires that the therapist be more than ordinarily skilled in facilitating communication. The third step is the establishment of causal relations, with consideration given to the probability of overdetermination.

The fourth step is the choice of intervention. Having determined the cause of the symptoms relative to the presenting problem, the therapist proceeds to the task of undoing. The therapist must specifically identify those factors which demand change or lend themselves most readily to it. Interventions which are based essentially upon talk between patient and therapist are considered the primary techniques; the others constitute secondary or adjunctive measures. Bellak and I employ an assessment of ego functions to guide the choice of interventions, selecting approaches carefully with a view toward achieving either the strengthening of an ego function or the lessening of an overreliance upon that function.

The fifth phase is the working-through period. Here the problem is further resolved through the achievement of reinforcement of the learning of new behavior and the extinction of ineffective modes of adjustment.

Finally, the sixth and last phase is the ending of treatment. Care must be taken to leave the patient with a carefully cultivated positive transference and a clear understanding that he is welcome to return.

On the Need for Speed in the Treatment of Crises

Kardiner observes quite correctly that the goal in treating traumatic situations is to prevent stabilization of new, inadequate ego states—hence, the need for speed. Also this is precisely why crises of recent origin have a more favorable outcome than do chronic states. This important concept, temporal proximity and availability of treatment, highlights the social responsibility for providing facilities to meet human crises. The community is inadequately supplied with twenty-four–hour, seven-day-a-week, walk-in facilities where individuals may get help without delay to cope with otherwise overwhelming situations.

The telephone extends the influence of a limited supply of psychotherapists. Suicide-prevention services in Sweden, London,

Berlin, Vienna, Frankfurt, Zurich, Birmingham, Paris, Seattle, New York, Los Angeles, San Francisco, Brooklyn, and Sydney, Australia, employ this device. In some places, professional staff support unpaid volunteers who are available twenty-four hours a day, seven days a week. In other operations, volunteers screen calls, handle those they can, refer elsewhere as needed, or initiate contact between the caller and a professional person. Gwartney[12] observes that the very presence of a therapeutic personality is a stabilizing factor in most acute emotional episodes. His colleague, Nelken, gives sensitive expression to the way in which the presence of a therapist may help to combat a patient's despair in an emergency. The emergency, he notes, is "something which isolates him from the fellowship of other men. Imagine what it is like to have your most valued relationships collapsing, a gulf of helpless misunderstanding widening between you and others, and even your esteem for yourself turning to abhorrence."

The availability of the therapist should be an important guiding concept throughout the treatment of many patients. The availability of the therapist on short notice at any time of the day or night is a critical necessity in suicidal dangers or in the threat of severe decompensation. Giving a patient a telephone number to call at unusual hours of the day or night provides him with a support that may make the call unnecessary or may save a life.

Laing[15] likens the psychotic experience to a journey or voyage fraught with tremendous anxiety and uncertainty, a journey the person must make to find his new reality and end his alienation from the preceding reality. I find Laing's description applicable to only a small percentage of psychotic episodes and psychotic individuals I have known. I find, however, a greater applicability of the idea of an imperative voyage to certain types of crises which are necessary for growth. Even greater is the applicability of his admonition that society supply companions for such voyages to the general principle of availability of the therapist during critical episodes. We cannot help if we are not there, and we can be there in open clinics or at the telephone.

Laing interviewed a most unusual man who had gone through a ten-day psychotic experience and had reestablished himself in reality. He asked what principles the man felt should guide the care provided a person during such episodes and reflects on what the man told him: "So there should be other people to sort of look after your. . . ." The man continued: "Other people who you trust, and who know that you are to be looked after, but they won't let you go adrift and sink."

Ventilation

Ventilation here is a metaphor describing the act of freely expressing one's emotions, feelings, and thoughts. Similar to the cathartic experience, it differs in having less structured anticipation that incidents of the past will be relived and the tension associated with them discharged. Often ventilation is an important first order of business in the treatment of crisis situations. As we shall see, a sharp psychodiagnostic formulation is imperative in crisis treatment, but often clarity and fullness of diagnostic conceptualization must wait until the pressure upon the patient has been relieved. Ventilation not only clears the air, but it also establishes the working relationship between the patient and therapist and identifies the therapist as a listening, sympathetic, comprehending individual. Ventilation relieves affective pressure sufficiently for the patient to engage in the necessary cognitive tasks of psychotherapy; it has the effect of increasing ego strength.

Sedation

Where the personality is overwhelmed and both verbal and affective ventilation produce no strengthening of the ego, sedation may be the only way to provide rest and distance from the pressure of the crisis. The implication, of course, is that a crisis-intervention center must have medical facilities available for prescribing and control of sedation when it is so indicated.

The Expectation of Improvement

Optimism breeds optimism. The therapist's expectation of improvement creates expectation in the patient of movement and change for the better. One technique for creating such expectancy is to announce a limit to the number of sessions assigned to the therapeutic work. The effectiveness of the limitation may depend upon the patient's comprehension of psychotherapy. A sophisticated, upper-middle-class individual may scorn the concept of short-term psychotherapy for, say, alienation; he is likely, however, to hope for the rapid amelioration of a crisis. By and large, less-educated people expect and hope for nothing else but rapid progress.

The therapist's expression of his expectation that the present crisis can be resolved and that the patient will feel better is a powerful force for producing exactly such change. The expectation elevates the self-esteem of the individual and employs the positive transference to create an optimism that in turn influences mood, allays anxiety, and thereby improves cognition.

These expressions, of course, must be meaningful; they must be founded in reason, not merely in hope, and certainly not in reliance upon magic or fortuitous circumstance. This requirement predicates our next concept.

The Psychodiagnostic Formulation

Comprehensive understanding of the patient's situation, how he got to be that way, and what can be done to unburden him is essential to progress in crises. Nosology is inadequate; it states nothing about etiology, about treatment, or about prognosis, and has little or no role in the resolution of crisis situations.

Alexander[18] and Bellak and I[3] are among those psychoanalytically trained therapists who argue that the precision of our knowledge about the psychodynamics of each individual relates directly to our ability to adapt therapeutic interventions to his specific needs. Current knowledge enables psychodiagnosis to be comprehensive. It permits determination of the relationship between the patient today and the important events in his life, past and contemporary. Comprehension of a patient's psychodynamics requires knowledge about the stage of development at which he had a given experience. The therapist must remain always mindful of the organismic equipment of the individual in as much detail as it is discernible. In a crisis, the intervention cannot be haphazard; it must be rooted in and guided by a definitive understanding that permits the therapist to ascribe the patient's complaints to the dynamics of the precipitating circumstances and in turn to relevant historical factors. To be useful, such a formulation must enable the therapist to identify those factors in the patient which are most susceptible to change and to select and apply methods for effecting change.

The dynamic diagnosis is made more difficult because we are no longer permitted rigid determinism but can think only in terms of the most probable effects of a given cause. Diagnostic psychodynamic hypotheses today must be cast in terms of probability. These demands for breadth and scope of knowledge make the term "psychodiagnostic formulation" preferable to "diagnosis."

For some time I have been developing a series of guides to the psychodiagnostic formulation. They consist of a set of implicit questions which the therapist keeps in mind and uses as a sieve through which the data he obtains from the patient are constantly being sifted. The questions are as follows: (1) What is the complaint? (2) What is the precipitating cause of the complaint? (3) What are the antecedent analogues of the present situation? (4) What are the meanings of the symptoms? their origins? their generic dynamics and their individual dynamics? (5) What is the state of the ego system and the strengths and weaknesses of the various functions? (Bellak[2] has contributed enormously to semantic clarification in this area by delineation, definition, and measurement of twelve such ego functions.) (6) What is the prognosis? (7) What dynamic shifts are needed to restore homeostasis? (8) What interventions are most likely to produce the required shift? (9) What therapeutic allies are available? (10) What shall be the general procedure of this specific therapy? (11) What are the organismic factors which could contribute to or aggravate the present situation? How do they affect the ego? What shall be the course of treatment and the prognosis?

Focal Technique

Crisis intervention mandates concentration on selected problems or symptoms. Such concentration is favored by brief psychotherapies of both psychoanalytic and behavioral orientation. Wolberg[23] speaks of "target" symptoms. Malan[16] provides the most thoroughgoing presentation of focal techniques based upon psychoanalytic theory. He urges that the therapist keep in mind an aim that ideally is formulated as "an essential interpretation on which therapy is to be based." The focus is pursued throughout the course of the treatment; the patient is guided to it by partial interpretations, selective attention, and selective neglect. The therapist reinforces the patient's attention along a selected direction by responding with either verbal or nonverbal communications of approval when the patient's associations or insights follow a path congruent with the one predetermined by the therapist. Conversely, the reinforcing communication is withheld when the patient takes a tack or direction that is not so congruent.

Interpretation

The interpretation is the universal technique of psychotherapy. Its widespread use is based upon its observable effectiveness in producing insight that promotes a dynamic realignment of the personality forces, resulting in more effective ego functioning. The achievement of insight may be pursued in crisis situations, but with caution.

Usually, simultaneous change in several personality variables is required for success in psychotherapy, so the interpretation must not be oversimplified through singleness of purpose. The therapist must attempt to predict the effect of his interpretation and incorporate necessary safeguards. The uncritical encouragement of uncovering instinctual impulses is a misapplication of the technique of interpretation.

In some situations limiting the depth of interpretation is not feasible; Rosenthal[19] believes that the traumatized patient in particular must be helped to comprehend the symbolic meaning of the situation in which he finds himself, that repression must be avoided and dissolved. However, she speaks of *steering* the patient to an insight. The use of interpretation to achieve insight, particularly its application to dreams, is probably best made dependent upon evaluation of the patient's ego strengths and his response to initial and partial efforts to illuminate his conflicts.

Coleman[6] makes a most interesting point about the relationship—a mutually excluding one—between interpretation and gratification. He observes that in acute depressions of recent origin where the lost object can be identified, effective use of interpretation decreases the severe superego, deflects aggressive drives from the ego, and lessens the pressure or oral demands. He noted that the actual relationship of the patient with the therapist, the giving of drugs or of advice may so gratify oral wishes that it is not necessary to interpret them. This seems a clear example of how seemingly superficial moves, predicated upon psychoanalytic comprehension of a person and his disturbance, may be singularly effective.

Bellak and I[3] suggest that the rapidity of intervention necessary in crises requires care in the use of interpretations so that they do not precipitate a cathartic experience, the dimensions of which cannot be predicted by the therapist. We advocate an approach which we call "mediate catharsis." The technique modifies the impact of the usual interpretation: (1) it tempers its uncovering potential by substituting moderate words for those stronger ones that might be used in a cathartic interpretation; (2) it reassures the patient at the same time that uncovering goes on; (3) it provides an acceptable outlet for the drive so that, even though it is not confronted fully, it will not be dammed up; (4) it seeks to alienate the patient somewhat from the drive at the same time that the drive is made more acceptable to the personality; and (5) it lends the therapist's ego strength to the patient to help him combat his own more punitive superego.

The Role of Transference

One must distinguish between general transference phenomena and the sharply defined psychoanalytic concept of a transference neurosis. Obviously, severely critical episodes permit no time for the development of a transference neurosis, even if such a technique were thought to be desirable. To help the patient within the necessarily short time allowed in critical events, positive transference is essential. The therapist must be viewed as likable, reliable, understanding, and accepting; the patient must have the expectation that the therapist will be able to help him. Negative features are handled promptly as they arise, effectively and with good grace.

The Role of Self-esteem

The loss of ability to cope and master is a tremendous blow to our self-esteem. For many individuals even the need to ask for help is viewed in a similar way. The necessity to increase self-esteem is an almost universal requirement in psychotherapy. The person may have his positive qualities pointed out to him; recognition may be given to the fact that he has accomplished something, that he has been especially reasonable in seeking help for his problem.

Environmental Manipulation

This technique, basic to the quick adjustment of many human situations, requires of the therapist the greatest departure from the traditional model of the nonintervening psychoanalyst. Family and friends may have to be called upon, particularly where the patient's life is in danger. Recommendations of job training and referral for proper job placement may be necessary to increase self-esteem or to permit sublimated expression of drives. Rehabilitation procedures may help stabilized psychotic individuals to overcome doubts and anxieties about their ability to sustain the demands of a work schedule. Recommendation of activities such as sports, body mechanics, dancing, painting, sculpture, ceramics, and music may all be made in an effort to provide proper expression of drives. Certain types of social-service volunteer activities may provide outlets for effeminate needs which otherwise would be unacceptable to the individual. Great care must be exercised that these recommendations do not create conflict at the same time they seek to ameliorate it. And almost everyone has had the experience of making adjustments in the arrangements of living patterns in the family of children in crisis.

Sometimes it is advisable to permit, even encourage, dependency in a patient if he is badly traumatized, by having the therapist himself actively engaged in bringing about the change in the patient's environment. In other individuals, where growth and mastery are being encouraged, teaching of new styles of coping with the environment may be indicated. An example is the man who comes to a clinic for help because he is enraged and beating his wife. Foreign born, his English poor, he is terrified of his inability to use the telephone to call the department of welfare to make some needed adjustments. Interpretation, however correct, of his fear of his passivity, which he must deny by identification with the aggressor, will be of no help. What is effective and long-lasting is to teach him to use the telephone to deal with bureaucracy.

Theoretical Grounding and Therapeutic Flexibility

Technique must be rooted in theory, and, as is evident, theoretical allegiances are numerous and diverse. The psychoanalytic allegiance is prominent. In more recent years the advocates of learning theory, the behavior therapists, have appeared on the scene. There are approaches to treatment that stress activity and nonactivity, directiveness and nondirectiveness, anxiety arousal and anxiety mitigation; some are affect-centered, others are cognition-centered.

Unfortunately, we sometimes tend to confound a theory of personality with a specific therapeutic technique that has become identified with that theory of personality. Yet to find that your comprehension of human behavior is best facilitated by psychoanalytic theory of personality, its development and vicissitudes, does not mean that the only therapeutic technique available to you is psychoanalysis. So-called behavioral techniques are not the sole property of the behavioral theorist. Relaxation methods were employed long ago by Stekel[21] and Ferenczi,[8] and a recent paper[22] describes the use of free association in the establishment of hierarchies in a behavioral therapy program. Over the decades, many psychoanalytically trained therapists have used their theoretical grounding to select and apply interventions that depart markedly from classical analytical procedures. The traumatized patient—the patient overwhelmed, unable to cope, unable to exercise mastery—is not a suitable candidate for psychoanalysis at that time. However, his situation may be explicable by psychoanalytic theory. Beyond that, the crisis therapist requires flexibility of approach and the knowledge of and willingness to use a highly diversified therapeutic armamentarium.

Crisis and Community

Effective crisis intervention enables the disturbed person to remain in his community. (In the Netherlands, the much-admired mental health system is based upon this aim.[20]) There are very few situations in which removal of a patient from his neighborhood and home makes therapeutic sense. Removal and hospitalization is always an onus and damaging, and the possible good must be carefully weighed against the predictable harm.

Resolution of a human crisis within the community is a proliferative humanizing experience. The visibility of another human as disturbed and then as functional gives dimensions to crises for everyone who observes the process; it destroys the irrationalities about troubled emotional behavior, it promotes optimism about oneself and others, it creates a favorable set for accepting the crisis victim as a peer at work or at school, it has preventive value in encouraging observers to use therapeutic services for themselves and to recommend them to others, and it enables the community to become related to the total mental health effort.

REFERENCES

1. Baker, E.: Brief psychotherapy. *J. Med. Soc. New Jersey, 44*:260-261, 1947.
2. Bellak, L.: Research on ego function patterns: A progress report. In Bellak, L., and Loeb, L. (Eds.) : *The Schizophrenic Syndrome.* New York, Grune & Stratton, 1969.
3. Bellak, L., and Small, L.: *Emergency Psychotherapy and Brief Psychotherapy.* New York, Grune & Stratton, 1965.
4. Cohn, J. U.: The psychiatric emergency. *Southern Med. J., 52*:533-547, May, 1969.
5. Coleman, J. U., and Errera, P.: The general hospital emergency room and its psychiatric problems. *Amer. J. Public Health, 53*:1294-1301, August, 1963.

6. Coleman, M. D.: Methods of psychotherapy: Emergency psychotherapy. *Progress in Psychotherapy*. New York, Grune & Stratton, 1960.
7. Fenichel, O.: Brief psychotherapy. *The Collected Papers of Otto Fenichel*. New York, Norton, 1954.
8. Ferenczi, S.: Contra-indication to the 'active' psychoanalytic technique. *Further Contributions to the Theory and Technique of Psychoanalysis*. New York, Basic Books, 1951.
9. Forer, B. R.: The therapeutic value of crisis. *LASCP News, 5,* 8, December, 1963.
10. Garetz, F.: The psychiatric emergency. *Med. Times, 88*:1066-1070, September, 1960.
11. Greenblatt, M., Moore, R., and Albert, R.: *The Prevention of Hospitalization*. New York, Grune & Stratton, 1963.
12. Gwartney, R., Auerback, A., Nelken, S., and Goshen, C.: Panel discussion of psychiatric emergencies in general practice. *JAMH, 170:* 1022-1030, 1959.
13. How to conduct 6-session crisis-oriented psychotherapy. *Roche Report: Frontiers of Hospital Psychiatry, 4*:9, May 1, 1967.
14. Kardiner, A.: *The Traumatic Neuroses of War*. New York, Hoeber, 1941.
15. Laing, R. D.: *The Politics of Experience*. London, Penguin, 1967.
16. Malan, D. H.: *A Study of Brief Psychotherapy*. London, Travistock, 1963.
17. Miller, A.: A report on psychiatric emergencies. *Canadian Hospital, 36:* 36-37, December, 1959.
18. *Proceeding of the Brief Psychotherapy Council*. Chicago, the Institute for Psychoanalysis, October, 1942 (mimeographed).
19. Rosenthal, H. R.: Emergency psychotherapy: A crucial need. *Psychoanal. Rev., 52*:446, 1965.
20. Ross, M.: Holland's social psychiatry service. *Mental Hospitals, 14*:375-376, July, 1963.
21. Stekel, W.: *Technique of Analytical Psychotherapy*. London, Bodley Head, 1950.
22. Wilson, A., and Smith, F. J.: Counterconditioning therapy using free association: A pilot study. *J. Abnormal Psychol., 73*:5, October, 1968.
23. Wolberg, L. R.: The technique of short-term psychotherapy. *Short-Term Psychotherapy*. New York, Grune & Stratton, 1965.
24. Wolk, R. L.: The Kernal interview. *J. Long Island Consultation Center, 5*:1, 1967.

IN HIS USUAL SPONTANEOUS and vivid style Dr. Emanuel K. Schwartz covers a great deal of territory. At times he whets your appetite for further intellectual food; at other times he provides sufficient nourishment for many days of cerebral digestion. First, in a broad approach he touches on the many intruding facets of forces at work in our society, from the influence of TV in modeling behavior of dress to consideration of broad cultural concerns such as the problems of aggression and alienation. From these panoramic views he manages also to zero in quite concretely and specifically on the proliferating interest in groups and grouping and the widely disparate points of view and approaches that are in evidence in modern practice.

His review of traditional approaches in group therapy is juxtaposed against some of the newer inventions in the same interest area. He clearly explicates those forces at work within the more traditional or analytically based approaches. With an incisive review of the structure and meaning of the different aspects of group therapy, he clarifies the basic issues. One can see most succinctly the value and limits of the groups in the way he views them. The utility of transference in group therapy and concomitant increased problems of countertransference are fully detailed in a manner that is both lively and enlightening. These issues are presented as positive forces at work in therapy and as an oppositional position to the trends that Dr. Schwartz sees evolving in some of the newer group approaches. His excellent presentation of the psychogenetic factors in neurosis and the rational forces that must be set in motion to effect change are also contrasted to newer techniques and their conceptions which he feels will not and cannot be productive in the healing process. At the end of the paper, he directs us to possible innovations that might be attempted within the context of his prescription for group treatment.

G.D.G.
D.S.M.

Chapter 3

IS THERE PLACE FOR THE
TRADITIONAL IN GROUP THERAPY?

Emanuel K. Schwartz

T HE TITLE listed in your printed program is not the one I submitted. If you look at it you will see that it says something about "in-group" therapy. There is only one person I know who is really expert on "in-group" therapy and that is George Bach[5] of Los Angeles. He is a specialist in "in-group" fighting among marital partners. Anything can happen out in California. Bach has an institute there for training married couples in jungle warfare. Obviously you must be married before you can fight properly. Bach is convinced that marriages break up because husband and wife do not know how to really fight with each other. He claims to be very skilled in infighting in marriage because he calculates that he and his wife have had some three thousand fights at the last count.

Some of you may have been misled by the title, and I want to set matters right. In addition, this is supposed to be a weekend workshop on innovations in psychotherapy. To those for whom there may be some snob appeal, you will note that I put reverse emphasis on the topic and suggested we talk about the traditional. I am quite serious about wanting to talk about the traditional in contemporary psychotherapy and especially group psychotherapy, which is, at this moment, submerged in a wild explosion of novelty in form, structure, and method.

There are, I notice, some hard-minded psychologists in the audience. They will have to bear with me. I am not going to try to present quantitative evidence to demonstrate that there is usefulness in the traditional approaches to psychotherapy or even to persuade you that psychotherapy has usefulness—whether it is traditional or innovative. Nor do I wish to suggest that innova-

40

tions have or do not have usefulness. You may with some justification hold all this up to question and ask for facts, data to demonstrate the goodness or badness of any technique or of psychotherapy in general. Nevertheless what I plan to do is simply to present my convictions, my value system, and my point of view about the nature of psychotherapy (specifically group therapy and more particularly, analytic group therapy) because I have a commitment to psychoanalytic psychology. On the basis of many years of clinical experience and some hard thinking—not hard facts—I must say that I do think that the traditional is important. Certainly I shall have to expose something of my own social and psychological conceptualizations for you to understand the small but hopefully nonetheless meaningful message I want to leave with you this afternoon.

I am convinced that the big movement toward grouping—a new word in our everyday vocabulary—is a response to personal and social necessity. There is more grouping going on in this country today than ever before in its history. I say this without hesitation. I doubt any of you will be able to come up with data to refute that statement. Despite our tradition of widespread joinerism, there is quantitatively more group activity in industry, in school, at home, in social settings, on stage, and in private and public life than ever before.

McLuhan[7] suggests that we have a deep longing to return to the tribe and to tribal living. I do not believe this nostalgia lies at the root of the grouping fad. The factors involved on the social scene at least look something like this. To begin with, we are now deeply into a postindustrial society. Ours is no longer an industrial one; we live in an electronic age. Under such a social condition one of the ubiquitous problems is isolation, alienation, *anomie*—the loss of identity. You and I play with these words all the time. A cause of this pathosocial phenomenon is the fact that on the contemporary American scene the nuclear family model is, by and large, the prototype. In the old-fashioned extended family there were grandparents, aunts, uncles, cousins, and in-laws. A variety of roles were available for a child to identify with, to emulate, and to rehearse. A large number of problems could be acted out with others. I use the term "acted out" advisedly because one major function of parents and other relatives in the family circle is to be buffers for the aggression of the growing child—buffers to receive, work out, and work through some of the child's aggression instead of having him take it outside the home.

We have been witnessing urbanization trends that sponsor housing, which in turn encourages smaller and smaller family units. The typical unit in urban America is the nuclear family, consisting of father, mother, and a child or sometimes several children. In some of the poverty areas you will find in the usual apartment two families with three to eight children all living in two or three rooms. You who live at a distance from the city may not know this at first hand, but visit Spanish or black Harlem and you will see this condition as a fact of everyday life. Regardless of its size, in the nuclear family we have limited for the child the role opportunities—the experiential possibilities.

The hard-minded research behavioral scientists would do well to investigate this issue. If a child is brought up in a nuclear family, is he more limited in his areas of relatedness and in his freedom to relate socially than a child brought up in an extended family? In my experience, the child brought up in the nuclear family shows greater social anxieties, and his ability to communicate or contact is much more limited. The studies of the kibbutz child which I did in Israel in 1951, recently confirmed by Bettelheim,[2] would indicate that my conjecture may be correct. Children brought up in the kibbutz crèches showed little anxiety in the group. That does not tell you about their very real problems in the dyadic situation, but in the group they were not anxious. They showed clear-cut, solid group membership; in the group they could face authority with little or no anxiety.

I could always pick out a foreign (non-Israeli) child in 1951. These were largely refugee children who had been recovered from institutions, orphanages, and families in Europe and North Africa and brought to a kibbutz. If a stranger like myself visited one of these children's age-level groups, the more recent arrivals moved off to the side by themselves. But the children brought up in these groups walked over, shook hands, and made some conversation.

They did not exhibit the kinds of social anxiety the other children did. The nuclear family then represents a new kind of institution for child rearing and, though it probably has benefits as well, in some ways encourages isolation, difficulties in human relationships and in role ascription, perhaps even in sex identification.

I would like to offer as a second proposition that in our present-day culture, and particularly in urban areas, psychotherapy represents in part a substitute for the extended family. There are great varieties of group activity going on everywhere, in places like Esalen, Oreon, and many of the other "eons." When I was a boy—and that is long ago—we used to call the moving picture house down the street the "nickelodeon." A nickel could get you into the movies. But the new theatres of group operations, if you will, are attempts to provide opportunities for persons to find relationships, to find a clan, to find the extended family, to find other persons with whom to work out problems.

I brought along some of the programs of offerings of the institutes on the West Coast. It is said that anything is possible on the West Coast. I thought I would read some of a table of contents to you. There are dozens of institutes like Esalen on the West Coast. Esalen is not unique in the group experiences being promoted there. From the titles and descriptions it is often not possible to deduce what actually goes on in the group. Reports of participants are often quite different from what the programs state. I have just written a review of "Joy" by William Schutz of Esalen. He emphasizes the necessity for the group to experience physical contact, physical exercises and activities; but sex does not appear in his book. In my review I asked whether an author could be held responsible for what his disciples do or for what he himself does, or whether a reviewer is limited by what the author writes. Obviously, different things go on in these groups than are reflected in the writings. I thought the titles of some of these encounter opportunities might set the tone for why I would today opt for the traditional, why I would play square.

The present catalog of the Oreon Institute lists its offerings. These are group experiences to which many go for "therapeutic" purposes. Indeed there is some legitimacy in a person's seeking a beneficial experience, even if not therapy. Some of these groups are as follows: "Inner Grouping, Outer Youth," "Hypnosis and Tantric Yoga," "A Seminar on Intimacy," "On Inner Being," "Learning to Look," "Learning to See," "Learning to Touch," "Learning to Feel," "Group and Non-group," "Adventures into Being," "Learning to Believe Together," "Learning to Live Together," "Learning to be Together," "Psychodrama and Hypnosis," "Cultivating Peak Experience" (There are in California, at least, groups in the nude, so maybe there are peek experiences, too.), "Being Open," "Being Closed," "Zen Meditation," "Marathon Group Experience," "Creative Photography and Personal Growth," "Being Intimate in a Large Group," "Workshop on Myopia" (I wondered about that. Once I heard of a method in which you rub your eyes, you palm your eyeballs, and it cures myopia.), "The Transparent Self" (Why do they not have a group on The Nontransparent Self? After all, you must offer the opposite; that is part of the dialectics of it.), "The Sentiency Workshop in Love and Life Issues."

To be sure, I do not wish to diminish the social meaningfulness of these groupings. They must be responsive to need. I am concerned, however, about who is served by these group experiences and how well. Can we call such experiences psychotherapy in my sense, in the traditional sense? I do not think so. For me, treatment has to do with causal therapy, with facilitation of decision making.

There is one other social phenomenon I want to discuss in setting the frame, the context for my presentation. Recently we have been seeing more open expression of, if you will allow me to use a "bad" analytic word, id forces—sex and aggression—in personal living and in the community. I do not think we need psychological techniques directed to "uncovering" in the sense that Freud meant it in 1900 in his highly repressed, inhibited, controlled society. We are much more open, much less repressed. We still have a great deal of inhibition, Schutz would assure you. However, we are living in a society in which the players have left the stage, exited the theatre, and gone out into the streets. The costumes are everywhere. You will remember when the hippies were very visible. They are now nearly dead and gone as a movement, as a population segment. It was not unusual a few years ago to go down to St. Mark's Place in the East Village and see a large group of hippies sitting in a circle in the middle of the street singing mantras, Indian chants of meaningless sounds. They did not understand a word but they sang, and in some way they were together.[11]

I am suggesting, therefore, that the forces of irrationality are very much at the forefront of our society. Not only is there violence at home, on the streets, and in the community, strange kinds of personal and interpersonal violences, but also violence on the international scene—war and strange kinds of war. I use my experience as a psychotherapist as only one sample, a very limited and specialized sampling to be sure, although I have a very large number of students from whom I draw additional information, though that is always less direct.

There are two major forms of presenting complaints. Either the person says he has never experienced love (that is, loving or being loved) or he is experiencing uncontrollable interpersonal violence. These may be two aspects of the same set of dynamics, but violence seems to be rampant. You might with some validity say it is due to television. McLuhan[7] calls this the first TV generation. All psychopathologic as well as normal human development employs imitation, uses modeling, at least for the manifest content of behavior. This has always been true. Look at the manifest content of the costumes worn by the youth of the last ten years—the headband and wampum, cowboy and Indian suits, or uniforms of the U.S. Cavalry. They come directly from the video tube. These costumes and styles of dress reflect modeling, and the modeling comes largely from television. But that is a subject for another lengthy debate.

It is in this social context that I should like us to examine what I think are some of the values in traditional group therapy and especially analytic group therapy. I will come to my conclusion first by saying that the function of group therapy—whether analytic or nonanalytic, so long as it is psychotherapy—is to provide a rational explanation for behavior. If we cannot ultimately offer a patient a rational explanation for his behavior no matter how irrational it appears, if he cannot enter into the therapeutic relationship with the assumption that we will help him find a rational explanation for his behavior, our usefulness as scientific psychologists, as psychotherapists, is in grave question. I do not mean merely a pointing out of behavior and labeling it, such as, "That's resistance!", "That's acting out!", "That's pathological!", "That's neurotic!" I mean offering to the person who comes for help in the individual or group setting a rational explanation for his behavior.

Only if we can commit ourselves to a search for rational explanations are we on the road to a meaningful psychotherapy. This implies that we have a theory of behavior, an understanding of causality, a conviction about psychic determinism, and that we believe that the nature of human behavior is knowable. A viable theory of human behavior must provide the bases for explaining past behavior, predicting future behavior, and modifying present behavior within certain limits, within the laws of chance. By the way, that is what an interpretation is, whether you are an analytic or a nonanalytic therapist; namely, offering a tentative, rational explanation for behavior.

Certain psychological consequences follow these assumptions. In the group the therapist is required to be more observing than interacting. It requires that he be noninterfering with the individual patient or the group of individuals that present themselves for help. The usual term used to describe the therapist's posture, "nonjudgmental," is bad. I prefer "nonretaliative" to "nonjudgmental." We are not retaliative nor are we demanding of reciprocity. These represent some of the traditional stances of the psychoanalytic psychotherapist. He is dedicated to understanding the patient. He is committed to consciousness, to meaningfulness in his interventions and activity. Thus he tends to be noninterfering, nonretaliative, and noninteractional because he is committed to looking for, looking at, and observing the behavior of a person so as to discover a possible rational explanation for it.

Since my own theoretic preference is psychoanalytic, obviously

I have a few additional psychological "values." For instance, I am committed to the idea that human behavior cannot be taken at face value. Perhaps this is my choice of the paranoid alternative. It was Gardner Murphy, I believe, who said that human beings have the choice of one of two positions—the catatonic or the paranoid. Given such a choice he would prefer the paranoid. Perhaps the paranoid is the traditional, the necessary, the required position for the psychotherapist. He starts with the assumption that "he is from Missouri," that he has to be shown. He has no fixed preconception about the person but wants mutually to pursue the truth, to examine, to explore. He does not accept the manifest, the phenomenological, the given at face value.

That is the major difference between the nonanalytic and the analytic psychologist treating patients in a group. The nonanalytic therapist takes the phenomenology, the sociology as central. The analytic therapist wants to go beyond the sociology, the phenomenology, the group dynamics. That does not mean that they do not exist, that they are not present or that we do not use them in our understanding and interactions. It means that the analytic therapist wishes to go beyond because he knows that there is material out of awareness—latent behavior, latent causation, latent motivation for the phenomenology.

Another principle that I as an analytic group therapist respect is that thought and action, if they are temporally related, if they appear together, probably come from a common source. This is an old Thorndikian view. If a patient shakes his fist, picks up an ashtray, and throws it across the room at a patient opposite him and says, "Drop dead!", there is a connection between what he is saying and what he is doing. Generally we assume that concurrent thought and action are causally related.

As I have already mentioned, the analytic group therapist is committed to the principles of psychic determinism and causality; that is, behavior is understandable, and the cause of a particular phenomenon or happening in the *here and now*, at this moment, has historical origins, probably in the nuclear family. In one sense we might say that all the experience a human being has had up to now is condensed in this moment, in this phenomenon, in this complex of behavior. Should you wish to undo the condensation, you would have to review, rebuild, or construct anew the person's life history.

I offer that idea as an interesting innovative variation; namely, to *construct anew*. It represents a change in analytic psychology that I wish to explore for a moment. Analytic treatment has been identified with reconstructive therapy. An attempt is made to reconstruct the past, to discover the historical origins of present behavior, symptom formation, conflicts, style of life. A more recent view holds that perhaps the psychoanalyst does not make a reconstruction at all, but a new construction. For example, some years ago I visited the city of Ephesus in Asia Minor. That is where Paul talked to the Ephesians (the Epistles to the Ephesians) from his prison, which still stands there on a promonotory. Well, it seems to me that the archeologists found some pieces of stone and they built a whole city. Certainly we do not know that this is a reconstruction of the original city of Ephesus. It is much more probably a new construction, a construction that makes sense, into which these extant pieces of building material fit and work with the remainder of the new city.

Perhaps we psychoanalysts have misled ourselves into assuming that when we get a dream and the attendant associations, a piece of history, or a series of memories, we utilize these materials in reconstructing the past. It may very well be that what we are offering the patient is a new construction which is a rational explanation of the past—one upon which the individual may now rebuild, begin to build, or attempt new alternatives in the present. This is a somewhat different view of our concern with the *then and there*.

Furthermore, the analytic therapist assumes certain mental mechanisms, observable psychological phenomena such as repression, displacement, projection, and denial. These mental mechanisms work; that is, they serve a function. Their major purpose seems to be to keep the latent out of the way, to keep what is hidden, what is forgotten, out of awareness, to keep out of consciousness that which is disturbing. Behavior then is often unconsciously motivated by emotional forces. Symptom formation is generally the result of a crisis in which what is wished to be forgotten breaks through. It creates much anxiety which must be bound by a symptom, otherwise the anxiety becomes intolerable. These mental mechanisms defend the ego, the self, the organism against being overwhelmed by anxiety. They control the level of anxiety.

One of the main functions of the therapist is to help make manifest what is latent, to try to make what is forgotten remembered, to try to help the patient look at that which is brushed under the carpet, to bring to the light of day the kinds of feelings and actions from which we would rather hide. Freud once said to a patient, "Life is not easy." One of my young, rebellious students translated that into, "How to be happy though alive." If we can offer a rational explanation or provide the patient with the hope that there is a rational explanation or basis for current behavior, the possibility of change is enhanced. It supports the possibility of new alternatives, a break-away from the repetitive patterns of living, the repetition compulsion. The therapist continually looks for what is hidden to bring it out into the open. The principle is that consciousness is curative.

One of the most important single factors that we use in the group or with the individual and his history are the transactions between patient and therapist. The distorted elements are called transference phenomena. Transference reactions in a group are directed not only to the leader (that is, in the vertical vector) but also to the other members (in the horizontal vector). In a sense this is a redefinition of transference. The traditional view of transference holds that it is the unconscious reaction of the patient always and only to the analyst, to the therapist, to the leader. The analytic group therapist assumes that such reactions not only occur in the hierarchical direction (that is, to authority) but also to the peers. Perhaps transference projections in the horizontal vector are not as intense or attenuated, but they exist nevertheless. These may be what Sullivan[13] called parataxic distortions, which exist in all directional vectors; in fact, one may assume that they exist in all personal and interpersonal aspects of life.

All of us must find ways of gratifying our transference needs.

In every transference reaction, there is a demand. If I make a symbolic mother out of someone, I want that person to play mother to the symbolic child in me. I demand that he or she behave in the way that I anticipate, in the way I have experienced it before, the way I remember my mother having responded. Every time I transfer, every time I distort who you are and the objective nature of the social interaction between us, I also project, I also demand how you are to behave.

By the way, expectations lie at the root of many problems in interpersonal relations. We expect one another to fulfill reciprocally archaic as well as current demands. There is no man who does not want to be mothered by his wife. There is no woman who does not need mothering from her man. You will recall last year's Adelphi weekend seminar where I discussed the meaning of pregnancy and the nature of breakdown after pregnancy.[9] This is due partly to the fact that the woman who has now delivered the baby no longer has an important role. The baby takes over, takes center stage. However, the mother needs mothering as well. One of the factors in postpregnancy depression seems to be insufficient mothering of the new mother.

In every transference reaction there is an implicit demand that the other person fulfill our transferential needs. We go through life hoping that our infantile, fantastic, symbolic, unconscious needs will be met. These are needs which we are not willing to look at consciously, needs which we are not ready to accept because they may be infantile and bring with them great anxiety out of childhood. This is what Ezriel[4] calls the calamitous relationship; that is, we do a required thing because we want to avoid something else, because calamity is involved, is anticipated. It is another way of saying that we make adjustments to reality because if we act in terms of our unconscious drives and motivations we may get into trouble. Our anxieties may become too great. Even in treatment, transference needs have to be gratified to some extent. It was Freud's theoretical view that in psychoanalysis the analyst was supposed to frustrate all transference demands, all of the archaic, the infantile expectations of the patient. You and I know that this is not possible; and even if possible, it is not necessarily desirable. To be sure, Freud also recommended that the patient be frustrated, but only more or less.

The more disturbed the patient, the more the therapist will have to gratify archaic needs until the patient can be calmed, can develop more mature needs and more mature ways of relating. One of the values of the group treatment setting is the possibility that some of the archaic needs, the transferences, can be fulfilled by other members, the copatients. It is not unusual to find some patient playing the role of mother to other members of the group; it matters little whether it is a male or female patient. It is also not unusual to find some member playing the domineering father when the therapist leaves, as for example, in the alternate session (that is, the meeting of a treatment group in which the therapist is not physically present). Patients in a group play alternating roles.

Berne[1] very schematically and perhaps somewhat too simply defined all human beings as ever seeking three kinds of symbolic relationships: parent, child, and adult. He says we want to play parent to the child in another, we want to play child to the parent in the other, and we want to play adult to the adult in some other person. These wishes are a part of all of us; we play these three roles all the time—sometimes with the same person, sometimes with several others. Often we get antagonistic responses. If, for example, I want to play mother to your child and you want to play mother to my child, we are in trouble. We have antagonistic expectations, we make antagonistic demands, and so we clash. We may struggle to see who is going to play the mother and who the child. Who will accept my wish to mother—be the child and play the reciprocal responding role? Berne's schemata offer us a rational basis for explaining human behavior in terms of symbolic role expectations, but it is merely one and not the only rational basis.

The processes I have just been describing are not transference and countertransference as they appear exclusively in the treatment setting, but are distortions as they may appear in all human relations.[12] Countertransference is traditionally the unconscious response of the therapist to the archaic needs of a patient. When the therapist fulfills the infantile demands of the patient, he is in countertransference. One of the basic prescriptions and proscriptions of the traditionalist might be expressed as the therapist's commitment to frustrate these archaic demands of the patient. The function of the traditional group therapist is not to fulfill, not to satisfy the irrational wishes of the patient to suck, to be dependent, to control, to be conquered, to fuse, and the like. The therapist resists satisfying such demands; he analyzes them.

I believe that there is value in this traditional position. The kind of group therapy being done by many nontraditional group leaders does not produce significant change. If there is evidence to the contrary, I should like to see it and be convinced. Even good clinical evidence would be acceptable. But experience points in the opposite direction. Most neotherapists, experimental group leaders, tend not to frustrate and not to analyze but to gratify and intensify the transference regression to irrationality. This is a definition for noncure. At best, under such circumstances no change takes place.[6] There is in these experiential approaches an overevaluation of the significance of interpersonal relations concomitant with a mistaken underevaluation of intrapsychic factors.

Most nonanalytic therapies and most medical arts are based upon transference, on the need of a patient to have transference reactions, to symbolize, to build a fantasy around the doctor. It is this factor that can be used for good or for bad even in social situations. Recently I received a copy of a paper by a Brazilian colleague,[3] a group therapist who did a review of the literature on group therapy in the international journals. He found that the word "transference," the concept, or anything that could be identified as transference occurred in relation to "countertransference" in the proportion of eight hundred to one. That is a staggering fact—eight hundred references to transference for each reference to countertransference. In other words, professional persons are perfectly willing to look at the irrationality of their patients, but they are not eager to examine irrationality on their own parts. I hope some day there will be enough time to share with you some of my ideas about why this is true, why we therapists want to brush our own irrationality under the rug; but that subject is really not for now.

One of the traditional values in group therapy is that the presence of several observers, eight or ten other pairs of eyes, tends in some way to attenuate, to counteract, to neutralize the irrationality of the therapist. When I am alone with a patient, and the patient says, "You were angry with me last time," it is too easy for me to respond, "Who, me? Why, I haven't a hostile feeling in my bones. You must be projecting. Examine yourself! I wonder why you needed to see me that way last session!" I could get away with it. In the group, however, if that same patient says, "Last session you were angry with me," and I say, "Who, me?", eight or ten others say, "Oh yes, you were!" Then I have to stop and look at myself. It is difficult for anyone to resist that kind of pressure. There is an old saying that if one person says you are drunk, don't worry about it. If two say you are drunk, stop and think. If three persons say you are drunk, lie down.

I want to leave some opportunity for discussion. Certainly I have provoked some questions and reactions in you. However, I cannot close without affirming that innovations can take place within the traditional frame. It is not necessary to be square. One can be a swinger and still be committed to the traditional values of psychotherapy: reason, rationality, science, systematic thinking, a theory, consciousness, the wish to put the needs of the other before your own, the freedom of choice in thinking, feeling, and doing, a willingness to accept the limitation and transiency of all human endeavor. There are variations, modifications, and innovations that may be introduced even within such a matrix.[10] If innovations seem demonstrably to work or to be helpful, we must respect them and incorporate them into our therapeutic armamentarium. Let us not be closed-minded. But I urge you to be hard-minded about what you do choose to do when patients pay you a fee to be helpful to them. You have a traditional necessity to be responsible—*primum non nocere*. Within that traditional frame, however, there is ample opportunity for innovation if we are ingenious enough.

For example, we do not need to restrict ourselves to a set

number of patients in any setting. We can have groups of eight or ten persons, such as Alexander Wolf and I describe in our book on psychoanalysis in groups.[14] But it may also be possible to conduct groups of fifty, seventy-five, or even a hundred persons and still do good work. It may not be as intensive or extensive, but I believe effective work can be done. I have seen, for example in England, groups of nearly one hundred patients with four cotherapists.

Very often in group therapy we use either an observer or a cotherapist. We do this in part because it relieves us of the necessity of taking notes. We have an additional pair of eyes that are more objective. He can help us observe. The therapist can be free to be the therapist. He does not have to take note of everything that is going on or try to remember everything. We can use himself more freely to interact, when appropriate. However, I have never heard an individual therapist ever say he would like to have an observer in the dyadic treatment setting. Most will not permit even an observer, much less a cotherapist, in one-to-one therapy. But in the group we permit it, and I think it is a good thing. I know that we get anxious about having somebody in. I see this all the time when we put groups of patients or even individual patients behind the one-way mirror. There is sure to be anxiety, but it is one of the ways of trying to better understand what goes on, of having the possibility of introducing greater objectivity.

However, let me return to the group in England where a leader and three cotherapists conducted a group of seventy-five to a hundred patients. The sessions were three hours long, and I attended a number of them. All of these patients had concurrently each week at least one other session of individual or small group therapy. I was impressed by what I saw. Surely there are some kinds of patients, selected patients, perhaps with limited kinds of goals (if, for example, you do not want to make a new person in your own image out of the patient) such as crisis intervention, educational information giving, and certain kinds of attitudinal change, who may derive benefits in groups running up to a hundred.

We must be open about the fact that group size is not a holy matter. We have tried this kind of treatment in the Social Re-habilitation Clinic at the Postgraduate Center for Mental Health. We find that we get good interaction and good insights. Rational explanations can be provided in the experience of large groups ranging from fifty to seventy-five patients. Of course we really do not know the outcomes or the implications of such efforts be-cause we need more experience, more experimentation, and more objective evaluation.

Furthermore, we also need to do some experimenting with time-limited therapies—not short-term, but time-limited. In such an arrangement, even if you decided on a ten-year stint of therapy, in ten years you must stop the treatment. However, it could be ten sessions. After ten sessions the therapy is over. For example, plan a group treatment program lasting six months. After six months the group ends with no ands, ifs, ors, or buts. If a patient needs more therapy, send him elsewhere. Let us see if we can try to use the time available more efficiently and effectively. If you have not been able to accomplish the goals bilaterally set for the time period, examine yourself, examine him, analyze the situation; learn what you can about the success and failure and then send the patient elsewhere.

I wonder about the validity of a group or an individual ther-apy experience going beyond three years without the intervention of a good supervisor. Of course I have patients who have been in analysis with me five or six years, but is there not some type of law of diminishing returns that is applicable to therapy? Pelz' study[8] about research teams and the diminishing usefulness or creativity of members after three years is an interesting idea worth thinking about.

I am suggesting that we try time-limited therapies of three weeks or three months or three years. Such an arrangement agreed upon in advance by both patient and therapist would compel them to face the problems of economy and hygiene; that is, get-ting the best results with the least expenditure of time and effort. As we begin to nationalize medical and social services, as health insurance plans set limits on the number of hours, time, or money available for psychotherapy, we will have to face this issue squarely. We shall not be able to escape behind the usual defense that we cannot be held accountable for the time and energy invested in the outcomes we hope to achieve.

I believe these are some of the directions in which we can and must go and still retain what has been a proven value in the traditional forms of treatment modalities. Keep in mind that for a large segment of the professional population, even considering seeing more than one patient at a time for psychotherapy is still perceived as a radical departure.[14]

REFERENCES

1. Berne, E.: *Transactional Analysis in Psychotherapy.* New York, Grove Press, 1961.
2. Bettelheim, B.: *The Children of the Dream.* New York, Macmillan, 1968.
3. Blay Neto, B.: Some Aspects of Counter-Transference in Group Psychotherapy. Unpublished study presented at the Second Seminar in Group Psychotherapy, Sao Paolo, December, 1963.
4. Ezriel, H.: A psychoanalytic approach to group treatment. *Brit. J. Med. Psychol., 23:*59-74, 1950.
5. Bach, G., cited by Keats, J.: Lets you and her fight. *Quest, 1* (3) :10ff, July, 1969.
6. Lamott, K.: Marathon therapy is a psychological pressure cooker. *The New York Times Magazine,* 28ff, July 13, 1969.
7. McLuhan, M.: *Understanding Media: The Extensions of Man.* New York, McGraw-Hill, 1964.
8. Pelz, D. C.: Creative tensions in the research development climate. *Science, 157:*160-165, 1961.
9. Schwartz, E. K.: Discussion. In Goldman, G. D., and Milman, D. S. (Eds.) : *Modern Woman.* Springfield, Thomas, 1969, pp. 151-160.
10. Schwartz, E. K.: Non-Freudian analytic methods. In Wolman, B. B. (Ed.) : *Handbook of Clinical Psychology.* New York, McGraw-Hill, 1965, pp. 1200-1214.
11. Schwartz, E. K., and Leder, R.: The hippie or what makes groovy tick? In Riess, B. F. (Ed.) : *New Directions in Mental Health,* New York, Grune & Stratton, 1969, Vol. II, pp. 227-241.
12. Schwartz, E. K., and Wolf, A.: On countertransference in group therapy. In Riess, B. F. (Ed.) : *New Directions in Mental Health,* Vol. II. New York, Grune & Stratton, 1969, Vol. II, pp. 21-32.
13. Sullivan, H. S.: *The Interpersonal Theory of Psychitary.* New York, Norton, 1953.
14. Wolf, A., and Schwartz, E. K.: *Psychoanalysis in Groups.* New York, Grune & Stratton, 1962.

Family therapy is intimately connected to group therapy in both its development and conception and certainly owes a great deal to group therapy for its present impetus. As with the majority of modern techniques of therapy, there is the usual debt to Freud and psychoanalysis. Aspects of both marital therapy and the use of multiple therapists have also been part of the mainstream of the factors influencing its development. The late Asya L. Kadis, who was a practicing psychoanalyst and outstanding group therapist, brought to this paper her extensive experience with all of these trends, and was thus particularly well equipped to assess and elucidate the many diverse forces in effect in this rapidly developing sector. Her knowledge and experience were clearly apparent in the scope of her paper, in which she conceptualized and blended together in a coherent picture the seemingly disparate developments in family treatment.

She began with a historical perspective on family therapy that provides us with a conception of the roots of this new approach and the different directions it has taken. (The lack of developments in the area of lower-class and disadvantaged populations is also indicated, plus the differences in family structure that one encounters in dealing with different groups.) Because this is a relatively new and very complicated treatment sphere, it is also of utmost importance that we perceive how the different systems of family treatment are related, overlap, and diverge. It requires the utmost skill in organizing the material of a particular theoretical position to make the essence of that particular stance understandable. Mrs. Kadis accomplished this, not only in a skeletal fashion, but with a great deal of theoretical and technical flesh added to each approach she considered. With her as a guide it is readily apparent how the various theoreticians approach family treatment, from the viewpoint not only of family dynamics, but also of their therapeutic systems of intervention.

57

In addition to her analysis of the entire field, she also provided us with a thorough introduction to the approach to family therapy that she had evolved with Markowitz. She described in detail the intricacies and complexities of psychoanalytic family therapy and the utility of the intrapersonal in family settings.

Mrs. Kadis was concerned not only with where family therapy is at present, but also with where it can and will go. With her warmth, flexibility, and experimental vigor, she gave us an excellent model to direct us on the path to the future in this new territory of treatment.

G.D.G.

D.S.M.

Chapter 4

CURRENT THEORIES AND
BASIC CONCEPTS IN FAMILY THERAPY

ASYA L. KADIS

THE LITERATURE on various approaches to family therapy has grown by leaps and bounds, making it impossible to cover all the developmental trends. Family agencies and child guidance clinics were interested in family welfare and counseling long before psychologists and psychiatrists became concerned with the family as an entity.

My first experience with family treatment as an entity began in Vienna in the early thirties. At that time, Alfred Adler was interviewing a father, mother, and their son who was about to go to jail. It was a most unusual event, inasmuch as at that time an analyst would not even talk to the parent of a child who was in treatment with him.

PIONEERS IN FAMILY THERAPY

Among the major contributors to family therapy in the last fifteen years were Nathan Ackerman,[2,3] Gregory Bateson,[8] J. E. Bell,[9-12] Ivan Boszormenyi-Nagy,[13] James Framo,[14,15] Jay Haley,[19] Donald Jackson,[20] Salvador Minuchin,[29] Virginia Satir,[34] Gerald Zuk,[37] and others. Their theories will be discussed briefly, since they are representative of family therapists from coast to coast.

Ackerman and Bell were the first psychiatrists to stress the importance of recognizing and handling the family as a unit. Ackerman, in particular, in his prolific writing over the past fifteen years, encompassed significant principles of family treatment. He delineated goals of family therapy, pinpointing critical issues in the field. He conceptualized the roles with ever-widening frames of reference, starting from the analytic point of view and integrating this into a broader sociocultural spectrum.

59

Bell indicates that more attention should be paid to scientists in genetics and epidemiology and that more recognition should be given to the impact of such methods as control group, replication, generalized activity, and operational definitions. The most troublesome aspect is to define the components of the system or systems with which we must be concerned.

Sorrells and Ford[35] also make us aware that the concepts are lacking in experimental validation. Their origins have been in the therapist's office rather than in the laboratory, making them more clinical than experimental.

Comprehensive Review of Family Therapy

Clifford Sager and co-workers[33] published an excellent review entitled "Dimensions of Family Therapy." They point out that understanding of the individual's psychological disturbance must include consideration of his network of social systems, the interpersonal systems through which he is related to others. Only when these are explored is there hope for effective treatment. The most influential of these systems is, of course, the family itself. It is the principal transmitter of cultural patterns and the primary arena for development of personality and satisfaction of basic needs. For the mental health professional this existing natural group can foster the psychological growth of its members. On the other side of the coin, serious emotional disturbances may arise and flourish when the family patterns and interactions are disordered. Viewed from this angle, mental illness of one family member may be regarded as a symptom of a psychopathologic process within an ongoing system, and alleviation of psychological disturbance may result from shifts in family relationships.

It may be well at the outset to emphasize that forms of psychopathology prevalent in a very low-income population may be quite different from those commonly found in middle-class patients. Unfortunately, the existing techniques of family therapy were developed and refined largely on the basis of studies conducted among middle-class patients and schizophrenic families. When the family therapist works with community groups, these discrepancies are increasingly evident.

There has been considerable publicity about the high percentage of black families headed by women, about 25 percent, as compared to 10 percent of white families, according to a survey by Glaser and Moynihan.[16] Auerswald[7] and Minuchin *et al.*[29] reported that youngsters in such families tend to lack a sense of capacity to influence events, a feeling for causality and the chronology of events, the ability to respond with differentiated behavior, the verbal skill to communicate nuances of feeling, and the ability to appraise and control their own destinies realistically. As a result they tend to be restlessly on the move, sometimes ganging together to obtain "kicks" from wanton destruction, drugs, or stealing, joining militant groups, finding excitement in the here and now. This behavior is, of course, not the monopoly of the ghetto but is shared by many middle-class and upper-class young people who are alienated from society, their families, and themselves.

How does the therapist approach a family which can receive public assistance only if the father lives elsewhere? There is a danger in pigeonholing any group. Perhaps too much attention has been focused on fragmented black families; there are more unbroken than broken homes among Negroes, more responsible than irresponsible parents, more nonworking than working mothers, more good homes for children than poor ones. We have focused attention on blacks and Puerto Ricans in ghetto areas because this is the most dispossessed and depressed of all groups, the segment most alienated from the "in" structure, and the one in greatest need of opportunities to develop a sense of self-worth and the vision of a meaningful future. Family therapy of non-intact black and Puerto Rican families can help furnish solutions to problems of vital social importance which have too long been ignored.

Implicit in the practice of traditional family therapy are certain assumptions, such as regard who should be responsible for earning the living, who should care for the children, and who should enforce discipline. These assumptions have been woven into treatment procedures though they may not fit in with the practices of certain cultural subgroups. In low-income families with multiple problems, mere survival takes precedence over other factors. For example, Grey[17] found that 56 percent of his sample of lower-class men in adolescence had had to care for their younger siblings, as compared with 25 percent in a comparable middle-class population. These examples are cited to show that rigid adherence to certain concepts may only increase the difficulties of families in need of psychotherapeutic "bolstering" or reality help.

Rather than try to instill uniform values, the therapist is asked to openly attempt to ascertain each family member's feelings about the role he plays, the amount of satisfaction he gains from it, and to assess the realistic possibilities for change. In this country we have long believed that the father should be the head of the household and bear the major responsibility for its financial stability. However, a tour of depressed areas (from urban ghetto regions to Appalachia) shows that, while their women have gone off to work, the Navajo Indians, the Mexican migrant farm workers, the Chinese shopkeepers, and numerous other groups have their own familial patterns which must be taken into account if we are to deal with the families in helpful ways. Indeed, Sager's group[33] has outlined some of the multiple problems inherent in family therapy.

RESPONSIBILITY TO TOTAL FAMILY

In the clinical approach of most leading therapists, a child, an adolescent, or an adult referred because of emotional disorder is regarded as an indicator of family psychopathology. A therapist may treat one or more family members individually or collectively, but his orientation is to the total family and his responsibility is to all family members, not to one at the expense of the others. This calls for procedures to study the psychodynamics of the whole family in its social and cultural setting and offer treatment on a family basis.

Family treatment focuses on the interactional field as well as on the intrapsychic experience. The interrelationship must be clarified and each person's mode of functioning explored, as an individual and in the dual roles of father-husband, mother-wife, brother-son, and sister-daughter. The family can then be helped to recognize how each member contributes to the positive and negative aspects of their relationships, and helped to change communication patterns, resulting in more open channels and less contradictory messages, as well as to evaluate and structure the goals as realistic, desirable, or desired. The family therapist's aim is to use the entire family as an instrument to help each member, without the improvements' being made at the expense of the others.

Accent on Family Homeostasis

Virginia Satir,[34] a pioneer in conjoint family therapy, also feels strongly that the therapist's responsibility is to the total family. She believes the therapist should determine the role of family members and help them develop less rigid roles that will lead to better balance in relationships, or family homeostasis. For example, it is important for the husband and father to be made to feel as essential to the therapy process as to the family itself, and the same is true of the wife-mother and the children. It is her conviction that a family showing symptoms of disturbance is in actual pain, which the therapist should try to understand and help to alleviate. By compassionately allying himself with the total family, the therapist can help the unit work through painful rigidity that threatens its balance. The parents are considered architects of the family. If their marital relationship is pained, the unit inevitably becomes dysfunctioning. She uses role-playing techniques, among others, to relieve the painful, flawed family relationships.

Markowitz and Kadis[28] consider the parents as the architects of the family. Treating couples in groups for about ten years has convinced us that changing their rigid interaction patterns can alter the family climate, bring about family homeostasis, and often eliminate the need for total-family therapy or therapy of the children.

Treatment of the Family as a Unit and in Subsystems

Salvador Minuchin[29] focuses mainly on slum families on the lowest income level. Unlike the therapists mentioned previously, he sees the family not only as a unit but also in what he calls "subsystems," which may be further divided. For example, he may see the marital couple or the siblings alone, or even in groups comprised of siblings from different families.

With use of the one-way screen, family members often observe and hear (with the therapist) the interaction between other family members. For example, a woman who fiercely protected her son against his father observed and heard a dialogue between them. Minuchin, who felt that her fear of the husband's harming the son was groundless, instructed her to join them and back up her husband in the discussion. He sometimes invites children to observe and listen to their parents who are discussing a problem, or the parents to do the same, by means of the one-way screen.

When working with the family of a schizophrenic child, Minuchin and others first see the identified patient (IP) alone a few times before meeting with the entire family. Their aim is to develop a strong dyadic relationship with the IP so that he can better cope with the spirited family therapy sessions.

The Eastern Psychiatric Group and, to my knowledge, Lee Hammer of the East Hampton Child Guidance Clinic are now developing teams of psychiatrists, social workers, and psychologists to treat schizophrenic and other severely disturbed families in their own homes. It is perhaps too soon to evaluate this new project, but it certainly presents a challenge that calls for all the courage and skills of the team members.

Communication and transactional theories are contributing significantly to our understanding of the family as an entity, and it seems important for us to delve into them in more detail.

Communication Theory

Jay Haley[19] and the late Don Jackson[20] of the Mental Research Institute, Palo Alto, California, were influenced by Ruesch[32] and Bateson[8] in formulating their communication theory. They regarded the relationship between any two people in interpersonal terms only—whether communication was between husband and wife, each sibling and the parent with whom he identified, or the total family. This interpersonal communication involving family members was the only focus. While accepting the idea of intra-psychic conflicts, these therapists never dealt with them in treating a family. "You don't deal with the oedipal problem or material in a family therapy session," Haley says, "You just go with the interpersonal movements, back and forth."

According to Haley, the core of the problem is how a relationship is being defined. People are continuously in the process of defining their relationships to one another; this works out well if the two people accept and have a reciprocal relationship. He distinguishes two kinds of relationships: (1) symmetrical (more or less between equals, such as a peer relationship) and (2) complementary (in which one gives and the other receives, such as a parent-child relationship).

When do such relationships run into snags? One person may want to control the other, or change may occur; for example, an adolescent may maneuver to form a symmetrical relationship (e.g. obtain the family automobile), but the parent may maneuver to maintain the former complementary one (e.g. withhold this privilege).

A third type, which Haley calls the metacomplementary relationship, develops when one person maneuvers the other into a controlling position and, through his complaints, covertly controls it himself. Haley also identifies different types of messages, e.g. those given back and forth on different levels—ambiguous, conflicting, or maneuver messages. Unstable relationships are characterized by constant maneuvering of all kinds. Psychopathology is viewed as a method of gaining control in human relationships; in other words, psychopathologic symptoms are used as tactics for this purpose. Haley presents a clear alternative to the insight-centered analytic model.

Transactional Theory

The transactional theory of the Eastern Psychiatric School in Philadelphia, represented by Boszormenyi-Nagy[13] and Framo,[14] differs greatly from the communication theory. It emphasizes both internal and external relationships and focuses on the object relations encountered in any interpersonal relationship. For example, a husband responds to his wife the way he would to his internalized object (e.g. his mother) or the wife responds to the husband as she would to some internalized object of her own (e.g. her father). In either event, they are interacting and the transaction is readily grasped. Each member is responding to his internalized reality.

However, the therapist focuses on the relationship regardless of whether or not the family members are dealing with internalized objects. Introjects are based not only on a one-to-one relationship to the mother and father as individuals, but also on the nature of their marriage relationship, on the psychological parents, and on the family itself (including the sibling subsystem). In the view of Nagy and Framo, a whole family system can be introjected.

The following points illustrate the rationale of the transactional theory:

1. The substance of psychiatric disorder in one member can be, and generally is, a family manifestation; the IP, or identified patient, is only the most obvious system through which the family system manifests its pathology.

2. The system of the family has regulating mechanisms of its own which control the collective mechanisms of its individual members. More is involved than the unconscious dynamics of each person; the complicated processes of the ongoing system govern the individual motivations. Despite numerous plots and subplots, the family remains a unity. Any one person can affect the whole transactional structure.

3. Each member of the family has to fit in with the rules of the family game.[19] Deviation from this on the part of any one member leads to a graduated series of injunctions, the most extreme of which is threatened abandonment. The members of an undifferentiated family have never learned that it is better to have the voluntary love of a free, separate human being than the "love" resulting from emotional enslavement.

4. In a poorly differentiated family, the parents are more likely to see or act toward their children or each other not as they really are but as screens to project on or as images through whom

they can work through past, unsatisfied longings and so on, which stem from original experiences with their own families.

5. The IP half willingly accepts his role as the scapegoat and sacrifices his autonomy in order to fill in gaps and voids in the lives of his parents or their marriage relationship. The IP often is subjected to the "Yo-Yo" syndrome—pulled toward parents when they need him and pushed away or ignored when not needed.

6. SOS signals sent out by the IP, such as car stealing or re-curring stomach aches, should be looked on not as requiring treatment per se, but rather as part and parcel of the transactional system in a family, and so diagnosed. In families where the individual members' ego boundaries are diffuse, one member can wish or will the satisfaction of a need, and, as if by magic, it will be met. For example, if a mother feeds a child when she herself is hungry, the child can become "addicted" to responding to her unspoken needs.

7. Whenever there are disturbed children, there is a disturbed marriage, although disturbed marriages do not always create disturbed children.

8. From the point of view of the transpersonal family concept, schizophrenia or any other mental illness can be looked upon as the only logical, adaptive response to a deranged, illogical family system (the same is true for delinquency).

9. The most powerful obstacle to successful treatment is the individual member's libidinal attachments to their parental introjects, no matter what the parents were like in real life. In the family concept, introjects are based not only on a one-to-one relationship to the mother and father as individuals, but on the nature of the parents' marriage relationship, on the psychological mother and father of the family, and on the family itself (including the sibling subsystem). A whole family system can be introjected.

10. Therapists have sensed that a patient in individual treatment does not change and develops great resistance because the transactional elements of his family life (reality problems) are not under direct observation or dealt with directly. The "resistance"

of the patient often resides, in part, in someone else. For example, a patient may argue, "You can say what you like, but I have too much to lose from somebody important to me if I really change."

Evaluation sessions. These should follow the guidelines listed below:

1. All designated members of the family must agree to come to the sessions at a convenient time.

2. The family has to express willingness to give more than lip service to family problems other than those having to do with the designated patient. The therapist should ask each family member, "What changes would you like to see in the family that would benefit you?" or, "What changes would you like to see in yourself that would make your life better?" (This helps to get the IP off the hook.)

3. The greater the family's resistance to bringing in one family member, the more that member's presence is necessary to understand the total family system.

Nagy and Framo are representative of those who hold that the family cannot be regarded only as an entity, but must be understood in the framework of the total family system.

PSYCHOANALYTIC APPROACH

At the other end of the spectrum we have the representatives of the psychoanalytic approach to the treatment of families. Ackerman,[3] Grotjahn,[18] Kadis and Markowitz,[21-23,28] and others represent, as I understand it, the psychoanalytic position. We are concerned not merely with changing the behavior transactions among family members, but with "insight-centered" analytic principles. One of our main goals is to change the intrapsychic processes. We are also concerned with the flow of affect among family members and with their motivational patterns. We try to correlate intrapsychic and interpersonal processes so as to change the pathogenic prospects of family life—something much easier said than done. We believe that intrapsychic conflicts interfere with interpersonal relationships; thus, resolving some of them may help resolve the defenses of different family members. When seeing a whole family together, for example, we may be able to resolve the father's sibling rivalry within his nuclear family by bringing to light actions toward his children that are similar to earlier actions toward his own siblings. We can sometimes gain insight and the ability to act upon it in only a few sessions.

Lacking a truly global concept of intrapsychic mechanisms, we therapists strive constantly to understand the *meaning* of the situation. Everything that happens, or does not happen, at all times has a purpose and meaning. We who are psychoanalytically oriented stress the intrapsychic process though not, of course, at the expense of the interpersonal processes.

In this approach, the therapist tries to understand the patient's character structure (e.g. passive-aggressiveness or submissiveness) due to his identification and projections, his past that still is operative in the present, his transference resistance and its working through. Ackerman[3] is unusually successful in bringing to the fore with ease interpersonal conflicts, sexual material, family secrets, and the like, which bear on the couple-parents' problems and are, in turn, reflected in disorders of the children-family. Ackerman, who has greatly broadened his analytic position, emphasizes the importance of family treatment for the mental health and welfare of the entire community.

The Role of Family Therapist

Family therapy is a distinct modality. The family by its very nature is a biosocial closed unit; the therapist relates to it as a whole and also to its separate members. Virtually snowed under with interactions of the parents and children, the family therapist is expected to immediately absorb the numerous actions, gestures, and situations—many of them overlapping and conflicting—and cope with the individuals all clamoring for attention.

He tries to listen attentively to each member of the group (but is often unable to do so), to gather and integrate the material, to gauge the relative importance of various interactions and select one for prompt discussion by the family. He goes "all out" to see that each member takes part and also listens to the others—not always easy, for they may have lost their ability to "hear" each other or may fail to listen because they are too absorbed in their own problems and eager to speak for themselves. Feeling that they know each other's stories all too well, they are interested mainly in impressing the therapist. The success of family therapy depends to a great degree on the therapist's willingness and readiness to assume leadership, to engage the members in discussion of a common theme, to see that they stay with it, and, in general, to evoke in them a sense of concern and responsibility for each other and for the family as a whole.

Gerald Zuk[37] defines family therapy as "the technique that explores and attempts to shift the balance of pathogenic relating among family members so that new forms of relating become possible." In family therapy (in what he calls the "go-between" process) , the therapist may be very active, intrusive, and confronting, or inactive and passive. He may move into the role of go-between by (1) attacking two parties he hopes to make into principals or (2) calmly pointing out a difference between them. Conversely, he may refuse to take sides in a dispute that has erupted or may become a go-between by presenting a new point of view in a dispute. He assumes that conflict is a characteristic and inevitable phase of group life whose magnitude can be checked by steps taken overtly or covertly in the interest of the principals.

Ackerman[2,3] stresses the therapist's role as an instrument of reality testing and as an educator and personifier of the range of models of family health. The therapist enters into the role of a real parent figure, as a source of support and controller of interpersonal danger. He also can provide emotional elements which the family lacks but sorely needs.

The Cotherapist's Roles in Family Treatment

When we consider the therapist's taxing role in handling an entire family, it is easy to see why MacGregor[27] and others advocate not one therapist but a large team to help the individual members and the family in both the diagnostic and assessment phases. Proponents of the Eastern Psychiatric School feel that cotherapists are essential in the treatment not only of marital couples but also of the whole family, which has a very strong impact. The E. P. group do not specify a male and a female co-therapist, although their experience with two females has not been successful. They believe that cotherapists are also needed in dealing with quite sick patients; if one therapist becomes tired enough to blank out for a minute or two, no matter what the reason, the other can take over. In such cases, having another person to "carry the ball" is enormously helpful. Many years ago, the Atlanta Psychiatric Clinic (headed by Whitaker, Felder, and Warkentin[36]), recognizing the difficulties encountered by one therapist, initiated treatment throughout the whole clinic by multiple therapists with individual patients, couples, or families.

I agree wholeheartedly with Celia Mitchell[30] of the Jewish Family Service that the presence of a cotherapist calls for more intensive work with transference and crosstransference elements, oedipal material, and such; I also agree with her that abuses are quite possible. However, the advantages of a cotherapist in couples or family therapy seem to greatly outweigh any disadvantages, especially when both therapists are at the same level of experience.

I first thought of a cotherapist for a marital couples group. It had become apparent that each patient was projecting onto me the ego ideal of a magical, all-powerful mother. I felt that a male cotherapist would have a salutary effect in countering certain obvious factors: (1) lack of male identification in the husbands, (2) lack of an adequate father prototype in the wives, and (3) tardy psychosexual maturation in both husbands and wives, with fixation in the symbolic pregenital period (i.e. an early undifferentiated child-mother relationship).

Max Markowitz became a cotherapist, and this was the beginning of a fruitful and zesty relationship. We anticipated that we would both be free in the interaction to assert our separate feelings, attitudes, and values. We hoped that our acceptance of this freedom in each other would provide a model for couple interaction, permitting separateness and self-expression.

We recognized the importance of overt expressions of his "fatherly" or self-assertive position in the group (to promote growth and to reduce the dyadic, symbiotic relatedness between myself and my "children"). This recognition helped to frustrate the members' alliance fantasies with me.

We consider the ideal situation a male and a female cotherapist with virtually the same status and level of development. We are convinced that all therapists from time to time fall into countertransferences, and a cotherapist is of incalculable help. The demonstration of a healthy, realistic alliance between cotherapists sanctions the spouses' separateness and frees them from their interlocking reactions.

Like others in the field, we have been shifting from what may be an obsessive preoccupation with the mother-child dyad toward a broader focus on the child-parent interaction. We believe that parental interaction can promote or impede the development of healthy family relationships.

By a healthy family we mean one in which the members act independently as well as interdependently. Each member learns to exert self-discipline ("I can wait for that"). Separateness or individuation is emphasized and valued in the context of togetherness. This permits the individual to move freely both within and beyond his family circle. All members work productively ("I do it for the good of all of us"), a context permitting the evolution and fruition of their needs. In contrast, by an unhealthy family we mean one in which each member regards himself as central ("I must be fed now without regard for any reality other than myself").

Our methodology in couples therapy takes into account here-and-now effects of the spouses' characterological problems that arose in their early familial experiences. In most instances, we have found that breaking the compulsive strife between husband and wife depends on making them see that they are perceiving each other and expecting things of each other in much the same way as of a significant parental figure in their past.

In our experience, a male and a female cotherapist can help to alter fixed transferential patterns. We find that patients tend to become quickly involved in the transference production and can be directly confronted with transference manifestations. The male cotherapist acts not only as a father prototype but also as a husband prototype who can survive stormy disagreements with the cotherapist while they remain on the best of terms.

We have found it effective to concentrate on challenging the ubiquitous fantasy of the "good mother," eliciting a "bad mother" transference when needed to challenge or frustrate and otherwise represent reality and limitations. We have both noted that the resulting transferences are sharply delineated and more amenable to ultimate correction.

MULTIPLE FAMILY THERAPY: A NEW APPROACH

Psychiatric hospitals with a large patient load have slowly become convinced that the patient's optimal long-term benefits from hospitalization depend to a great extent on integrating the spouse and/or family into the treatment plan. We who have worked in such hospitals know well the patient's often disturbed behavior after weekends at home or occasional family visitation in the hospital.

Laqueur, La Burt, and Morong,[24,25] and others describe the principal aims, procedures, rationale, and impressions in the treatment of families in groups in city hospitals. The principal aims of multiple family therapy are to improve communication between the spouses and all family members and to help them achieve better understanding of their disturbed behavior toward each other. Many of us have observed that a schizophrenic patient in a peer group engenders a great deal of narcissistic soliloquy.

Four or five families usually meet with a therapist once a week. The setting offers maximal opportunities for them to learn from each other directly and through analogy, interpretation, interaction, and identification, directly or by proxy. Members of one family often see their problems and behavior mirrored in other families and can better face and cope with them in this less highly charged climate. More often than not, confrontation of the hospital patient with his own family mobilizes strong defensive and protective mechanisms (such as denial, avoidance, and resistance) in all of them and winds up in discussion and accusation (e.g. "You always do so and so," "You never do so and so"). The psychotic patient's behavior is observed simultaneously with the sometimes bizarre symbiotic reaction patterns of his family members, who cling to their pathologic responses and refuse to allow him to learn new and more useful ways of coping with his life.

Symbiosis is ultimately expressed in reciprocal control by the patient and his family. He frequently exerts the most profound control over his parents by employing various means to maintain dependency and passivity. Thus the nonhospitalized parent and the patient may be engaged in an active identification struggle. Multiple family therapy provides a unique situation for them to help resolve such conflicts and also provides support as they attempt to develop new interpersonal relationships with parental and other family prototypes who are less threatening than their own nuclear family. "Pooling" of families broadens the base for trying out new adaptive behavior patterns for the IP and the family members.

I would like to point out that families are usually more tolerant of bizarre behavior in the IP of another family than in their own IP. Also, when two families who are in multiple therapy are joined by a third family, they may be even more helpful and responsive toward the newcomers than the therapist himself.

In general, therapists treating families in this fashion agree that they must be more active than in peer group or couples therapy. Dreams tend to evoke more spontaneous group interaction and invite projection on a safe level. The therapist needs to use various strategies to keep the communication on a meaningful level.

An important characteristic of this setting is the presence of many authority prototypes (the hierarchiacal system of our society, father, mother, and other authority figures), with the therapists assuming any of these roles to aid the patient in dealing with and working through any immediate unresolved authority conflict. As the group progresses, the patient's behavior is seen only as a symptom of his interaction with "family" members.

This treatment method, which began in city hospitals, is already gaining favor elsewhere. I foresee its widespread application in outpatient clinics and private institutions in the near future. Leichter and Shulman[26] use the family interview as an integrative device in group therapy with families.

VIDEOTAPE RECORDING — A NEW TOOL

Videotape recording is still in the exploratory stage for use in group, marital, and family therapy. Ian Alger and Peter Hogan[6] report that this adjunct facilitates the study of communication patterns and levels by providing visual and auditory feedback of therapeutic interaction and transaction. They describe its use in private group therapy, family therapy in private practice, individual psychotherapy, and in the conjoint treatment of marital couples. The patients' reactions fall mainly into three categories: (1) the "image impact"—his immediate reaction to seeing the tape, (2) his reactions during the remainder of the playback, and (3) his overall response, including residual and subsequent reactions related to the videotape experience. The image impact may be a significant factor in estimating the value of the technique for a particular patient. Once this impact is over, the patients begin to pay attention to other aspects of the playback, especially in relation to their own activity and the others' reactions to it. One woman said to her husband, "'Didn't notice it during the session, but now I see that you looked bored while I was talking."

Alger and Hogan cite advantages of the technique for research and teaching; its value in supervision is obvious. Videotape recording has so far been confined mainly to hospitals and other large institutions. However, the therapist can now obtain a machine for his private office at a low cost and have a permanent record and feedback for individual patients or groups. The total feedback is especially illuminating in terms of (1) heightening perception of the self and of others and (2) revealing how empathy influences perception of others.

SUMMARY

As you can see, the field of family psychotherapy is opening on all sides. The literature is beginning to report more and more experiences; people are talking and arguing about methods—always a sign of something good and yeasty in the air.

Since it is obviously impossible to cover all the theoretical approaches, I chose to concentrate on representative ones and only wish more could have been mentioned. Those who feel convinced of the value of this form of therapy may wish to study the different rationales, weigh the alternatives, and choose the approach that seems the most "comfortable." The watchword is flexibility. As therapists we hope to help those families who want to remain intact learn *how* to do so and in the meantime to increase the individual members' usefulness and sense of well-being. Most important of all, we must guard against imposing on families our own value systems and personal needs as determined by our cultural backgrounds. Let us realize that we are there to serve these families and can do so only if we are guided by their unique needs, which may be determined by vastly different cultures and customs. It has become increasingly evident that family psychotherapy promotes improved interpersonal family relationships and thus fosters a healthier and better-functioning community. We should therefore realize our definite obligation to the total community in this important and basic aspect of its fiber.

REFERENCES

1. Ackerman, N. W.: *Expanding Theory and Practice in Family Therapy.* Family Service Association, 1967.
2. Ackerman, N. W.: Family psychotherapy and psychoanalysis: Implications of difference. *Family Process, 1*:30-43, 1962
3. Ackerman, N. W.: Family psychotherapy today: Some areas of controversy. *Compr. Psychiat., 7*:375-387, 1966.
4. Ackerman, N. W.: *Psychodynamics of Family Life: Diagnosis and Treatment of Family Relationships.* New York, Basic Books, 1955.
4. Ackerman, N. W.: *Treating the Troubled Family.* New York, Basic Books, 1966.
6. Alger, I., and Hogan, P.: Enduring effects of videotape playback in family and marital relationships. *Amer. J. Orthopsychiat., 139*:86-98, 1969.
7. Auerswald, E. H.: Cognitive development and psychopathology in the urban environment. In Graubard, P. (Ed.): *Children in Schools.* In press.
8. Bateson, G., Jackson, D. D., Haley, J., and Weakland, J. H.: A note on the double bind 1962. *Family Process, 2*:154-161, 1963.
9. Bell, J. E.: Extended family relations of disturbed and well families. *Family Process, 1*:175-193, 1962.
10. Bell, J. E.: *Family Group Therapy.* Washington, D. C., Public Health

Monograph No. 64, U.S. Dept. of Health, Education, and Welfare, 1961.

11. Bell, J. E.: Recent advances in family group therapy. *J. Child Psychol. Psychiat., 3:*1-15, 1962.

12. Bell, J. E.: A theoretical position for family group therapy. *Family Process, 2:*1-14, 1963.

13. Boszormeny-Nagy, I.: The concept of schizophrenia from the perspective of family treatment. *Family Process, 1:*103-113, 1962.

14. Framo, J. L.: *Intensive Family Therapy.* New York, Harper & Row, 1965, pp. 143-177.

15. Framo, J. L.: The theory of the technique of family treatment of schizophrenia. *Family Process, 1:*119-131, 1962.

16. Glaser, N., and Moynihan, D. P.: *Beyond the Melting Pot.* Cambridge, Mass., MIT Press and Harvard University Press, 1963.

17. Grey, A.: Social class and the psychiatric patient: A study in composite character. *Contemp. Psychoanal., 2:*1-35, 1966.

18. Grotjahn, M.: Analytic family therapy: A survey of trends in research and practice. In Masserman, J. H. (Ed.): *Individual and Family Dynamics.* New York, Grune & Stratton, 1959, p. 90.

19. Haley, J.: Family experiment: A new type of experimentation. *Family Process, 1:*265-293, 1962.

20. Jackson, D. D., and Weakland, J. H.: Conjoint family therapy: Some considerations on theory, technique, and results. *Psychiatry, 24:*30-45, 1961.

21. Kadis, A. L., and Markowitz, M.: Psychoanalysis and Multiple Contact Forms of Therapy. Paper presented at meeting of American Orthopsychiatric Association, March, 1968.

22. Kadis, A. L., and Markowitz, M.: Short-term analytic treatment of married couples in a group by a therapist couple. In *New Directions in Mental Health.* New York, Grune & Stratton, 1968, pp. 50-68.

23. Kadis, A. L., and Markowitz, M.: The therapeutic impact of co-therapist interaction in a couples group. In Moreno, J. L. (Ed.): *International Handbook of Group Psychotherapy.* New York, Philosophical Library, 1966, pp. 446-455.

24. Laqueur, H. P., La Burt, H. A., and Morong, E.: Multiple family therapy. In Masserman, J. H. (Ed.): *Current Psychiatric Therapies.* New York, Grune & Stratton, 1964, Vol. IV, pp. 150-154.

25. Laqueur, H. P., La Burt, H. A., and Morong, E.: Multiple family therapy: Further developments. *Int. J. Soc. Psychiat., Special Ed., 2:*70-80, 1964.

26. Leichter, E., and Shulman, G.: The family interview as an integrative device in group therapy with families. *Int. J. Group Psychother., 13:*335-345, 1963.

27. MacGregor, R.: Multiple impact psychotherapy with families. *Family Process, 1*:15-29, 1962.

28. Markowitz, M., and Kadis, A. L.: Parental interaction as a determining factor in social growth of the individual in the family. *Int. J. Soc. Psychiat., Special Ed.,* 81-89, 1964.

29. Minuchin, S., Montalvo, B. G., Rosman, B. I., and Schumer, F.: *Families of the Slums.* New York, Basic Books, 1967.

30. Mitchell, C.: The uses and abuses of co-therapy as a technique in family unit therapy. Bulletin of the Family Mental Health Clinic of Jewish Family Service, *1*, New York, Spring, 1969.

31. Paul, N. L., and Grosser, G. H.: Famly resistance to change in schizophrenia patients. *Family Process, 3*, 377-401, 1964.

32. Ruesch, J., and Bateson, G.: *Communication: The Social Matrix of Society.* New York, Norton, 1951.

33. Sager, C. J., Waxenberg, S. E., Brayboy, T., Slipp, S., and Waxenberg, B.: Dimensions of family therapy. *Progress in Community Mental Health, 1*:137-165, 1969.

34. Satir, V.: *Conjoint Family Therapy.* Palo Alto, Calif., Science & Behavior Books, Inc., 1967.

35. Sorrells, J. M., and Ford, F. R.: Toward an integrated theory of families and family therapy. *Psychotherapy: Theory, Research and Practice, 6*:150-160, 1969.

36. Whitaker, C. A., Felder, R. E., and Warkentin, J.: Countertransference in the family treatment of schizophrenia. In Boszormenyi-Nagy, I., and Framo, J. L. (Eds.): *Intensive Family Therapy.* New York, Hoeber-Harper, 1965, pp. 323-341.

37. Zuk, G. H.: Family therapy. *Arch. Gen. Psychiat., 16*:71-79, 1967.

D<small>R. C</small>ARL A. W<small>HITAKER</small> <small>PIONEERED</small> in the use of multiple therapy at the Atlanta Psychiatric Clinic. Presently at the University of Wisconsin Medical School, Dr. Whitaker has presented in a concise, direct, and very open manner a very interesting paper on his ideas of how to, when to, and why to use multiple therapy. Because the paper is a condensation of his ideas for this volume, he whets our appetites and makes us wish that the paper had been a monograph wherein we could have obtained more of his very real and personal opinions on the uses of multiple therapy. Specifically, his section on multiple therapy as a research tool introduces us to the many exciting ramifications that this technique offers for research in therapy.

In this paper Dr. Whitaker initially provides a history of his introduction to the use of multiple therapy and its extension to others as well. His section on this technique as a training aid cites innovative and, for some individuals, startling suggestions. He proposes that residents in training should proceed from multiple therapy with a couple or group to individual treatment. Dr. Whitaker's ideas are provocative and provide a new perspective and as such can lead to growth and change in therapists and in the field. In this chapter he compares multiple therapy to real life and indicates that it can be the growing edge for the therapist. If one is concerned that the presence of another therapist could interfere with the beginning therapist, just as the supervisor might, he also has an answer to that. For him, multiple therapy gives one much greater freedom emotionally to be oneself as a therapist and makes for greater and easier learning of therapy.

There are interesting and provocative sections on choosing cases for multiple therapy as well as choosing one's cotherapist. If one is a Carl Whitaker, with his ease, coolness, and great self-assurance, it is not hard to imagine that the choice of cotherapist has the latitude that he describes, but for many this could be one of the most difficult of professional collaborations. Dr. Whitaker's illustrative cases are interesting and this chapter, written in his slightly ironic style, makes for a good overall introduction and summary of the use of multiple therapists in therapy, yielding many and new thoughts and interesting innovations for both beginning and experienced therapists.

G.D.G.
D.S.M.

Chapter 5

MULTIPLE THERAPY AND ITS VARIATIONS

Carl A. Whitaker

D R. SPAFORD ACKERLEY ONCE SAID many years ago that Freud held psychotherapy back fifty years. He was pointing out by this rather radical statement that Freud's devotion to research in and understanding of the intrapsychic aspects of the individual made progress in the understanding of the process of treatment, of patient recovery, and of therapist function a much delayed and little studied procedure for many years. It was only in very recent years that the American Psychiatric Association had a section on psychotherapy. Part of this delay arose after the discovery that research with individual patients many times was very therapeutic. Thus the pragmatic study of psychotherapy as such was delayed until more recent years.

Probably the biggest breakthrough was in the mid-forties when Rudolph Dreikurs began to bring his young trainees into his own interviews with individual patients. The author's work in multiple psychotherapy began in 1945 at Oakridge with Dr. John Warkentin. Whereas Dr. Dreikurs began his innovation as a training technique, we began ours in an effort to increase our communication. When one of us burst out of a one-to-one interview with great excitement, the other one was not interested in hearing the story. He had not been part of the live experience. Thus we decided that the two of us would treat a patient together.

The new freedom to communicate created a better understanding of our bilateral experiences and facilitated many gains in our relationship to each other and our treatment of patients. A second important gain from multiple therapy was the development of more power in the therapist and confidence in his functioning. With a second therapist present, each therapist was more free to be a person and not just a symbol. Much of the research approach to patient treatment suffered from the fact that the therapist became a symbol and, to some extent, the patient also became a symbol. Thereby these two communicated by a kind of secondary process which kept them at some distance from each other. This not only limited the interaction between the two people but also prevented each of them from being themselves.

One other gain from multiple therapy was the therapeutic and professional protection and the increased flexibility thereby available for response to the patient. Each person could get a feedback not only from one other person but from two people and had the opportunity to compare the two feedbacks. In multiple therapy the legal protection also avoided those disturbing episodes which happen from time to time in any psychotherapist's practice.

COTHERAPY AS A TRAINING AIDE

Jim began his psychiatric residency with a great deal of insecurity. He had gone into the field partly because his mother had been mentally ill in years past and he was anxious not only to find ways of being helpful to her but to try to make sure that he himself did not suffer a psychiatric breakdown. The first week on service he was put into a state hospital ward, and although he had supervision he was immediately plunged into a personal relationship with two new, acutely psychotic female patients. He spent his regular hours interviewing them and feeling increasingly frightened. His discussions with the supervisor and with the ward chief psychiatrist only served to prove to him how little he knew about what was going on and how responsible he should be for their care and their recovery.

He began to develop nightmares and shortly started taking tranquilizers so that he could sit through the interviews each day without having to be in a tremor and acute panic. One of these women looked remarkably like his mother; the other one had an incisive way of digging at his own personal anxieties until he was literally beside himself. He gradually increased the number of tranquilizers until he was comfortable and casual about the interviews and thus began his development toward becoming the kind of psychotherapist who can say, "Who listens?"

In order to avoid the kind of tragedy outlined above, there is a need to protect the new trainee from his own tender feelings, to teach him in a personal and comfortable way how to respond to very sick patients, and to give him some sense that he can make a contribution to their recovery. One way is to teach him psychotherapy by having him sit in with someone who is comfortable, someone who is competent; he can then participate to the degree possible for him in the ongoing therapy conducted by the more experienced man. The two of them, having lived through a common experience, can also talk in a much more significant and personal way about the ongoing process in the patient and in the interpersonal relationship that is psychotherapy. Once the trainee has had the experience of working in a safe setting with even disturbed patients, he can begin to develop his own pattern of interaction.

Although psychotherapy is usually taught in very small groups, it is possible to have four or five residents plus two or three medical students plus two staff persons making up the therapeutic team for the treatment of even one patient. Such a process is vastly more efficient than the use of movies or the one hour of supervision for each hour of interview system. There, words become the means by which individuals play games with each other about an experience that one of them replays in his mind while the other one is trying to get the picture from words alone.

Multiple therapy or cotherapy as a training method has an extra advantage. It produces a different quality in the "as if" relationship so characteristic of one-to-one therapy. The characteristics of a triangular or multiperson group are much different than the secretive and highly symbolic quality of the one-to-one relationship.

Ideally the new trainee might be introduced to psychotherapy by sitting in with an experienced colleague in the treatment of a married couple. The married couple is probably the least demanding therapeutic unit. The husband and wife, newly married or within the first few years, are largely transferred to each other. The therapist is free to move into and out of the relationship without particular strain and without the grave responsibility involved in other types of therapeutic intervention.

Once having gone through the treatment of a couple with an experienced colleague, the young trainee will be in a position either to do the same thing with a peer or to move on to treating an individual with a more experienced colleague as cotherapist or to the treatment of a group with a more experienced colleague. With this background the trainee can comfortably and efficiently go on to the treatment of an individual with a peer and at that point is ready to treat his first couple without a cotherapist.

Once he has had the experience of treating a couple alone and possibly running a group alone, he is ready to treat an individual patient in a one-to-one relationship without either undue panic or the distortions in perception which are so typical of the beginning psychotherapist. With a peer as cotherapist he should then be ready to take on a couples group. Maybe then he can inaugurate the more difficult procedure of treating a family with one of the senior therapists of the training staff. It is the author's contention that training should always begin with patients who are less seriously disturbed, although there are some who feel this is not true.

Parenthetically, the author must confess that one of the great gains in the use of multiple therapy for training is the feedback he gets from young trainees whose knowledge of such modern additions as systems theory, information sets, and existentialism is a tremendous asset in his effort to grow and to expand his understanding of the therapeutic process. That we learn from these young trainees must of course be kept secret from them lest they lose their reverence for the establishment. The author has been consistently amazed at how comfortably VIP private patients take the introduction of a young resident into their personal psychotherapy. It is as though the only real problem is whether the supervisor is willing to take the chance of being one-upped by the wisdom of the novitiate.

THE USE OF MULTIPLE THERAPY FOR THE GROWTH OF THE THERAPIST

Although every therapist is a mature person, some of us recognize that there are bits of growth we can still gain. In the one-to-one relationship such feedback to the therapist is fairly limited. In the first years we suffer the strange experience of the patient growing past us, and we learn from some of the things they experience how to be different in our own living. However, as we become more experienced, patients do not have that much significance for us and do not ordinarily rock us to such a degree that we are forced to change.

Multiple therapy changes all that. The presence of a triangle— even in the treatment of one patient, or several triangles in the treatment of a couple—makes possible certain unique things characteristic of triangles which are not true of dyadic relationships. In a triangle, one can have the formation of an alliance when two members team up to help the third or all three members team up together. A triangle also can and frequently does make possible the development of collusion, when two people team up against the third. This can have some very painful and sometimes very growthful reverberations in the therapist. When both the cotherapist and the patient agree that the other therapist is off base or is distorted in his perception, it is very difficult for him to use ordinary rationalizations and excuse making about how immature the patient is, and certainly he would not be able to challenge both.

A third factor characteristic of triangles is the possibility of mediation. The mediator in this case may be one of the therapists or it may be the patient. The experience of having a patient resolve discrepancies between the two therapists or having one therapist mediate the painful struggle between you and a patient is a very growthful one.

Further facilitation of the growth of the young therapist (of course, the older therapist has no need for such experience) is brought about by the unique advantages of seeing yourself in the other therapist. It is very disconcerting to be in the middle of a profound interpretation or a very cogent observation and have both the patient and the cotherapist agree that you are out of order or that you are playing some fancy game that they can both see and you had not been aware of.

Although these dynamic factors and the experience of collusion, mediation, and alliance are all of great help, one of the most obvious gains in the multiple therapy setting is the mere fact that the experience is closer to everyday reality living. This not only necessitates that the therapist be more himself, but it also makes the patient more responsible for his living process rather than just responsible for telling it all to good old mother.

THE USE OF MULTIPLE THERAPY AS A RESEARCH TOOL

Dr. Al Scheflen first pointed out to the author that in the extensive use of multiple therapy he reported the process of the interview with a greater proximity to the actual experience as seen in the camera than most other therapists they had seen in the Temple Research Project. In the one-to-one relationship the therapist must be a supportive, nutrient mother figure offering intimacy and understanding while he simultaneously carries administrative, reality-oriented, and structured father-function. This double role can be split between the two therapists.

The use of multiple therapy enables each therapist to function on the intermittent time base. Dr. Scheflen discovered that the therapist ordinarily works on a six- to eight-minute schedule, and after this period he withdraws his affect from the patient for a short period before starting another six- to eight-minute episode. In the multiple therapy setting the two therapists alternate so that it is possible to continuously interrelate with the patient. Simultaneously, during the period when the one therapist is carrying the initiative, it is possible to study the ongoing process between the patient and the other therapist or to reflect upon the experience you and the patient have just completed.

It is also of great use to the patient for the two colleagues to discuss their joint experience openly during the interview by checking out their observations with each other and with the patient. This freedom to do research—or, if you will, clinical observation—with a live interaction and a present-tense communication gives the multiple therapy setting many advantages for upgrading the therapeutic process.

The patient may make great contributions to this study because, in his involvement with the two therapists who serve as prototype, he will report back his adaptation of the therapeutic experience in his own living. For example, if the two therapists are free to fight with each other, the patient may well return and describe the relationship between the fight he had with his wife last night and the fight the two therapists had during the last interview. This gives the therapist a very exact extrapolation of the interface between them and an opportunity to evaluate their own relationship to each other, the changes in it, and the use of it in the therapeutic process with the patient.

THE USE OF MULTIPLE THERAPY IN TREATMENT

We have been discussing the use of multiple therapy for training, for the growth of the therapist, and for research. It also has unique advantages in the specific problems that come up in the treatment of patients. One of the most obvious ones, as implied above, is the entrance of the therapist into any new territory. Whereas work with psychotic patients on an outpatient basis is very rewarding, it is also very arduous and particularly difficult during those first few years as a psychotherapist. The use of two therapists in this setting makes for a greater freedom and a greater learning experience; once one has become comfortable in treating such patients, then the multiple therapy need not be continued.

Cotherapy or multiple therapy is also useful in other expansions of the therapeutic territory; for example, the development of a couples group, working with families, working with adolescents, working with severe alcoholics, as well as the intensive personal involvement necessary for work with serious psychosomatic illnesses. The newer work with several families in a group or with a friendship network, à la Ross Speck, also suggests two therapists. The advantages of taking on a cotherapist for working with seriously ill patients for its obvious gains in the freedom for creative innovations in your own therapeutic development is only one of the gains that the author believes to be unique to multiple therapy.

CHOICE OF CASES

One of the serious challenges for a psychotherapist is how to treat a patient who has been to two or three other therapists, each of whom failed. The treatment of such a failure is always tricky. Each time the patient fails he gets twice as cynical about psychotherapy. It is exciting to think that you could take on this woman who has had ten years of treatment with an expert in a distant city, but it is more painful to discover that ten years later you are right where he left off. It is simpler to start out with the humble admission that you are probably not any better and that maybe you would be smarter to start out with all you can get on your side rather than trying to test your mettle.

Parenthetically, multiple therapy is also a way to inaugurate the treatment of those VIP's who are frightening when they first arrive; be it another psychotherapist, the mayor of your town, a beautiful woman, a millionaire playboy, or your old college chum —each can be a hidden threat to your own daily equanimity. An ounce of real-life significance can outweigh five pounds of your therapeutic competence.

We have all had experiences also with those loaded combinations sometimes called "the gruesome twosome." The hysterical woman and her latent homosexual husband make a good combination for the first few interviews, but it is very difficult not to get caught in the throes of their triangulation so that you are on the bottom and in trouble. The alcoholic wife and the hypertensive husband can be just as dangerous. Beware also of the schizophrenic and his widowed mother.

When one is deciding what cases to treat with multiple therapy, there are many factors to take into account. Most of the above are obvious. It is not so obvious that if you are planning to see the patient in multiple therapy, it is better to make the decision before the first interview.

CHOICE OF COTHERAPIST

The choice of cotherapist is even more crucial than the cases. The most obvious thing is to choose a psychotherapist who is personally compatible and whose training and personality are complementary to your own. However this is not always available, and in some settings discovering any cotherapist who is willing to work with you is a difficult process.

My residents have taught me that my presumption of years past was equaled only by my assumption that I knew the answer. They have shown that it is not necessary for the therapists to be deeply personal in their relationship to each other. In the beginning the cotherapy relationship may be like a pseudomutual family. After the first fight, which certainly should take place in front of the patient or the couple, the cotherapists then may deal with each other in a respectful but personal interaction which does not necessitate intimacy or even profound compatibility outside the interview. Cotherapy can be a time-limited "affair." However, if a cotherapist is available with whom one becomes gradually more established, this is most helpful. Surprisingly, almost any two therapists can work together, although it is equally true that any two therapists can be phony with each other and therefore of little help to the patient.

In using the cotherapy pattern as a way of supervision, compatibility certainly is not a requirement. However, there are some people with whom a cotherapy relationship is very difficult. This seems to be related to a difference in basic philosophical convictions about life rather than technical differences in treatment. For example, since the author tends to work on a base of paradoxical intention, any effort to do cotherapy with a therapist who tries to do psychotherapy on a base of education is apt to be self-canceling.

VARIATIONS OF COTHERAPY

We have been discussing some of the characteristics and uses of cotherapy as a process. There are many variations which should be mentioned in passing. One of the most obvious is the use of the second therapist as a consultant in the ongoing therapeutic process. The pattern utilized by the Atlanta Psychiatric Clinic during their years of developing multiple therapy is fairly routine. The therapist who is going to see the patient takes the initial history. The second interview is joint. A second therapist comes in as a consultant. The first interview is reviewed with him. He expands the history, and the two therapists then, either in front of the patient or after the patient has left, staff the situation and make variations on a plan for treatment.

The original therapist then presents this plan in the third interview, and the patient or patients are informed of the alternative plans. It is suggested that they consider the situation, and if they decide to go on in treatment they may reapply. This use of the second therapist as a consultant also has the advantage of completing the initial diagnostic contract, and renegotiating a new contract will set a new framework for ongoing treatment. If the decision is to have the treatment done by one therapist, the consultant is still symbolically in on the continuing treatment and can be brought back as consultant either at the request of the therapist or at the request of the patient. This use of the consultant in the ongoing process of psychotherapy is also of great value whatever the need.

Dr. A., in the seventh interview with his beautiful adolescent patient, began to be suspicious that he was not free to be fully honest and that he indeed was probably overinvolved. He asked the supervisor in, presented his problem in front of the patient, and in the presentation of it the three were able to work through to another level of relating, such that she was clear she needed a therapist, not a boyfriend, and he was clear that he could treat her as a patient and not get her confused with his own girlfriend.

Dr. B. did not discover until near the end of the second interview that the young man he was seeing was actively suicidal. At this point he interrupted the interview, went out and found a peer who was not actively involved in an interview, brought him into the interview, and presented him with the problem they were facing; the three of them were able to arrive at a decision that this suicidal impulse was indeed of such character that outpatient treatment would be feasible. Dr. B. was, of course, also able to sleep that night.

Dr. C. had been seeing Mary Zilch for six months and although in the beginning he had dreams of converting this somewhat dried-up old maid into a live, vivid human being, he sensed during the last six interviews that he was becoming more and more bored. Because of this he asked his supervisor to come into the interview with him. The supervisor helped the two of them face the situation for what it was. They developed more realistic plans for the on-going treatment and the expansion of the one-to-one interviews to include group therapy. This helped Dr. C. get out of the rather awe-some corner of being the only man in this forty-year-old woman's life.

One of the implications in the consultation episodes just presented is the usefulness of multiple therapy or the consultant interview as a method of supervision. *In vivo* supervision, either by the regular supervisor or by a peer, allows for an expanded experience as well as learning about psychotherapy. We have talked casually about the relationship of the consultant therapist to the therapist in one-to-one therapy as though it were a one-interview solution. Sometimes this is not possible; the second therapist may continue to stay in the therapy, or he may come back for every other interview, every fourth interview, or when invited. In some patient settings it becomes quite clear that the initial contract between the patient or patients and the individual therapist is quite untenable.

For example, Dr. Joe had agreed to see Mr. and Mrs. Q. because of Mrs. Q's severe body symptoms, which included intestinal cramps, rapid heart action, insomnia, and episodes of heart pain. He assumed that her rather passive husband would be a kind of helper in the psychotherapy. Within a matter of three or four interviews it became clear that the husband was actively suicidal and a fairly severe alcoholic, both of which had been concealed. At this point it was clear that they should be seen in multiple therapy because of the severity of the situation.

One of the most efficient uses of the second therapist is in the facilitation of the ending process. The author some years ago was seeing a psychotherapist and wife, each of whom had had considerable previous treatment, yet the relationship between them was still quite stormy. Over the course of a year the therapeutic process was intense and fairly effective, but the patients showed no inclination to break loose and continue without further treatment. At this point the author invited one of his colleagues into the interview without any prewarning. Halfway through the interview this colleague suggested that they sounded as though they were both bored with psychotherapy and he thought they should give it up as hopeless. They accepted this a bit wryly but in the two years since have been very happy about the resolution.

As one becomes more comfortable with custom tailoring the psychotherapeutic process rather than having to follow a preestablished plan, it seems very useful to also utilize a second therapist whenever one is expanding the treatment base. If treatment is begun with a couple, it is advantageous as treatment goes along to add a second therapist for the initial interview with the children present. If one is doing family therapy, it is useful to have a second therapist in for such different episodes as a home visit, an open interview with the extended family, or an interview to which the family invites the husband's colleague or the wife's best girlfriend.

CONCLUSION

We have discussed the use of multiple therapy as a methodology for expanding the power, the safety, and the creative freedom available to the therapist during his workaday world. We have tried to point out some of its advantages in the realm of training and in the growth of the more experienced therapist, its technical efficiency in the treatment process, and variations in the use of a second therapist in the ordinary ongoing practice of psychotherapy. The days when psychotherapy had to be secretive because it was concerned with the sinful aspects of the patient's life are past. Our basic concern now is with therapeutic efficiency and the discovery of more effective methods for helping individuals find their own life as well as learn how to function in this game-playing world we live in.

THIS PAPER is a very thorough evaluation of the forces of change in effect in the present evolution of psychotherapeutic practice. It begins with an extensive discussion of the reasons why there is a marked discrepancy between many of the theories of personality and their application in practice. For Dr. Basescu this discrepancy raises a series of questions and the answers to these questions are essential to an understanding of the changes evolving in the treatment sphere. However, he warns against the usual solution, which is a criticism of existing practice resulting in a negative reaction to what exists rather than a positive movement toward growth. He argues for developments that are active attempts to narrow the gap between notions about the way people function in life and the way people actually function in therapy.

With these ideas as a background for his discussion Dr. Basescu proceeds to an extensive evaluation of the theoretical difficulties and attitudes involved in a position based primarily on the phenomenology of experience. He traces the importance of Freud's concern with transference and its limits in the relationship with the patient. His contrast of the more classical position of the neutral role of the therapist in the therapeutic interaction with emerging interaction patterns of some newer approaches brings these differences into sharp focus. Additionally, it provides him with a springboard for further discussion and clarification of how the relationship between the therapist and patient might be made more meaningful. Using such areas as physical contact and the therapist's disclosure of personal aspects of his life as points of departure, he explores in depth the transference and countertransference aspects of these and similar issues. There is an honesty, integrity, and a search for further ways to promote healing that are characteristic of Dr. Basescu's entire paper and serve as excellent models for his existential humanism.

G.D.G.
D.S.M.

Chapter 6

EXISTENCE AND EXPERIENCE

Sabert Basescu

T HE INNOVATION in psychotherapeutic practice that I am going to discuss is intensive individual psychotherapy. Describing it as an innovation applies in two ways. First, in these days of rapidly proliferating techniques, methods, and experiences of instant personality change, the traditional one-to-one talking therapy may indeed appear as unique. Second, the nature of individual therapy itself has been changing and continues to change.

Critics from a number of sources would do away with it altogether. For example, the community mental health movement considers individual therapy irrelevant to the immense task at hand. Behavior therapists evaluate it as inefficient at best and ineffectual more often than not. And the sensitivity training people relegate it to the realm of the intellectual and nonexperiential. Each of these criticisms could be discussed at some length, but it is important to note that dissatisfaction with traditional ways sometimes leads to a couple of dangerous errors. "One is that what is good about the past may be thrown out along with what is bad. The second is that newness and innovation may be embraced for their own sake, rather than for any intrinsic merit, and without consideration for their potential harm."[7] For example, while intensive individual psychotherapy is clearly not a solution to the large public health problem, it may be the desirable or necessary way of working with a great many troubled people. Similarly, language may be used in the service of concealment. The antidote to this is not the elimination of talk. In any case:

> Rather than an orderly and appropriate development of knowledge and concepts leading into a new phase, much of what we see now has originated in a disavowal of the past because of the displeasure with it. Change has occurred on a negative basis rather than on the basis of growth. Most of what was taken for granted before has been opened to question.[7]

Perhaps some of the most important and relevant questioning has been done by those committed to the theory and practice of individual psychotherapy themselves. It has been noted, for example, that gross discrepancies exist between therapeutic functioning and the personality theories upon which the therapeutic approach is presumably based.[1,3] This is true no matter what personality theory or psychodynamic theory one selects. The practitioners of the therapy that is presumed to be based upon and originate in a personality theory more or less function in contradiction to major tenets of the theory itself. Much therapy is done in spite of the personality theory on which it is based rather than because of it. There are also theories of therapy that are relatively independent of any theories of personality. Ellis[5] and Rogers,[9] for example, have therapeutic approaches that are not essentially based on personality theories.

One of the implications of these facts is that something is missing from our personality theories that tends to come into focus when we begin to function in clinical and professional settings. In other words, something is missing that comes into focus in interpersonal experience. It may be that our personality theories have not sufficiently dealt with man in his world, but have dealt with man as a psychodynamic entity and not paid sufficient attention to what happens in interpersonal experience. Laing,[8] for example, writes: "It is the relation between persons that is central in theory and in practice. Persons are related to one another through their experience and through their behavior."

In our research and theorizing much attention has been paid to behavior primarily because behavior is observable. Experience which may underlie behavior is only inferable, not observable; therefore, particularly in the traditional academic settings, experience is relegated to the realm of the untouchable. There is relatively little study of the relationship of experience and behavior.

In a recent article, James Deese,[4] an experimental psychologist, writes:

Psychology is the science of behavior only in a trivial sense. . . .
Yet any concept without direct 'behavioral implications' seems to have dubious status in the current market for psychological theory.

. . . When we limit ourselves to the study of behavior, we make it difficult or even impossible for psychological theory.

He goes on to say:

> In short, we have been badly oversold on the classical experimental model as the means of studying such central aspects of human psychology as cognition. Too much evidence—obvious and available evidence—is ignored because it fails to conform to our prejudices about how empirical information arises. We have insisted upon the measurement of behavior to the extent that most of the things we observe in experiments have no relevance for the process of thinking, other than the empty observation that thinking, like most processes, takes a measurable period of time. . . . Thinking does not occur as a reaction to a stimulus but as the result of activity, within an almost totally unmapped system, obeying instructions from within the system itself.

That system is the experiencing human being. Laing[8] describes the human being as an experiential-behavioral system, and describing man as such, points to what may be a most severe lack in our existing psychological knowledge; namely, a phenomenology of experience—including even unconscious experience. There is relatively little research, even relatively little thought, in the whole area of the nature of human experience.

In psychotherapy our primary concern is with experience that enables change in the modes of existence. In the history of psychotherapy the initial focus with Freud was on what was essentially a cognitive uncovering process, an examination of the experiences of repressed childhood traumas. Freud initially felt that when the puzzle was laid bare, the analyst would be in a position to instruct the patient and that would provide the needed impetus for changed modes of experience. But Freud found very early in his work that cognitive uncovering and instruction were not enough. Then his focus shifted to the transference neurosis. Freud's emphasis on transference and the transference neurosis was essentially his early recognition of the role of the relationship in the psychotherapeutic enterprise. With the recognition of the importance of the relationship one of the major trends in the transformation of the nature of individual psychotherapy began. That trend might be described as the humanizing of the therapist.

Initially the therapist's role was to be silent, unmoved, non-reactive—the mirror for the patient's emotional projections. The next step in the process of humanizing the therapist involved the therapist as participant-observer. Our current conception of the therapist is that of an interactive, involved, confrontational member of a two-person relationship. Although many therapists continue to describe the therapist's function as essentially to maintain himself in a nonreactive role, we find that, currently, therapists—even traditional therapists—often step outside of the nonreactive role and involve themselves very much as human beings in their relationships with their patients. Sometimes the therapist involves himself to the point of preempting the role of the patient. That is, some writers[10] justify the therapist's assuming the role of the patient for himself.

Having embarked on the process of humanizing the therapist, we are confronted with the need to specify the particular attributes of relatedness that are important for change. A number of these attributes have been described in the psychotherapeutic literature. For example, Rogers[9] highlights the need for the therapist's unconditional positive regard for the patient. Leslie Farber[6] claims that the essential quality is the I-thou relationship. Farber writes:

> Listening requires something more than remaining mute while looking attentive. Namely, it requires the ability to attend imaginatively to another's language. . . .Interpretation, then, would express the analyst's own reworking in language of that attention to the other's existence out of which relation might arise. . . .Certainly it is only when a Thou relation arises out of interpretation that the patient will risk the pain of applying the interpretation to further exploration of his disorder.

This raises many questions: How does an I-thou relation arise between two people? What about an I-thou relation that becomes enabling of change, and to what extent will somebody open himself to the experience of pain in the context of such a relation?

Binswanger[2] refers to caring as the essential quality that characterizes man and his relationships. If we take seriously the possibility that the therapist may be very much involved in a relationship with a patient, a number of problems and questions arise. Even in the traditional analytic model where the therapist maintains a nonreactive, analyzing role, the experience of trust must be present. The patient must experience the therapist as interested, concerned, and caring. How does this develop? What is there that goes on in a therapeutic relationship or in any relationship that results in the experience of being cared for or even the experience of caring for someone else? One might ask, What are the minimum behavioral ways of caring and of experiencing oneself as cared for? How does the inner experience get communicated? How do the minimal behavioral ways vary from person to person and even from era to era? That is, one can conceive of different cultural periods or even different societal groups as having the kind of early childhood and later adult interpersonal environments that would make their experience of a caring relationship dependent upon quite different behavioral patterns.

We operate within a traditional professional therapist's role that may impose constrictions on us that impede the growth or even the introduction of a caring relationship or a relationship in which the patient and the therapist experience a more open kind of relatedness. As we commit ourselves to humanizing the therapist, where do we draw the line?

Some of the innovative techniques currently in vogue may cater to the needs of the therapist or cater to unexamined needs of all participants. Involvement in some kinds of interactions may be in the service of creating experience but may not be in the service of dealing with the characterological resistances which allow that experience to result in change. Although one may be wary of some of the growth-potential–movement kinds of experience, that does not excuse us from examining the question of how far we go in humanizing the therapist. For example, we might consider the issue of physical contact. The traditional professional role attaches a good deal of prohibition to physical contact between patient and therapist. Why is this so? What does it mean? What consequences does it have for what develops in therapy?

In my own work I have not avoided all physical contact. I have shaken hands with patients, and that is physical contact; I have put my arm around patients; I have kissed patients; I have been kissed! I have held patients, and the holding was mutual. I did these things—particularly initially—with a great deal of anxiety because I was not supposed to, and I felt I was not supposed to. Yet there were many times when I felt such behavior was emotionally appropriate. The dilemma left me very conflicted and distracted. On a number of occasions when I decided to ignore the prohibition, I felt much better. In fact, on some occasions when I decided not to be constrained, I no longer felt the need to do what I had been feeling very much the need to do up to that point. But the therapeutic relationship does not exist for the sake of the gratification of the therapist's needs. However, patients have reported that they felt they responded to such times as these by feeling a letdown in the barriers that they experienced within themselves.

The question of physical contact remains an unresolved one for me. There have been times that contact has been detrimental to the therapeutic process because it has been a response to a transference demand or a countertransference need. However, one might question to what extent the frustration of the transference demand is in the service of the therapist's needs. We cannot resolve the question of what goes on in relationships in which there is demand by saying we stay out of them. That leads us back into the mirror role, which I no longer find a satisfactory kind of therapeutic posture. On the other hand, it is even more dangerous to say you should go ahead and act impulsively and do anything you feel like doing. Either extreme position is an unsatisfactory one to adopt.

A connected issue is to what extent we legitimatize kinds of relatedness, contact, and behavior in therapeutic groups that are not professionally acceptable in one-to-one therapeutic relationships. In the traditional group therapy situation, the therapist justifies the group members gratifying a transference demand that he would avoid responding to. To what extent is this a way of avoiding an anxious situation? To what extent are we neglecting the kind of interaction that ought to go on in a one-to-one relationship because of our commitment to a traditional professional role—the violation of which makes us uneasy—or because of our own anxieties about intimacy? Perhaps we refer patients to groups so that they can get the needed gratification from somebody else. It is interesting in this connection that, contrary to what is expected, we seem to find certain kinds of behavior (nudity, for example) more culturally acceptable in groups than we do in individual therapy.

Another question that arises out of such considerations of the nature of human relationships has to do with the role of self-disclosure. By self-disclosure I do not mean primarily the facts of one's life such as place of birth, age, marital status, and the like, but more importantly, the disclosure of one's immediate experience in the therapeutic transaction. I have heard it said to me often enough, "If only you'd even get angry so I'd know you were feeling something." That seems to mean that it is more important to the patient to know that the therapist responds to him than to elicit a particular kind of response.

Perhaps what we most importantly convey to our patients is not always what we had in mind. I have been surprised on a number of occasions—following what I thought was a good session because I had pulled things together in a cogent, moving, and illuminating way—to have a patient tell me it was a great session because I emptied the ashtray and made him feel that I cared enough for him to get up and do that. I am not content to take such expressions simply at face value and conclude that the patient's experience of a good session was solely a function of my emptying the ashtray; on the other hand, I am not willing to dismiss that as a very important transaction and maybe even the most important transaction.

Often, in revealing our own experience in a therapeutic relationship, what we may be conveying is not so much something about ourselves as the way we feel about the person to whom we are disclosing ourselves. We may be communicating that we feel enough is going on between the two of us for me (therapist) to want to tell you (patient) something about myself, and what I tell you about myself is considerably less important for your own experience in this relationship than the fact that I am telling you something about myself.

In thinking about all kinds of relationships, not simply therapeutic ones, it does seem to me that I do feel closest to people to whom I have disclosed something about myself and with whom I have shared my experience. The feeling of closeness arises out of the self-disclosure and does not precede it. We assume that a person opens up to somebody else because he feels close to him, and to some extent, I am sure that is true. But the very process of revealing oneself to another person creates the experience of closeness in the relationship.

The therapeutic relationship has been compared to marriage in that only the people inside the relationship can really experience what it is like. I think I would describe the therapeutic relationship as like an extramarital affair rather than like a marriage. In the therapeutic relationship there is an exclusive focus on the personalities and interaction of the participants and not on the everyday problems of living. That is what makes extramarital affairs uniquely attractive. Two people may involve themselves in what may be a meaningful relationship, and they do not have to take care of the kids, pay the bills, worry about jobs or the many details of everyday living that married people have to attend to. That makes a difference.

One can note that difference even without having extramarital affairs by examining what happens when a couple goes on a vacation. Their experience with each other tends to be different on a vacation, precisely because the vacation is designed to relieve people of the attention to the everyday concerns of living. But even a vacation rarely relieves a person of these concerns to the extent that an outside relationship sometimes does. This is what we have in some kinds of therapeutic relationships.

The primary concern of both patient and therapist is with the relationship itself. This can facilitate an intense experience of intimacy and closeness, which may result in unusual openness and alleviation of interpersonal anxieties. However, these attitudes are often not sustained when the patient leaves the therapeutic environment and goes back to the maintenance of relationships in the face of the everyday demands of living. This raises the question of the effect the circumscribed nature of the therapeutic relationship may have on the experience of caring and on the experience of intimacy in therapy.

I realize I have raised questions in this paper and not given answers. I make no apology for this. I hope it is clear that I am not advocating "touch-y-feel-y" psychotherapy as opposed to a more traditional examination and analysis of behavior. However, I do feel quite concerned about some of the issues that are raised in expanding the limits of the therapist's role in the therapeutic experience. At this point in our understanding of human experience and our experience of relationships in particular, I think that our state of knowledge is best represented by questions rather than answers.

REFERENCES

1. Basescu, S.: Human nature and psychotherapy: An existential view. *Rev. Existential Psychol. Psychiat.*, 2:149, 1962.
2. Binswanger, L.: *Being-in-the-World.* New York, Basic Books, 1963.
3. Boss, M.: *Psychoanalysis & Daseinsanalysis.* New York, Basic Books, 1963.
4. Deese, J.: Behavior and fact. *Amer. Psychol.*, 24:517-518, 1969.
5. Ellis, A.: *Reason and Emotion in Psychotherapy.* New York, Lyle Stuart, 1963.
6. Farber, L.: *The Ways of the Will.* New York, Basic Books, 1966.
7. Hersch, C.: The discontent explosion in mental health. *Amer. Psychol.*, 23:504, 1968.
8. Laing, R.: *The Politics of Experience.* New York, Pantheon, 1967.
9. Rogers, C.: The process equation of psychotherapy. *Amer. J. Psychother.*, 15:27-45, 1961.
10. Whitaker, C., and Malone, T.: *The Roots of Psychotherapy.* New York, Blakiston, 1953.

In RECENT years there has been increasing emphasis on the dichotomy within our culture between the humanistic and scientific forces in effect. Many of man's problems are indicated as arising from this dualism. Theoretical conceptions of man's needs and inability to actualize these needs within our society have multiplied, and consequent to this there has developed an increasing emphasis on new approaches to solve modern man's dilemma. Dr. Denes also looks at the problem of our cultural conflicts and traces the threads that led her to the conclusion that there was a cultural conflict. However, her brilliant analysis of the mainstreams of our society, drawing on the wellsprings of diverse sources including history, philosophy, psychology, and literature, enables her to arrive at her own synthesis and interpretation. She concludes—and with considerable evidence—that the major emphasis in present-day society is a scientific one.

As part of her analysis of the issues we face she has outlined the broad differences between more traditional approaches to psychotherapy and the Gestalt technique. With the broad panorama of both cultural and technical theory as a background setting she clearly delineates in center stage the concrete aspects of Gestalt approaches that focus on dealing with neurosis. Thus, her paper is an original synthesis of the Gestalt approaches and their relevance in dealing with the issues that confront mankind in modern society.

G.D.G.
D.S.M.

Chapter 7

THE CONTEXT OF PSYCHOTHERAPEUTIC INNOVATIONS: A GESTALT THERAPIST'S VIEW

MAGDA DENES-RADOMISLI

GESTALT THERAPY[6] is an essentially humanistic and existential movement rooted in the firm belief that man is basically a forward-striving, growth-seeking, self-regulating, and self-affirming organism who is in possession of inherent progressive potentialities which, in a state of health, he is capable of fulfilling with excitement and joy. Conversely, neurosis and psychosis in Gestalt therapy are understood to be emergency measures—in a sense also creative—on the part of the organism in the service of meeting catastrophic situations.

Man, then, is seen both in health and in illness as striver, as actor, as chooser, and as doer. Therefore, what distinguishes health from illness is the *direction* in which these activities take place, the *locus* where the activity occurs, and the *consciousness* with which the activity is chosen and affirmed. Man in health is in possession of his faculties. He is in readiness for contact with the stimuli affecting him at any given time (both extroceptive and proprioceptive). He is capable of sensing his internal and external environment; he forms periodic and adequate Gestalten through easily accessible and directed awareness of himself and of his world. Man in health is vital, immediate, spontaneous, authentic, and active. Rather than truncating his own powers, he creatively confronts his milieu and makes it yield him satisfactions that are further food for his continuing growth.

Unfortunately, man in health does not exist. The catastrophic situation does. Gestalt therapy then is the arduous and optimistic attempt to help man to recapture his own nature so that he may fulfill what is potentially his privileged grandeur.

I say the catastrophic situation does exist because it is my contention—by no means unique to me or even to Gestalt thinking—that we live in and are witness to a disintegrating culture in which the human state itself has become neurotic. Let me for a moment examine this proposition. A great deal has been said of late about a chasm in the culture introduced by the Industrial Revolution, which is said to have divided society into two conflicting and, to each other, hostile factions, whose difference centers around the image of man. One group, representing what is called "traditional culture," is said to be comprised of literary men, other intellectuals, and artists; the other group is said to consist of the scientists, both the pure scientist and the technician.

Each culture (the general-humanistic and the scientific) is in possession of a private language, unintelligible and, in any case, uninteresting to the other. Each presumably has its distinctive tools: the scientists, specialized tools aimed at mastery and manipulation of mostly the world of matter; the artists, intellectuals, and literary men, general tools aimed at representation and manipulation of mostly the world of spirit. Each seemingly lives within the confines of a characteristic status hierarchy and each holds idiosyncratic moral commitments that reflect great divergence on such a variety of issues as, for example, religion, the nature of man, the good life, and time-space perception and orientation, to name a few. This rift, this division, is the factor generally held accountable for the fragmentation of our society, with its attendant psychosocioeconomic and political troubles.

Now, among those who more or less seriously address themselves to this chasm, it is possible to delineate three kinds of generally held attitudes. First there is the primarily proscience, not expressly scientist group, typified by C. P. Snow,[8] whose remarkably nearsighted solution is that of appeasement by *reductio ad absurdum* and rapprochement through cross-education. In other words, he says that if only we would train our scientists in the humanities and our humanists in the sciences, we could reintegrate society and therefore people into a functional whole.

The second position, held in the opposing camp by a small number of very serious and committed artists and thinkers, is one of profound pessimism. While they subscribe to the existence of two cultures, they tend to feel that the humanistic culture is increasingly less influential, less fitting, and less appreciated. They believe that the arts and the intellect, in the humanistic sense, have been permanently defeated; that, whereas there might have been a chance to do battle against nineteenth century industrialization, twentieth century automation has definitely won. They may protest, but essentially they appear resigned to their own impending obsolescence.

The third position, whose most eloquent spokesman is the critic Susan Sontag,[9] advances the novel proposition that the conflict between the two cultures is in fact by now mere illusion. There is only *one* culture, the scientific one, and what we are witnessing is not a clash of cultures but a clash between *the* culture and the archaic sensibilities of a small segment of stick-in-the-mud artists, intellectuals, and humanists. As she puts it, and I quote: ". . . the 20th century intellectuals who talk of modern society as being in some new way incomprehensible, 'alienated,' are inevitably on the defensive. They know that the scientific culture, the coming of the machine, cannot be stopped." She goes on to say that, for example, the artists' concern has unquestionably ceased to be moral commentary or social criticism. The artist today "programs" mass senses. There is a new, unitary sensibility in the culture, based entirely on a mechanical model.

Now, of the three positions, I think Miss Sontag's is the most valid. I do believe that there is only one culture—the scientific-technological one (except for single bewildered voices opposing it here and there, the sum total of which can no longer be regarded as constituting any appreciable force; and also they *are* on the defensive). However, the meaning of the existence—for the first time in history—of the single culture is what I think needs reevaluation.

Now although the cultural chasm is ascribed to the influence of the Industrial Revolution, the truth of the matter is that, on examining history, one finds that men have held conflicting views about their own nature from the beginning of time. Bertrand Russell,[7] for example, in the introduction to his *History of*

Western Philosophy, delineates two distinct philosophical trends that in somewhat varying forms persist through the ages, and he dates their emergence back to sixth century B.C. Greece, prior even to the rise of what we traditionally recognize today as philosophy. The two categories he posits are represented: on one side by those philosophers whose aim has been to tighten social bonds, who have been sympathetic to some form of dogma, and who have to some degree been hostile to science and in tune with the more irrational parts of human nature; and on the other side by those philosophers whose aim has been to relax social bonds, whose sympathies have been directed toward the utilitarian, the scientific, away from the violent passions, and who have stood hostile to all of the more profound forms of religion.

Clearly, each of these philosophical trends represents the outcome of certain basic, underlying assumptions and presuppositions about man and his possibilities. Whether one opts for the tightening or relaxing of social bonds, for example, will depend on whether one sees man as primarily a creature of reason, or primarily a creature of passion. It will also depend on *where* one places one's values regarding man being either one or the other type of creature; in other words, which type of creature one regards as preferable.

Contrary then to the discussions of late, I am positing that with the Industrial Revolution there came a major, unifying cultural influence pushing western civilization toward a particular, unified direction—its own. We are not witnessing a clashing of cultures but a gradual obliteration of different views. Man is no longer to be seen from this and that angle, too; his destiny is no longer to be pondered by himself. His conclusions must not be various anymore. Science and its technical transmutation, the machine, provide the model answers. So art and the machine become tied up, music and engineering marry, the computer becomes the psychoanalyst, and at a slight fee it even acts as matchmaker these days.

Marshall McLuhan,[5] in his book *Understanding Media,* calls modern media the extensions of man. I think this is a very good point. What he fails to say, however, is that what has happened is that man, in western civilization in particular, has overextended himself. The concept of overextension is familiar to all of us. It is also familiar to the layman who refers to it by saying that someone "has bitten off more than he can chew."

Overextension in personality occurs when self-challenge unreasonably exceeds ability. To take risks is the mark of a healthy person; but to take risks beyond one's utmost power, outside one's remotest possibility, is to expose oneself to demands of such magnitude that the personality is put in danger of tearing through —stretching beyond size.

Kurt Goldstein has defined anxiety as the reaction that arises from the discrepancy between environmental challenge and the individual's ability to cope. He terms the resultant condition of such discrepancy "catastrophic reaction." From another angle, in Gestalt theory, anxiety is thought of as throttled excitement. When an organism is unable, by virtue of the discrepancy between its powers and the task, to confront the task with freedom and excitement (qualities which always accompany creative confrontation), the organism must truncate itself, cut its own powers, behave retroflectively rather than act. The result of this self-interruption is anxiety.

This, then, is what I think to be true of contemporary Western civilization: man, through his technological media and its attendant systems, has overextended himself to the point where he is no longer able to meet his self-imposed challenges; consequently, he is in a state that properly can only be termed catastrophic. It is this phenomenon that underlies the age of anxiety, the age of *anomie,* the age of alienation. Overextension of the civilization means that man's powers and his nature are no longer adequate to the demands of his productions. Thus, for example, levels of abstraction keep shifting upward, not only in matters of thought but in matters of the senses as well. Buckminster Fuller,[4] in dealing with this dilemma, has written:

> In World War I industries suddenly went from the visible to the invisible base, from the track to the trackless, from the wire to the wireless, from visible structuring to invisible structuring in alloys. The big thing about World War I is that man went off the sensorial spectrum forever as the prime criterion of accrediting innova-

tions. . . .All major advances since World War I have been in the infra- and ultra-sensorial frequencies of the electromagnetic spectrum. All the important technical affairs of man today are invisible. . . . The old masters, who were sensorialists, have unleashed a Pandora's box of non-sensorially controlled phenomena, which they have avoided accrediting up to that time. . . .Suddenly they lost their true mastery, because from then on they didn't personally understand what was going on. If you don't understand, you cannot master. . . .

One can also speculate, in this connection, as to whether the new drug cult among the young (and old), with its consciousness-expanding aims, perhaps really represents a desperate and doomed attempt not, as they claim, to do battle against the machine, but simply to keep up with it. Perhaps the recent proliferation of interest in the occult is really a testimony to the fact that man has succumbed to his helplessness in relation to his world. He can no longer consider his own nature as the proper locus of his powers. Things have become too vast for that, too invisible, too incomprehensible, too much beyond control. I say that it is from a mystifying technology and automation that this new, contaminated rebellion toward the mystic stems.

Throughout history man has turned to magic at those points when he has become terrified at the sight of the discrepancy between his nature and his fate. However, magic is as distant from and as degrading to man's wholeness as his machine models are, and so the hoped-for avenue of escape becomes a trap in disguise —a futile promise of power beyond merit, of strength beyond balance, of discipline beyond effort.

I regard these examples as symptoms of a declining age in which human organisms live under conditions that are so unfit for their nature that their inherent self-regulatory processes become impaired and their possibilities for self-fulfillment are hopelessly thwarted, conditions under which men are deprived of the opportunity (though hopefully not yet of the capacity) for creative action in the realms of their concerns. The result of such conditions is always symptom formation on an epidemic scale.

I am saying that what is happening to us is not altogether new; it is just worse. The Romans, for example, in the latter days of their empire watched, as we watch, the defection of the led from the leaders; they watched, as we watch, the vulgarization and decline of style in art, in clothing, in manners, and in education; they saw the boundaries between form and content merge; they saw the debasement of people into objects (I am thinking here of the gladiator plays then and "happenings" now) ; and they watched, as we watch, the increasing torpor of life, when the best hopes were pinned on revolutionary movements against the established order but which, since they were contaminated by that order, ended in truancy and promiscuity and a fateful sense of drift.

One could go on enlarging the parallel and enumerating the common symptoms of both eras, but I want to turn to a very alarming and exclusively modern phenomenon, and this will be my final, my last consideration of the culture. I wish to consider here three different but closely interrelated and, in practice, inseparable trends in the culture that I believe—in combination—seriously affect contemporary sanity. The first is the sudden proliferation of communication without real content; the second is the arbitrary fabrication of behavioral models without reference to actual persons—in other words, "image-making" or "image-projecting"; and the third is the resultant repression or denial of these cleavages between description and reality and between image and man.

I am using the word "image" here exclusively with reference to its popular meaning. I am using it to mean that fictional entity which is the product of advertising "brainstorms," the product of deliberately calculated verbal and visual distortions, which are willfully communicated to the masses with the conscious intent of achieving a desired aim, be it the sale of merchandise or the acceptance and approbation (not infrequently also referred to as "sale") of an individual, a group, an idea, or an event. Thus we have a national image, a public image, a presidential image, a housewife image, a hip image, ad infinitum. Now whatever an image is, the one thing it is not is real. It is, however, a composite fantasy, a verbal invention; it is an agreement on no degrees of freedom; it is an education in unreality; it is a fabricated mechanical model. It is based on a language that has lost its function of communication through meaning and is instead molded as far as possible into evocative symbols that elicit conditioned responses.

Whether we laugh at jokes such as, "My son, the doctor, is drowning," or weep that it is possible for today's press to focus on the Vietnamese war in terms of its giving us "a bad national image," or simply gasp incredulously at the fact that the only people in the world who suffer from constipation are beautiful females in evening gowns (or so our magazines lead us to believe), one crucial conclusion inescapably emerges; namely, that what we say and what actually exists has come to be disconnected, disjoined, separated, on a scale, and in matters of such variety and importance, that is unprecedented in history.

We are not dealing with mere suppression of information or simple distortion of facts, both of which are characteristic of all coercive political systems where there is a rift between the governed and the leaders. Propaganda is not a new vice. What is new, however, is the large-scale organized construction of behavioral models without reference to human beings. What is new is the sudden supremacy of words, the sanction of emphasis on communication, with full or partial knowledge that what is being communicated has no recognizable referent in reality. One is reminded of Camus' judge-penitent in *The Fall*,[3] who confesses: "Thus I progressed on the surface of life, in the realm of words, as it were, never in reality."

What these trends amount to is the emergence of the shaping of human consciousness toward a new style of being. Image and imagination are divorced. Man is no longer required or able to define himself and to create his world through the use of his own imagination. That function is now obsolete. Technology takes it over, prefabricating set images whose relation to human meaning is purely technical. The projected image (visual and verbal) is a manufactured product, it is marketable, and it is forged into a model. Under such conditions, man is no longer the source of his destiny and his creative vision; his transcending imagination, his readiness for action—in short, his best powers become alien to him.

It is in this context then that we therapists ply our trade, in this context that we must examine and reexamine our patient population, our traditional criteria of organismic health, and our methods of aiding persons in achieving it. Gestalt therapy is the outcome of such reexamination.

Let me then describe some of its salient features. As I said in my introduction, Gestalt therapy is firmly planted in the conviction that the human organism is forward-striving, self-regulating, and self-actualizing. The traditional Freudian assumption of the presence of inherent regressive tendencies in the organism is emphatically denied. Pathology then is *not* viewed as the result of a faulty reconciliation between inherent regressive strivings and reality demands; it is viewed as a compromise—to some measure creative, but unlucky—between inherently expansive strivings and the constrictions that reality imposes. Pathology then comprises the difference between what one is and what one might have become.

It is curious to note in this connection that Arieti[2] points out in a paper on manic-depressive psychosis, using Riessman's concept of "inner and outer directed," that in our outer-directed society, where the individual is no longer in control, manic-depressive psychosis is on the decline. Ackerman,[1] in a paper entitled "The Cultural Factor in Psychoanalytic Treatment," makes the corollary point that there is a contemporary shift toward a higher incidence of character disorders, presumably based on social compliance.

Most broadly stated, the goal of treatment in Gestalt therapy is to help the patient to recover those aspects of himself that have become alienated and lost during his battle with oppressive reality. The major tool toward this end is awareness, and the only possible starting point toward it is the *here* and *now*.

Gestalt therapy, therefore, is primarily focused on the phenomenology of the patient. Formulations about the patient based on theoretical considerations are replaced with phenomenological observation and description of the patient in the here and now by both therapist and patient.

It is assumed that the microcosm of the therapy session relevantly reflects the patient's habitual modes of dealing with himself and with another. The interaction, therefore, between patient and therapist is of primary concern. What I mean by this is that the bully will bully his therapist and the flatterer will flatter him. Those who swagger, swagger into the therapy room, and the bore will not spare his doctor.

The first subject of scrutiny then is all the stylistic messages the patient unawarely sends, the sum total of which add up to his characteristic mode of being. It is this mode which contains the neurotic (or for that matter, the psychotic, if that is the case) symptoms, the results of failed conquests of reality, the compromises, the alienations, and the self-curtailments. It is this mode, therefore, that needs altering. One technique of alteration in Gestalt therapy is that of confrontation, as opposed to the more traditional method of interpretation.

Traditionally, interpretation has been a rationalistic exposition offered by the analyst to the patient, based on the analyst's understanding and conceptualization of the patient's resistances and of the reason, usually instinctual conflict, for these resistances. Confrontation, on the other hand, is an attempt to bring the patient face-to-face with his own characterological modes. The emphasis shifts from *why* to *how* and *what*.

Confrontation neither analyzes character nor traces its historic origins. Rather it forcefully disrupts character with the aim of bringing the disruption into sharp focus and immediate awareness. Such disruption, of course, especially in the beginning of treatment, tends to elicit violent resistance, frequently accompanied by bewilderment or rage. Again, the resistance is not interpreted, but the patient is confronted once more with his new mode of being, his *here* and *now*, and this time is made aware of his rage or bewilderment or what have you.

This may sound to you like an endless sequence and it could be that, except that in practice, at one point or another, the patient catches on, has what has been referred to as an "Aha" reaction, and becomes genuinely interested in and excited by —himself. At this point he begins, to some extent, to take over the therapist's role in relation to himself. The neurotic feeling of emptiness disappears because he now has a vital field toward which to direct his concentration. The experience of emptiness itself becomes a mode of being. The questions, *What* am I doing?, *How* am I doing it?, *What* good or bad thing does what I am doing get me?, and so forth become relevant. Confrontation, then, is not knowledge imparted about the patient by the analyst; rather, it is a technique whereby the patient learns to learn about himself.

As is implied in the foregoing, the concept of transference is also seen differently in Gestalt therapy than in traditional analytic thought. From the orthodox point of view, transference is the reliving—in the therapeutic situation—on the part of the patient of his early interactions with significant figures. In other words, the patient reacts to the therapist as if he were someone from the past. Since the analyst keeps his own personality out of the therapeutic situation—insofar as is possible,—the projection of another personality onto him becomes inviting. The full-scale development of this projection is termed "transference neurosis," which is then analyzed in the traditional analytic fashion.

By contrast, what characterizes the Gestalt therapist in the therapeutic situation is his concentrated presence. Far from being a blank, he makes explicit use of his personality. A major part of his therapeutic tools are, in fact, not concepts, but his own reactions and experience in the therapeutic encounter. He acts both as catalyst (in the sense of precipitating reactions that might otherwise not occur) and as anchor (in the sense that he allows the patient insight into his own, that is the therapist's, relatedness to reality. Transference reactions, therefore, are treated as distorted reality perceptions in the *here* and *now,* whose resistive aims can and diligently must be uncovered through confrontation and experimentation.

Experimentation is a second technique, and I want to say a word here about its role in Gestalt therapy. Suppose, for example, that a patient comes in and I greet him with a friendly smile. He responds to the smile with a frown and says, "You are laughing at me." The first thing I will do is examine his proposition. Maybe he is right. On reaffirming that he is not, that I am in fact not laughing at him but smiling in a friendly fashion, or at any rate that I *was* smiling in a friendly fashion; as I say, on reaffirming this fact, I am left with a number of possible experimental avenues open to me. I may, for example, ask him to laugh at me; I may ask him to laugh at himself; I may ask him to imitate my laughing at him; I may ask him to please act ridiculous so that I may laugh at him; or I may end up asking all four in succession.

Now, although these requests represent different categories of possible experience for the patient and emanate from different assumptions on my part as to where his distortion originates, in practical terms it does not matter which request I choose to make. This is so for various reasons. It is so because whichever experiment I suggest, what I am after is the increase in the patient's awareness of the meaning to him of being laughed at. Whether he becomes aware of this meaning in the active mode through a reversal of his original experience (as when I ask him to laugh at me) or in the passive mode through recovery of the projection (as when I ask him to laugh at himself) matters little. What does matter is that he catch—that he experience his own emotional, muscular, and ideational state in relation to his original comment.

Also, whichever experiment is performed, it acts as a springboard for further experimental exploration. Although I said earlier that I might ask the patient to act out all four versions, in practice, most likely the first version (whichever one that may be) would suggest a new experiment which would allow the patient to contact his emerging experience of self in a more precise yet expanded way.

By saying that the therapist is free to choose from a variety of interchangeable experiments, I do not mean to imply that the experiments are evolved at random. They are inventions, but they must be organically rooted in the phenomenal field and in the analyst's intuitive and intellectual effort.

Since we assume that neurosis represents something "lost" in human nature, we devise experiments for its recovery. Incidentally, there are eighteen standard experiments in Gestalt therapy, all carefully designed for the mobilization and recovery of various alienated aspects of the self. However, since they are excellently and in great detail described in Fritz Perls' book,[6] there is no need for me to review them here.

A word about dream interpretation: Traditionally dream interpretation has been considered "the royal road to the unconscious," enabling the analyst to understand primarily the nature of drive derivatives and secondarily the nature of the counterforces that oppose the consciousness of these drive derivatives. In Gestalt therapy the dream is considered an existential message whose primary function is that of communicating to the dreamer his unaware, internal, experiential state.

Also, dreams are not interpreted. Instead, the patient is asked to act out every portion of his dream, with the assumption that each portion, be it mood or prop or person, is a projection and represents an alienated aspect of the dreamer's self. Through the acting out of these portions the patient is again dramatically confronted with lost aspects of himself that are novel to him and through whose recovery he is enabled to reintegrate at a higher level of functioning.

In conclusion, allow me to restate the goals of treatment in Gestalt therapy. They are, as I have said, to help the patient to recover those aspects of himself that have become alienated and lost during his battle with oppressive reality; to help the patient recover a sense of himself as an organism with the potentials of relevant action and genuine choice; to help the patient move from a sense of helplessness to self-support, from loneliness to a true acknowledgment of his aloneness as a human being, from self-throttling to a lustily aggressive confrontation of the world; to help him progress from his sense of meaninglessness and depression to the affirmation of himself as man—tragic and dignified.

REFERENCES

1. Ackerman, N. W.: The cultural factor in psychoanalytic treatment. *Bull. Amer. Psychoanal. Assoc.*, 7:319, 1951.
2. Arieti, S.: Manic-depressive psychosis. In Arieti, S. (Ed.): *Amer- Handbook of Psychiatry*. New York, Basic Books, 1959, Vol. I, p. 22.
3. Camus, A.: *The Fall*. New York, Knopf, 1957.
4. Fuller, B., quoted by Sontag, Susan: *Against Interpretation*. New York, Dell, 1961.

5. McLuhan, M.: *Understanding Media: The Extensions of Man.* New York, Signet Books, 1964.
6. Perls, F. S., Hefferline, R. F., and Goodman, P.: *Gestalt Therapy.* New York, The Sulian Press, 1951.
7. Russell, B.: *A History of Western Philosophy.* New York, Simon & Schuster, 1945.
8. Snow, C. P.: *The Two Cultures: And a Second Look.* New York, Cambridge University Press, 1964.
9. Sontag, Susan: *Against Interpretation.* New York, Dell, 1961.

DR. ALEXANDER LOWEN, by his extensive publications and through the many workshops which he has given throughout the United States, has attempted to familiarize the professional community with his concepts of bioenergetic analysis. His theories are "an extension and substantiation of the body-mind concepts developed by Wilhelm Reich."

In this chapter Dr. Lowen further explains the areas where he feels his theories and techniques can be most helpful, particularizing their efficacy as more beneficial for characterological problems than conventional analytic techniques. He contends that one must avoid the sterility of language and deal directly with feelings bottled up in the body of his patient, and thereby most effectively change very difficult-to-treat patients. In this exposition of Reichian theory, followed by his modifications of it, he provides his readers with the background necessary to understand his techniques and the reasons for their effectiveness. His translation of body language into personality descriptions is a truly fascinating conceptualization of complex material. Communication with one's body is the guiding principle of his theory of bioenergetic analysis. Since he feels that pleasure and joy depend upon good body feelings, a step towards mental health following Dr. Lowen's dictates, in these times of stress throughout the world, would include a soundness of the body as a basic requirement.

The paper consists mainly of his philosophy and as such is an excellent background for understanding some of his techniques. He illustrates one of the technical approaches in this paper with a remarkable case history exemplifying the advantages of encouraging a patient to scream. He theorizes that screaming "produces a total and unified body awareness." For those therapists who have found their conventional approaches less than successful, and for those with experimental inclination, Dr. Lowen recommends his therapeutic approach, which he feels "helps the character problems untouched by other methods."

G.D.G.
D.S.M.

Chapter 8

BIOENERGETIC ANALYSIS:
A DEVELOPMENT OF REICHIAN THERAPY

Alexander Lowen

THE CURRENT INTEREST in the body on the part of many psycho-therapists is laregly due to the growing influence of bioen-ergetic analysis. Through my writings and through the workshops which my associates and I have conducted at Esalen Institute and elsewhere, there has developed an increasing awareness of the need to incorporate immediate body experience in the thera-peutic situation. A large number of the procedures currently used by therapists working with the body are based on the principles of bioenergetic analysis. These principles provide the most rational explanation for the direct involvement of the body in the thera-peutic endeavor.

Bioenergetic analysis is an extension and systematization of the body-mind concepts developed by Wilhelm Reich. The fun-damental thesis underlying Reichian therapy is the functional identity of muscular armoring and character armoring or of an in-dividual's bodily attitude and his ego structure. This concept of physical and psychological unity allows a therapist to diagnose personality disturbances from the expression and motility of the body. One can, for example, recognize an "uptight" person from his bodily posture. This approach to the personality through the body is not new. Every person sees another as a body; that is, he has a picture of the other in which bodily form, movement, and gesture convey significant information about the other. Reich, however, was the first to integrate this information into the an-alytic procedure.

A second basic Reichian concept relates the inhibition of emo-tional responsiveness to the restriction of respiration. As early as

1935 Reich had observed that resistance to the analytic process was manifested physically by an unconscious holding of the breath. When the patient was encouraged to breathe deeply, his resistance fell apart, resulting in a flood of repressed material together with its accompanying affect or feeling. This observation led Reich to the realization that emotional responsiveness is dependent on the respiratory function. By limiting his oxygen intake a person reduces the metabolic process of his body and effectively depresses his energy level. Banking the metabolic fires cools the passions of the body. Children seem to know that holding the breath cuts off painful feelings and suppresses threatening impulses.

Apart from its effect upon metabolism, limiting respiration also restricts the natural motility of the body. The respiratory movements flow like a wave over the body, moving upward in inspiration and downward in expiration. These movements, which constitute the matrix for emotional expression, are blocked by chronic muscular tensions mainly in the throat, chest, diaphragm, and abdomen. The throat tension results from the inhibition of vocal expression. It constitutes an unconsciousness repression of impulses to cry, scream, and shout. Chronic tensions in the chest wall are closely associated with muscular spasticities in the shoulder girdle, which hold back the reaching out with the arms. Thoracic rigidity suppresses the feelings of longing for love which would seek expression in crying out and reaching out. These feelings are suppressed because repeated disappointments in childhood have made them too painful. Muscular tension or spasticity in any part of the body affects one's breathing because breathing is a total body activity. A set jaw or a tight ass reduce the respiratory movements and restrict the respiratory intake.

Broadly speaking, it can be said that if these tensions are predominantly in the superficial muscles of the body, the result is an overall rigidity that is both physical and psychological. When the main muscular tensions involve the deep and small muscles that surround the joints, the result is a flaccidity and fragmentation. These produce a loss of integrity on both the physical and psychological levels. Bioenergetic therapy aims to release the chronic muscular spasticities of the body and to restore, thereby, the natural motility and expressiveness of the organism.

The third basic tenet of Reichian therapy deals with the role of sexual fulfillment in regulating the energy economy of the body. Reich postulated that full orgastic gratification discharged all the excess energy of the organism and so left no energy available to support neurotic patterns of behavior. He recognized that this discharge fails to occur when energy is bound in chronic muscular tensions and that these must be eliminated if full orgasm is to be achieved. It was his belief that if an individual developed the capacity to discharge all his excess energy through orgasm—that is, if he became orgastically potent—this would guarantee his emotional health since there would be no energy available for neurotic attitudes. Orgastic potency thus became the goal of Reichian therapy and the criterion of emotional well-being.

These three concepts constitute the framework of Reich's character-analytic vegetotherapy, and they have become the foundation, with some important modifications, of bioenergetic analysis. Reich, however, moved further afield in his pursuance of his interest in the energetic processes of life. He developed the concept of orgone energy, which he called the special life energy. He did some work in cancer research where, I believe, he made important contributions. He investigated many physical phenomena in terms of his orgone energy theories. This development led him to change the name of his therapeutic approach to orgone therapy.

Bioenergetic analysis proceeded in a different direction. It focused all its attention upon the bodily functions, with the aim to integrate bodily processes and psychic phenomena in a more comprehensive way than Reich had done. The result is a deeper understanding of personality disturbances and the development of more effective techniques for treating these disturbances.

A good illustration of the effectiveness of bioenergetic techniques is the treatment of depression. Cinematic studies have shown that motility is markedly reduced in the depressed individual. Our observations clearly indicate that respiration is also severely limited in this disturbance. The effect of this reduction in the basic biological processes of the body is a decrease in emotional responsiveness. Ignoring for a moment whatever psychological factors are operative in this condition, the fact remains that any procedure that stimulates breathing and augments the body's motility must lift the person out of his depressed state. Using the special techniques of bioenergetic analysis it is often possible to produce a fairly quick temporary improvement in these basic functions. The result is often astonishing to the patient who had no idea that what he viewed as a mental disturbance was intimately and directly connected with the body's activities.

This immediate release from depression is only temporary since the dynamic factors that create a depressive tendency in the patient are still untouched. It can be anticipated, therefore, that depression will recur. Consequently, I advise these patients that recurrence is probable. But having experienced the release, they also know that continued work to improve the breathing and motility of the body will overcome the tendency to depression.

What is this tendency? I may surprise you when I say that depression occurs when an illusion that the patient entertained collapses. These illusions, which are just under the surface of consciousness, have the function of sustaining the spirit against an underlying feeling of despair. A child's mind cannot accept parental rejection and disapproval. It conceives the idea that the love which is not forthcoming could be earned by good behavior, success, achievements, intelligence, cuteness, and so forth. This leads to the illusion that if one could be different, everything might work out. The child rejects his own nature, his feelings, and his way of being to fulfill an ego image which was imposed by the demands of his parents.

The tendency to depression is based on the rejection and denial of the self and the attempt to gain approval by being what someone else wants. No matter how much acclaim one gets for success or achievement, it is not an adequate substitute for love. Love accepts the other wholeheartedly, without conditions or demands. The primary illusion is that one can earn this love. It is an illusion because a love that has to be earned is not true love. The illusion collapses when one senses that the goal is meaningless and the struggle was futile. Even without fully understanding what is happening, the individual gives up all effort and becomes depressed. Every depression indicates that a person has reached a position of "What's the use?" It signifies a return to the original despair, reinforced now by the failure of the conscious endeavor.

The sequence of despair, effort, failure, and depression must be worked through psychologically so that a patient can gain an understanding of the vicious circle in which he is trapped. I have found, however, that this understanding is generally incapable of overcoming the depressive tendency without a reversal of the self-rejection and self-denial that powers this tendency. To achieve this reversal, one must remove a secondary illusion—to the effect that one's attitudes are subject to ego control. Another aspect of this illusion equates the self with the mind and the ego image and ignores the body as the basis of one's being in the world. As we get older we realize that the ego is not master of the body. In our youth it had driven the body relentlessly in pursuit of its goals, and now the tired body cannot go on. We are beset with illness and we have a premonition of death. We feel somehow that we missed the boat. The pleasure and joy of living escaped us. We feel helpless and, again, a feeling of "What's the use?" overwhelms us. We become depressed.

The person who lives in terms of his body does not get depressed. He knows that pleasure and joy depend on good body feelings, and he is sufficiently in touch with his body to sense their absence and to take appropriate measures to restore them. He is aware of his bodily tensions; he knows that as long as they persist, they condition and determine his emotional responsiveness. Being in touch with the body means being in touch with reality, the basic reality of one's mode of existence. He has no illusions about himself or about life. He accepts his feelings as an expression of his personality, and he has no difficulty in voicing them. When a person can return to this way of being, the depressive tendency is eliminated. He may be disappointed and feel sad about events of his life, but he will not collapse into depression.

Being in touch with one's body is the guiding principle of bioenergetic analysis. The more emotionally disturbed a person is, the more out of touch he is with his body. Bioenergetic analysis attempts to bring a patient into contact with the fundamental relationships of his existence, his relationship to the ground on which he stands and his relationship to the gaseous environment in which he functions. The quality of contact between the feet and the ground determines how well grounded an individual is, whether his feet are firmly planted or whether he is "up in the air," whether he stands on his own feet or is a dependent person needing the support of others. Most patients soon become aware that they do not feel that their feet are fully in contact with the ground. Some even say that they are standing on their knees. But not to know how one stands is equivalent to not knowing where one stands or to having no standing as a person.

Poor contact with the ground is caused by chronic muscular tensions in the feet, in the legs, in the pelvic girdle, and throughout the rest of the body. High arches and narrow feet indicate a pulling away from the ground. Flat feet and collapsed arches signify an inability to move over the ground, or away from the ground. In addition to these tension areas one often finds chronic spasticities in the muscles of the legs and thighs, the calves, the hamstrings, abductors, and others. Each of these chronic tensions reflect a limitation of movement, and, by extension, represents a limitation of expression and of the self. Each has a history which must be elucidated psychologically if the tension is to be released.

The ground is always interpreted as a symbol for the mother. Ground equals earth equals mother is a basic concept of bioenergetic analysis. The way a person stands tells us much about his early relationship to his mother. The insecurity of that relationship becomes transferred to an insecurity in standing and becomes the basic insecurity of life.

The other major relationship is to the air, and the quality of that relationship is reflected in one's breathing. The air or breath is equivalent to the spirit, it is the pneuma of ancient religions, a symbol of the divine power residing in God, the father figure. Breathing is an aggressive act in that inspiration is an active process. The body sucks in the air. The way one breathes manifests one's feeling about his right to get what he wants from life. In breathing we are identified with the male principle, the active or aggressive principle of life. This concept shows the broad base upon which bioenergetic analysis rests. With this concept it is possible in many cases to analyze a person's relationship to his own father.

There are several kinds of respiratory disturbances that relate to personality function. Two are important enough to describe in this presentation. In the schizoid and schizophrenic patient, for example, one quickly finds that the chest is depressed in the expiratory position. Breathing in is severely constricted, as if the muscles of the chest walls, the diaphragm, and the throat were partially paralyzed. Actually in these patients there is a partial paralysis of all autonomic and involuntary functions of the body. This partial paralysis is related to a state of terror which is mainly unconscious in the schizoid patient but rises to consciousness in the schizophrenic. I have described these aspects of schizoid functioning in my book, *The Betrayal of the Body*.[1]

In the neurotic, on the other hand, one finds that the chest is held in the inspiratory position. It is generally overinflated and the patient has difficulty in breathing out fully. He holds on to the air as a security measure. Breathing out deeply often provokes a feeling of panic as if he would not be able to get more air. He holds in whereas the schizoid individual just holds on. In both cases working with the patient's breathing soon uncovers his basic anxieties and furthers the psychological working through of these anxieties.

This distinction between schizoid and neurotic breathing is not absolute. It is, in fact, no more absolute than the distinction between schizoid and neurotic behavior. What one can say is that a restricted inspiration denotes a schizoid tendency in the personality, whereas restricted expiration denotes a neurotic tendency. And even this distinction is less important than the fact that the patient is not breathing freely and fully.

It is beyond the scope of this presentation to describe the

bioenergetic techniques used to free the respiratory function from the chronic muscular tensions that restrict it. One of these techniques, however, merits some attention. It involves the use of the voice. The range and quality of sound production is a measure of personality. The word personality is derived from the expression per sona which means "by sound." By his sound you can recognize a person, and by the sounds he utters you can know what a person is feeling. Persons who are inhibited in crying, shouting, and screaming are restricted in their breathing by the tensions that block these expressions. Getting a patient to cry or to scream is one of the most effective ways of releasing the blocked emotion and freeing the respiratory function. Screaming can often be provoked by selective pressure on the anterior scalene muscles while the patient is making a sustained sound. The involuntary scream sends a flow of feeling through the body from the top of the head to the bottom of the feet and produces a total and unified body awareness.

Whatever the personality problem, it is reflected in a disturbance of the flow of feeling in the body. This flow of feeling is the basis of all emotional responses. If it is suppressed, the person's emotional responsiveness is flat. If it is fragmented, the emotional responses are conflicted and ambivalent. Only in the emotionally healthy person is the flow full, free, and rhythmical. Such a person is capable of expressing his feelings of love, anger, fear, and sadness easily and with complete ego control. He has self-possession.

When the flow of feeling is blocked by chronic muscular tensions, self-possession is limited. It becomes important, then, to remove these tensions. To accomplish this three steps are involved. First, the patient must become aware of the tension; that is, he must feel the tension and sense the impulse that is blocked from expression. For example, he must sense that his tight jaw holds back biting impulses, his tight shoulders hold back hitting and reaching impulses, and so on. Every chronic muscular tension represents an inhibition from expressing certain feelings. The tension is the physical counterpart of the psychological inhibition. But tensions are not isolated phenomena. They are interrelated and all together they determine the characterological attitude of the individual. The patient must become aware of this attitude and understand its role in determining his behavior. This is what Reich called character analysis.

Second, the patient must discover the origin and elucidate the history of the inhibition or tension. This is the analytic aspect of bioenergetic therapy. If this aspect is ignored, the patient remains unconnected with his past, and the underlying conflict that produced the tension is never fully resolved. In this step, too, the focus is never limited to the individual tension. The "why" of a particular tension is extended to include the "why" of the whole character structure. The patient must see himself as a product of a unique historical development. When he gets the full picture into focus, the jigsaw puzzle of his life makes sense. These concepts are developed in my book, *The Physical Dynamics of Character Structure*.[3]

Third, the blocked impulses must be released in appropriate movements. Unless this occurs, the analysis remains sterile and no significant changes occur in the total personality. The term appropriate movement means also appropriate circumstances. Acting out the blocked impulses in social relationships is a destructive form of behavior. Whether one feels guilty about such behavior or not, it negates the dignity and integrity of the self and the other. Bioenergetic therapy provides the means whereby these impulses can be expressed in the controlled setting of the therapeutic situation. Blocked anger can be released, for example, by pounding or kicking the bed. In this procedure there is no danger that the patient or anyone else will get hurt. In all the years of my practice I have never been hurt by a patient. The full range of emotion from the deepest longing to the most violent rage can be expressed in this way.

One advantage of working with these techniques is that the patient can do much to help himself. Gaining contact with the body is not a one-hour-a-week activity. Every waking moment and every movement provides the patient with an opportunity to increase his body awareness. The patient develops a feeling awareness of himself instead of the intellectual awareness that resulted from analyzing one's thoughts. In addition, my patients do many of the therapeutic exercises at home, thereby furthering their physical health at the same time that they promote their emotional well-being.

Among the many modifications which bioenergetic analysis made in Reichian therapy is the shift from orgastic potency to pleasure as the therapeutic goal. By pleasure I do not mean any momentary self-indulgence but the enjoyment of living. The aim of therapy is to help a patient gain the capacity for pleasure and joy. This is a broader aim than Reich formulated, for it includes sexual pleasure and orgastic satisfaction. While the analysis of sexual conflicts is still a focal point of the therapeutic endeavors in bioenergetic analysis, this therapy avoids the preoccupation with sex that characterized the Reichian approach.

At the beginning of this presentation I mentioned the growing interest in the body and in immediate experiences as the main features of the new psychotherapeutic approaches. The value of this focus is illustrated in the following short case history of one session.

> The patient, a young woman of twenty-five, consulted me because of a severe depressive reaction that culminated in an attempt at suicide. She was released from a hospital for the consultation. After discussuing her situation, I put her through some of the bioenergetic procedures designed to increase her breathing and motility and to promote the expression of feeling. At the end of the session her color was better, her eyes were more alive, and her body had more feeling. As she left she said to me, "Dr. Lowen, I came in feeling hopeless but I am leaving with a feeling of hope."

In psychotherapy the approach to personality through the body also provides a new hope for the understanding and amelioration of problems that verbal techniques leave untouched. These are the character disorders such as the schizoid personality, the oral dependent personality, the masochistic personality, and the rigid, compulsive personality. Verbal techniques are relatively impotent to affect these personality problems because they are structured in the body.

The schizoid personality, for example, is determined by the dissociation of the conscious mind from the body and based on a reduction of feeling in the body. Increasing bodily sensation and mobilizing body awareness are the immediate procedures which can overcome this mind-body dissociation. The oral dependent personality is determined by feelings of insecurity stemming from inadequate contact between the feet and the ground. Getting feelings into the legs and the feet overcomes the feeling of insecurity and reduces the dependency needs of this personality. Broadly speaking, the masochistic personality is determined by chronic muscular tensions that constrict the neck and the pelvic outlets. The masochist can be considered a bottled-up individual, one of whose main complaints is the fear of bursting. When these tensions are released the masochistic tendency to whine, complain, and suffer diminishes. Rigid, compulsive types are characterized by rigid, tight bodies and the psychological rigidity is only softened when the body rigidity is relaxed. The interested reader is referred to Reich's and my books for a fuller analysis of these personality structures.

Being in touch with the body offers to individuals a new hope for meaningful existence in these confused times. Every value but one can be questioned today. The one value that is beyond question is bodily health. The person who is in touch with his body is aware of its tensions. He senses when his breathing is disturbed and he can do what is necessary to restore his bodily function to its optimum state. Thus he can take the responsibility for his emotional and physical well-being. The person who is out of touch with his body projects his problems onto others and seeks a solution to his personal difficulties in radical social change. The illusion that society can change without a prior change in the character structure of its members was exposed by Reich in *The Mass Psychology of Fascism*. The inevitable collapse of this illusion will plunge the social radical into depression sooner or later.

REFERENCES

1. Lowen, A.: *The Betrayal of the Body*. New York, Macmillan, 1967.
2. Lowen, A.: *Love and Orgasm*. New York, Macmillan, 1965.
3. Lowen, A.: *Psychial Dynamics of Character Structure*. New York, Grune & Stratton, 1958.

4. Reich, W.: *Character Analysis,* 3rd ed. New York, Orgone Institute Press, 1949.

5. Reich, W.: *The Function of the Orgasm.* New York, Orgone Institute Press, 1942.

RESEARCH in the area of psychotherapy is a difficult and delicate task. Many of the studies have had difficulty defining and controlling the variables involved in this area, and this is true whether the studies deal with outcome or process in psychotherapy. Thus, the results of the research for the most part are inconclusive or at best suggestive. It is therefore very encouraging to see the programmatic project detailed by Drs. Grey, Ortmeyer, and Caligor. Their experimental design has imagination, thoroughness, and a scope which promises to make it a major contribution to this rather confused and hazy area. And although their project is directed at a very specific group, that of the blue-collar worker, the research has many implications for the entire field of therapy as well, for they have included more than simply an evaluation of lower-class therapy in their purview. When their work is completed we should begin to obtain answers to some of the major questions about therapist and patients and their interaction in that nebulous and many-faceted area called psychotherapy.

The problem of treatment of lower-class patients is a crucial one for our society, for even though these persons comprise a large percentage of our population, they receive a shamefully small percentage of treatment. Additionally, it is quite clear that the lower-class person, when emotionally upset, finds his way to the questionable treatment facilities of the mental hospital considerably more frequently than upper-class and middle-class patients.

The authors, however, do much more than just indicate a thorough research project in this sphere. In their detailing of the literature and the variables that must be considered in a thorough assessment of all the factors involved, they really have outlined all the therapy procedures and problems that are paramount for a

132

knowledge of this sector. Thus, their paper also provides an excellent perspective on the psychotherapeutic techniques useful in dealing with the blue-collar worker.

G.D.G.
D.S.M.

Chapter 9

RESEARCH ISSUES FOR PSYCHOTHERAPY WITH BLUE-COLLAR PATIENTS

ALAN GREY, DALE H. ORTMEYER, AND LEOPOLD CALIGOR

THE WILLIAM ALANSON WHITE INSTITUTE was asked in November 1963 by the president of a United Auto Worker's local whether we would be interested and able to provide prompt diagnostic and treatment service when needed by the union membership. The hope was to spare members the inevitably long delays on clinic waiting lists by providing a contract for a specific amount of service. All fees would be paid through a lump-sum grant from the union welfare fund.

The prospect of working with blue-collar patients offered a challenge to our analytic Institute which we gladly accepted. Our major theoretic orientation in Sullivan[17] and Fromm[2] posits an awareness of social problems in mental health and the assumption that treatment methods must be adapted to the needs of the patient population without adherence to *fixed* preconceptions about therapeutic techniques.

While rendering a sorely needed service over the last five years, we have continued peer group evaluations of varying therapy approaches to the blue-collar patient and undertaken a program of research. We would like to share with you some of the issues which our study of the literature and our clinical experience have made focal for us. (For a more detailed discussion of the history, scope, and goals of the Union Therapy Project, see Caligor and Zaphiropoulos.[1])

PREVIOUS STUDIES OF TREATMENT AND BLUE-COLLAR PATIENTS

Recent social changes have demanded that mental health needs be met for the *whole* community, not merely for the upper

134

and middle classes, as has been too much the case. There is an abundant accumulation of evidence that members of the blue-collar stratum have been too infrequently seen and too infrequently helped by psychotherapy. In explaining this fact, every major study to date has noted a socioeconomic influence, with patients of lower socioeconomic status receiving different diagnoses and treatment from those in the upper and middle classes, even if the problems were similar.

When the industrial worker seeks help for emotional distress he usually is institutionalized, in contrast to the predominant outpatient treatment for middle and upper classes. For example, Srole *et al.*[16] observe that considering psychotic patients only—for whom hospitalization rates would be expected to be more similar for all groups—it was found that 50 percent of "upper"-group patients were treated in the community on an outpatient basis, whereas only 10 percent of the lower-group patients remained in the community; 90 percent were institutionalized. Grey[3] notes that "middle class personnel of a psychiatric hospital were found to regard and treat middle class (male) patients more favorably than lower class (male). They judged the outcome of treatment to be more favorable for middle class patients."

Hollingshead and Redlich[5] report that one third of the neurotic patients in the lowest socioeconomic group receiving treatment for the first time were in a state, military, or VA hospital. Not a single neurotic patient in the upper classes was hospitalized. They concluded, "The state hospital is utilized in sharply increasing percentage as the class structure is descended." Their study clearly indicates the relationship between class and the type of treatment rendered. The lower-class patient, in contrast to the middle-class and upper-class patient, was given shock or drugs more frequently and tended to get the less-trained therapist assigned to him.

It is reported in the literature that there is a greater likelihood of failure in psychotherapy with the blue-collar patient when he comes for help, with the suggestion that it is more because of the middle-class therapist than the blue-collar patient. Miller and Swanson[7] state:

> In clinics which serve patients of both classes (blue-collar and middle), a disproportionate number of blue-collar workers drop out of therapy very early because of dissatisfaction with the therapeutic procedures. It is important that psychotherapists learn more about the characteristics of manual laborers and about conditions under which these people mature. . . .Our results indicated the desirability of exploring a variety of new psychotherapeutic techniques, particularly those in which words and concepts are subordinated to nonverbal and even motoric activities.

Note that all the above studies attempt to describe the blue-collar patient in terms of social class characteristics and rely heavily on sociological formulations. There is a remarkable dearth of psychodynamic conceptualization. The basic assertions which emerge are that (1) blue-collar and white-collar patients are significantly different, (2) middle-class therapy techniques do not work with blue-collar patients, and (3) blue-collar therapy techniques based upon blue-collar characteristics are needed.

According to Frank Riessman,[13,15] a leading authority in the field, it is clear that there are real differences in attitudes, values, goals, and life styles between the lower and higher classes. Riessman sees the blue-collar worker as action-oriented rather than verbal, extrospective rather than introspective, poorly educated, relatively unimaginative, and little given to fantasy compared with the middle-class individual. In a therapeutic relationship, Riessman observes that the lower-class patient is oriented towards problems and symptoms rather than towards personality change. He expects quick and direct results; for example, a specific improvement in his marriage or job. Riessman concludes that psychoanalytic procedures and psychodynamically oriented psychotherapy, in which great weight is placed on the use of introspection, fantasy, and dream material, as well as on long-range personality change, is of little value for the blue-collar patient.

Thus there have emerged a global picture of the blue-collar patient and a global picture of the therapy of choice for him which have become sufficiently pervasive and unquestioned to justify their being called stereotypes. The time has come to reexamine the findings in this new field for (a) the accuracy of the blue-collar portrait—the implication here is that certain widely reiterated patternings of social class, personality style, and their intercorrelation need to be reviewed—and (b) the polarization of treatment concepts into sociological and psychoanalytic formulations as if they were inherently opposed.

SOCIAL CLASS AND PERSONALITY STYLE

There is documentation of the existence of social class in our country; for instance, in the middle west (Lynd and Lynd[6]), metropolitan New York (Srole *et al.*[16]), and the industrial city of New Haven (Hollingshead and Redlich[5]). One of the more extensively used scales to differentiate social classes is Hollingshead's Index of Social Status,[5] which separates people into five social classes on the basis of ecological area of residence, occupation, and education.

On this scale the blue-collar worker falls in Class IV, where 48 percent of the total number of families were placed in the New Haven study. The blue-collar class thus encompasses approximately as many families as all the other classes combined. One anticipates, from a realistic appreciation of individual differences, that the more inclusive a category becomes, the greater the diversity of its members in various dimensions. Personality style is an important dimension for the mental health field, one that perhaps has been oversimplified for blue-collar patients. Indeed, it needs to be determined whether there are only one or two or many personality styles among blue-collar patients.

A second issue is that in many discussions it is Class V (irregularly employed) that has been portrayed in contrast with Classes II and/or III (business and professional). There has been a tendency to pool the blue-collar worker with the lowest class and then to characterize both in terms of the lowest class. It seems unlikely that the personality of patients who work at an assembly line in a large factory is the same as that of patients who do unskilled jobs and are not working steadily at any one job.

Much of the picture of social class and personality style in the literature is based on data of ten to fifteen years ago.[5,8,9,16] It seems time for a reappraisal to discover if there have been social class and personality style changes since then. With the rapid increase in automation and increasing educational and vocational opportunities which particularly affect the blue-collar group, it is possible that this stratum is in process of considerable change. The general issue posed here, therefore, is that there may be several personality styles of blue-collar patients and considerable variation within each style and over a period of time.

TREATMENT APPROACHES FOR THE BLUE-COLLAR PATIENT

There has been considerable criticism of the effectiveness of individual psychotherapy for the blue-collar patient. Reiff[12] states:

> Treatment methods which place a heavy reliance on the use of some *form of social process* as a technique of treatment rather than on individual face-to-face psychotherapy appear to be more effective with blue-collar and low income groups. We have in mind such techniques as group therapy of various kinds, role-playing, family treatment and work therapy programs.

Riessman said:[15]

> Nothing could point more sharply to the need for treatment agents (including social workers) to be exposed to and trained in a wide variety of techniques congenial to low-income people (conditioning approaches, sleep therapy, muscle relaxation techniques, role-playing, hypnosis, drugs, directive therapies, etc.). A further possible solution is the combination of some of these techniques with the more cognitive, psychodynamic approaches so attractive to the treatment agents.

Overall and Aronson[11] report lower socioeconomic patients expect physical modalities of diagnosis and treatment and expect the therapist to take an active but permissive role. Riessman, Cohen, and Pearl[14] state: "The failure of psychotherapy with low income groups may be in large measure due to the insistence on a particular model of treatment, namely the psychodynamic, insight and reconstructive oriented approach."

It is important to attempt to determine if this "failure of psychotherapy" has been largely or in part due to the limitations of psychodynamic theory, the related individual psychotherapy technique, the settings in which practitioners see patients, inadequate social process and community orientation of the psychotherapists, inadequate funding, inadequate sources of referral, inadequate education of the blue-collar worker toward mental health, or unconscious or conscious value orientation of practitioners toward blue-collar patients. To assign major responsibility to any one of these influences without adequate consideration of the others is to indulge a prejudice.

Possible strategy of research is to find out what treatment conditions actually are provided by practitioners who see blue-collar patients and their differential effectiveness with various kinds of symptoms and social adaptations. The neglect of issues raised above could lead to stereotypes in thinking, disadvantageous to the development of community mental health programs.

Like other new movements, community psychology and psychiatry have shown some tendency toward the precipitate dismissal of formulations which antedate them. Are leaders in the field throwing out a viable baby, the product of intense and creative clinical labor, because of its associated bathwater of sociological myopia? Careful investigation may provide a more judicious answer to the issue of whether psychoanalysis is indeed useless for socially oriented treatment programs or whether it continues to offer significant contributions.

A Research Program

To arrive at a reliable answer is no simple undertaking. In fact, the entire field of psychotherapy presents notoriously formidable obstacles to the researcher. The importance of the task, however, has led to the establishment of a Union Therapy Project at the White Institute and to a research program coordinated with it. If that program does not provide definitive answers to the issues raised, it may conceivably break some new ground. The investigative plan has at least four specific aims:

1. An overview of the socioeconomic population from which blue-collar patients are drawn. This calls for a survey of a substantial sample of the general membership of three United Auto Workers locals which have a psychotherapy service contract with the William Alanson White Clinic. This survey is designed to tap several kinds of information, including demographic characteristics of the union population and an estimate of their mental

status, employing the scale developed by Gurin *et al.*[4] in their nationwide sampling of emotional adjustment. There is remarkably little information available thus far on these purely descriptive matters.

2. A comparison of this general cross-section of all union members with those who emerge as the patient population. This may help to answer questions of great pertinence to public health planning. For instance, Are the patients those union members who are actually most in need of help or those who are more receptive to treatment because of middle-class orientation or some other predisposing characteristic?

3. An appraisal of the effects of a mental health educational program used with the union population. The timing and content of the educational activities are controlled systematically to trace any effects on patients of utilization of the treatment facilities.

4. An assessment of the relationship between various therapeutic techniques and outcome of treatment. For this purpose, union patients are assigned to one of two groups at termination of care: those showing more favorable outcomes versus the less successful cases. These groups can be compared for a variety of characteristics, including kinds of treatment techniques employed, diagnostic status, and so forth. As an additional control, a third category of middle-class private patients seen by the same Union Project therapists also is studied. They are matched with their blue-collar opposite numbers as to age, marital status, and other characteristics. It will be informative to learn the proportion of successful outcomes for this group as compared with blue-collar patients, as well as comparative information about matters like mental status and typical treatment methods employed.

The Psychotherapy Investigation

Obviously, the last research aim is the one most directly pertinent to the task of the therapist. It brings up a series of questions which confront him daily in his work and which seldom are simple to answer: What is the most useful way to define the patient's problem, to conceptualize the nature of the difficulties he presents? Tied in with this is the intimately connected issue of what treatment approach is most suitable for that patient. Finally, how do you assess what constitutes improvement or "success" in treatment? All of these thorny points arise to challenge the investigator into blue-collar therapy. Any critical estimate of the meaningfulness of his research requires at least a brief and explicit statement of how he copes with these matters.

Turning first to the question of how to define the nature of a patient's difficulties, it is a notorious fact that the conventional Kraepelin-derived psychiatric categories are less than adequate for treatment purposes, although they persist for a variety of other reasons. In the absence of a single completely satisfactory alternative, the White Institute study supplements the usual APA diagnosis with additional data directed toward a multidimensional approach. These data include the following:

1. The therapist's rating of the severity of the problem.
2. A mental status score (using the Gurin scale).
3. An explicit listing of symptoms presented at the outset of treatment.
4. Therapist's estimate of type and extent of interpersonal rigidity (uniform descriptive categories are provided for this purpose).
5. The patient's explanation of his motivation for treatment.
6. A characterization of the patient's value orientation.
7. A summary of the patient's previous medical history.
8. A summary of sundry sociological characteristics of the patient (such as age, marital status, education) which previous studies have found relevant to treatment outcome.

Since all of these facts are recorded on forms adapted to computer analysis, hopefully those criteria which best predict treatment outcome can be sorted out efficiently from the records accumulated, perhaps leading to new ways of identifying styles of blue-collar patients.

The evaluation of treatment outcome presents a second knotty problem, similar in many respects to that of estimating status at the outset of contact, so it may facilitate exposition to skip to that third major question at this point. A review of the various data collected for initial diagnosis of the patient suggests that while some of these facts cannot be expected to change as the result of treatment, others should be altered if he has become better or worse. Among such characteristics are these:

1. The therapist's rating of the severity of the problem.
2. Mental status score (using the Gurin Scale).
3. List of symptoms at termination of treatment.
4. Therapist's estimate of type and extent of interpersonal rigidity.
5. The patient's reported evaluation of satisfaction with treatment.
6. Observations of any shifts in the patient's value orientation.
7. The therapist's direct evaluation of extent of change during treatment.

Some indication of a shift, then, can be estimated from the therapist's initial assessment of his patient in each of these matters as compared with his entirely separate report made at the termination of treatment. Unavoidably, this procedure still is vulnerable to tendencies toward bias on the part of the therapist, whether or not he accurately recalls his initial impression when he writes his final statement. It is hoped, however, that the very specificity and variety of much of the information helps him to provide more objective data. Additional factual questions about any changes in the patient's occupational, marital, and educational status serve as further aids. A follow-up study of each patient by independent investigators, about a year after termination of contact, also is planned. This, in turn, can be collated with the social worker's intake report for a picture of patient change entirely separate from the information given by the treating professionals.

Early Indications

A most encouraging indication of the feasibility of these methods is that thus far we have found the participating therapists willing to report negative results. As a consequence, cases completed up to this time are separable into two approximately equal groups of more and less successful outcomes. It then becomes possible to determine whether particular kinds of treatment strategies and techniques are typically reported in connection with each type of result. To aid in this aspect of the study, every therapist indicates the extent to which he has relied on each of an extensive list of procedures for every one of his patients in the research sample.

Very pertinent to the investigation is the fact that the professionals cooperating in the project all have been trained in psychoanalysis at the White Institute. At the same time each analyst is free to use whatever approach he regards as in the best interest of his patient, who is seen in his private office whether blue-collar or white-collar. These analysts all are well aware that their customary psychoanalytic methods have been questioned by many experts on blue-collar treatment and are familiar with various recommended alternatives. The relatively limited number of sessions allowed by the insurance program of two participating locals (sixteen contacts per patient per year) serves as a further impetus to departures from strictly analytic procedures.

In their reports the analysts indicate how extensively they employ particular nonanalytic methods, such as direct advice, role playing, use of medication or placebos, direct intervention with community agencies, descriptions of their own experiences, and so forth. They also state how heavily they rely on more typically psychoanalytic procedures like explorations into childhood experiences, analysis of dreams, and analysis of transference reactions. Methods whose roots cut across many approaches, both psychoanalytic and nonpsychoanalytic, also are used and reported. These include explanations of psychological processes, group therapy, conjoint family interviews, and examination of the patient's emotional reactions.

In short, the research program places few restrictions on the therapist's freedom to choose his own approach, requiring only an explicit record of what he actually does. Nor is any great significance attached to the frequency with which a method is used. A highly favored approach may be merely a highly familiar one. What we hope eventually to discover is which combination of methods most often emerges in association with particular kinds of patients and outcomes.

Every mental health professional is keenly aware of the hazards which beset systematic research into psychotherapy. The complexity of the processes involved, the primary responsibility to the welfare of the patient, and the dearth of unequivocal measurement devices all act as formidable impediments. Nevertheless, we have had some encouraging signs that the evolving research design briefly sketched here may provide at least a few modest clues concerning the questions which motivated it.

Cumulatively, from November 1963 to March 1968, two hundred and sixty-six persons were seen, of whom forty-six had no more than three sessions and fifteen were referred elsewhere for appropriate services. Most of the others received from six to thirty sessions, with an average of about sixteen contacts. It is particularly interesting to note that patients from Local 259, whose program allows for an unlimited number of therapy hours, terminate voluntarily after an average of fifteen sessions. At the same time, some indication of range and flexibility in approach is suggested by the fact that one patient is now in his fourth year of treatment.[10] Perhaps a further indication can be found in the variety of therapy arrangements. Seventy-five patients have been seen individually, twenty as couples, one hundred and eight in family therapy, and eight by multiple therapists.

In summary, we have described an ongoing research program at the William Alanson White Psychoanalytic Institute which reexamines with theoretical implications the portrayal of the blue-collar mental health patient and the treatment of choice for him. The aims of the program are to inquire into the characteristics of a specific blue-collar patient group and the blue-collar population from which they come, mental health education with this population, and the techniques of treatment used in helping these patients.

REFERENCES

1. Caligor, L., and Zaphiropoulos, M.: History and scope of the Union Therapy Project. In Milman, D. S., and Goldman, G. D. (Eds.):

Psychoanalytic Contributions to Community Psychology. Springfield, Thomas, 1971.

2. Fromm, E.: *Escape From Freedom.* New York, Rinehart, 1941.

3. Grey, A.: Social class and the psychiatric patient: A study in composite character. *Contemporary Psychoanalysis, 2:*87-121, 1956.

4. Gurin, G., Veroff, J., and Feld, S.: *Americans View Their Mental Health: A Nationwide Interview Survey.* New York, Basic Books, 1960.

5. Hollingshead, A. B., and Redlich, F. C.: *Social Class and Mental Illness: A Community Study.* New York, Wiley, 1958.

6. Lynd, R., and Lynd, H. M.: *Middletown.* New York, Harcourt Brace, 1929.

7. Miller, D., and Swanson, G.: *Inner Conflict and Defense.* New York, Holt, 1960.

8. Myers, J. K., and Bean, L. L.: *A Decade Later: A Follow-up of Social Class and Mental Illness.* New York, Wiley, 1968.

9. Myers, J. K., and Roberts, B. H.: *Family and Class Dynamics in Mental Illness.* New York, Wiley, 1964.

10. Ortmeyer, D. H.: Clinical contribution. In Milman, D. S., and Goldman, G. D. (Eds.): *Psychoanalytic Contributions to Community Psychology.* Springfield, Thomas, 1971.

11. Overall, B., and Aronson, H.: Expectations of psychotherapy in patients of lower socio-economic class. In Riessman, F., Cohen, J., and Pearl, A. (Eds.): *Mental Health and the Poor.* New York, Free Press, 1964.

12. Reiff, R., and Scribner, S.: *Issues in the New National Mental Health Program Relating to Labor and Low Income Groups.* New York, N.I.L.E. Mental Health Program, 1963 (mimeographed).

13. Reissman, F.: *New Approaches to Mental Health Treatment for Labor and Low Income Groups,* Report 2. New York, N.I.L.E. Mental Health Program, 1964 (mimeographed).

14. Riessman, F., Cohen, J., and Pearl, A. (Eds.): *Mental Health and the Poor.* New York, Free Press, 1964.

15. Riessman, F., and Goldfarb, J.: Role playing and the lower socio-economic group. In Moreno, J. L. (Ed.): *Group Psychotherapy,* New York, Beacon House, 1964, Vol. XVII, No. 1.

16. Strole, L., Langner, T. S., Michael, S. T., Opler, M. K., and Rennie, T. A. C.: *Mental Health in the Metropolis: The Midtown Study.* New York, McGraw-Hill, 1962.

17. Sullivan, H. S.: *The Interpersonal Theory of Psychiatry.* New York, Norton, 1953.

A꜕T A MEETING of the American Psychological Association in 1956, Dr. Albert Ellis first introduced his rational-emotive psychotherapy as an effective innovation. This chapter summarizing his approach provides clinical examples of technique which illustrate its advantages and disadvantages, clearly indicating it to be a useful and stimulating addition to our psychotherapeutic armamentarium.

In this paper, Dr. Ellis indicates through a clinical example how "a shy, sexually backward client was emotively, behavioristically and cognitively treated." Concretely he analyzes the method, with its behavioristic and cognitive techniques that therapists are familiar with. There is reinforcement of adaptive and effective behavior, desensitization, and extinguishing maladaptive or inefficient reactions. He utilizes modeling through role-playing techniques as well as didactic *in vivo* homework assignments for practice of patterns of productive behavior. He teaches a new value system, directly and forcefully pointing up logical inconsistencies and contradictions in the client's behavior and thought. Thus, there is much direct information giving and teaching in Ellis' techniques as he describes them.

Dr. Ellis, the originator of rational-emotive psychotherapy, has very clearly and understandably outlined in this chapter how his is a comprehensive approach to therapy. Those of us who prior to reading Dr. Ellis' chapter knew nothing of his techniques will gain a knowledge of and familiarity with them after perusing it. For those more sophisticated in their knowledge of his work, this chapter is still fascinating and illuminating in its extension of his work for these other therapists and in its promise and concretization of the wide range of his methods and potential applications.

G.D.G.
D.S.M.

Chapter 10

RATIONAL-EMOTIVE PSYCHOTHERAPY: A COMPREHENSIVE APPROACH TO THERAPY

ALBERT ELLIS

ALL LEADING SYSTEMS of psychotherapy, as I[17] have shown in a recent article, are somewhat comprehensive in that they actually attack the individual's problems from a cognitive, an emotive, and a behavioristic standpoint. Thus, the expressive-experiential-existential school of therapy (as exemplified by the work of Bach,[3] Gendlin,[20] May,[24] Otto,[26] Perls,[27] Rogers,[32-34] Schutz,[35] and Whitaker and Malone [37]) includes a considerable amount of cognitive and behavior methodology. The practitioners of behavior therapy (such as Cautela,[5] Davison,[6] Lazarus,[40] and Wolpe[39,40]) wittingly or unwittingly embrace many emotive and cognitive techniques. As Potash and Taylor[30] have indicated, cognitive therapists (such as Adler,[1,2] Berne,[4] Ellis,[10-12,15,19] Kelly,[23] Philips,[28,29] and Wiener[38]) consciously or unconsciously include a good many aspects of behavioristic and emotive procedure in their individual and group therapy sessions.

Rational-emotive psychotherapy, as I shall show in this paper, is one of the few existing methods which not only openly and avowedly employs cognitive, emotive, and behavioristic approaches, but also does so on theoretical grounds. It hypothesizes that human beings normally think, emote, and act in an interrelated and inevitably pluralistic manner and that they do not get what are usually called "emotional reactions" unless they are simultaneously using their perceptual-cognitive and overt motor faculties. It particularly holds that what we term "emotional disturbances" are concomitants of their appraising or evaluating cognitions[25] and of their habituated motorial responses.[7] Consequently, rational-emotive therapy (or RET, for short) quite consciously and openly attempts to be a comprehensive system of psychotherapy, and it active-directively employs at least three major and interacting techniques.

Since I[8,9,13,16] have pointed out the comprehensive aspects of RET in several other recent papers, I shall not merely repeat this material here. Instead, I shall give the details of a typical recent client whom I treated with RET and shall thereby illustrate exactly what some of the cognitive, emotive, and behavioristic aspects of this kind of therapy are.

> The client was a thirty-year-old male who was exceptionally shy, who had not been able to speak up in front of even a small group of people, who was entirely virginal because he lacked the courage to date and make sexual overtures to girls, who thought that he might be basically homosexual, and who was making no progress in his would-be career as a novelist because he rarely sat himself down at his typewriter to do any actual writing. Five years prior to coming to see me he had suffered a so-called "nervous breakdown" and had been hospitalized in the phychiatric ward of a general hospital for one month; he then underwent nine months of psychoanalytically oriented psychotherapy which had not been very helpful to him. He was referred to me by one of my ex-clients who taught in the same school as he did and who had had several heart-to-heart talks with him about his problems. This client was seen by me for a total of five individual sessions and forty-two group therapy sessions.

RET EXPERIENTIAL-EMOTIVE TECHNIQUES

The main experiential-emotive methods that I employed with this shy teacher were as follows:

1. I began with the client's feelings and active-directively probed and reflected until I got him to see that he mainly felt like an inadequate, worthless individual who was born defective and who could not possibly succeed at virtually anything, including teaching, writing, and social-sexual relations with females. I also induced him to express his intense, though at first covered-up, hostility toward me, toward other members of his therapy group, and toward difficult and rejecting females. In group, he was directed to tell off one of the females about whom he previously had only made indirect snippy remarks and to admit that he really hated her guts.

2. I and the members of his therapy group kept the client mainly in the here and now. Whenever he tended to go off on an extended narration of the dismal events of his past life and to blame his parents and their overprotecting attitudes for his present state of inhibition, we said something like the following: "That's all very well, but it's quite irrelevant to the way you feel and act *today*. So you once felt that you had to give in to your parents' overprotecting ways. But you're a big boy now, and *you're* carrying on this inhibited feeling-state today. What are you feeling *right now?* Suppose, for example, you went out on a date with Judy, who is sitting next to you now, and you thought she would possibly react favorably to a sexual pass. How would you feel about approaching her?"

3. I directly and forthrightly directed the client to encounter others, to take emotional risks, and to do verbal or nonverbal exercises during the therapeutic sessions. On one occasion, I induced him to take the hand of a female member of his group and to try to talk her into kissing him. During his very first session of group therapy I forced him to speak up about his basic problems, even though he was most reluctant to do so and wanted to wait several more sessions until he knew the members of the group better and felt safer with them. On another occasion the group gave him the homework assignment of taking a promotion exam which he was terribly afraid to take.

4. I often used dramatic techniques—such as role playing, story telling, humor, and strong language—to make therapeutic points with the client in an intense, forceful, emotive manner. Once I deliberately forced him to go after another member of his therapy group who was not writing the plays he said he wanted to write and got him to laugh uproariously at this other member's attempts to evade his questioning and to give flimsy excuses for his not actually writing. I and the other group members also laughed, with the client, at the other nonwriter's rationalizations.

In the course of this session, the client confessed that he had written three novels but was having trouble in getting agents or publishers to consider them. He seemed to come out of himself while talking to the other group member and confessing his own problems (some of them for the first time in group). However, he shamefacedly and honestly confessed at the next session that he had entirely made up the story about finishing three novels himself; actually he had not even been able, yet, to finish a single chapter of one novel but had only done fragments of chapters. After this really honest confession he was able to do some concerted writing on a novel for the first time in his life.

5. I sometimes employed pleasure-giving methods with this client, to help him feel better, to give him learning experiences, and to make him more receptive to the harder-hitting, work-oriented aspects of therapy. Thus, I got him to go to a masseuse for several massage treatments to show him that he could enjoy a female's working on his body and could easily become sexually aroused by this procedure.

6. I, at times, emotively attacked the client's defense system to shake him up. Once, during an individual therapy session, I mimicked his evasive and namby-pamby manner with girls and had him hilariously laughing at himself during this session. Subsequently, whenever he attempted to revert to this defensive position he tended to remember my mimicking session and to challenge his own defensiveness and force himself to be more assertive with girls he dated.

7. I revealed many of my own authentic and personal feelings, desires, and responses to show him that I could empathize with his emotions and serve as a good model for him. Thus, I revealed that I myself had been very shy with girls up to my early twenties and that I had to force myself to pick them up in public places and make overtures toward them. I also showed him (during group therapy sessions) that I was not afraid to open myself up, to take chances in being attacked by other group members, and to persist in doing whatever I felt like doing even though at times there were unpleasant consequences.

8. I consistently tried to give the client unconditional positive regard—to fully accept him with his failings and to refrain from denigrating him as a person, in spite of his poor performances. I showed him on many occasions that although I deplored his *behavior,* I never despised *him* for displaying this behavior and that

I could always accept him as a human being, even when he did not accept himself.

RET BEHAVIORISTIC TECHNIQUES

Some of the main behavior therapy methods that I employed with this inhibited client were the following:

1. I kept frankly reinforcing his good or efficient changes during his time in therapy by verbally approving of them whenever he showed evidence of their occurrence; at the same time, I consistently helped extinguish his poor or inefficient reactions by showing him that they were unfortunate and that they would only produce self-defeating results. Whenever he made progress in asserting himself with a girl, I told him that was very good (but not that *he* was therefore a good *person*); whenever he fell back on passive behavior, I showed him that that was bad and that he could do better.

2. I used role playing with him, in both individual and group therapy sessions, to simulate someone's criticizing him severely and to train him in stopping his supersensitive reactions to criticism. I helped desensitize his catastrophizing about rejection during one group therapy session by having three female members of his group successively reject him, tell him his method of approach was terrible, and severely berate him while he tried to maintain his equilibrium. As a result of this and other desensitizing experiences during therapy, he became much better able to handle rejection by girls.

3. I and his therapy group continually gave him activity homework assignments to carry out in the course of his real-life situations. These *in vivo* homework assignments are one of the most important aspects of rational-emotive therapy; virtually all clients treated with this method are given a number of such assignments.

In this client's case, as I have noted in the previous section of this paper, the group once gave him the task of taking a promomotion exam at school which he was terribly afraid to take. At its behest, he took the exam and did very well in it. In addition, he was at various times given writing assignments, such as that of finishing ten pages of a novel every week. He was also given a series of graduated homework assignments in regard to dating girls: (a) making a date each week with at least one girl, (b) holding a girl's hand in the movies, (c) petting with a girl in a car, (d) trying to get a girl's clothes off while petting, and (e) attempting to have intercourse. After eight weeks of this type of assignment he was able to engage in coitus with a girl for the first time in his life. He then gave himself the additional assignment of spending an entire weekend with the same female and was quickly able to carry it out successfully.

4. I taught the client Premack's principle of reinforcement[21,22,31]—or how to permit himself easy and immediately rewarding behavior only after he had forced himself to perform more difficult, and subsequently rewarding, acts. For example, when he had difficulty studying for the promotion exam that his group induced him to take, I determined that he greatly enjoyed going swimming almost every day in a pool that was near his residence; I got him to allow himself to indulge in a half hour of swimming each day only on the condition that he had previously spent at least two hours that day studying for the exam. Under these conditions, he was able to study persistently and to pass the examination.

5. I forced this client to keep practicing new behaviors, particularly in the course of group therapy, until he began to automatically and enjoyably experience these behaviors. Thus, I forced him to keep speaking up about his own and others' problems in the course of group sessions, even though at first he was reluctant to do so. After about ten group sessions of this kind of forced performance, he found that he naturally enjoyed being an active group member and became, in point of fact, one of the most frequent and spontaneous talkers in the group.

RET COGNITIVE TECHNIQUES

Although, as I have just been showing, rational-emotive therapy employs many pronouncedly experiential-emotive and behavioristic methods, it is most known for its frankly cognitive techniques. Some cognitive approaches used with this shy client were these:

1. I actively showed the client that behind his emotional re-actions and his ineffective overt behavior lay a strong self-per-petuating value system or set of irrational philosophic assump-tions and that he largely created his own disordered emotions and actions by his vigorous, rigid beliefs in these assumptions. Thus, I showed him that his main premises were as follows: (a) "If I make a serious error in public, as in speaking up inadequately be-fore a group of people, I am a worthless individual and will never be able to act adequately under similar circumstances." (b) "I should be able to be perfectly successful in any overtures I make toward women; if I am so imperfect in this respect that any girl rejects me, that means that I am sexually inferior and that I shall never be able to succeed with a female." (c) "If I haven't succeeded with a woman during my first thirty years of life, I am most probably a homosexual who was born to fail with females." (d) "I have to quickly be one of the greatest novelists who ever lived and cannot risk writing a novel for fear that I will turn out to be a terrible bust in this respect." (e) "Almost any kind of risk taking will result in my experiencing awful trouble and pain, so I'd better not take any speaking, sexual, writing, or other risks, and in that way I will lead a happier existence."

2. I showed the client how and why his philosophic premises were illogical, inconsistent, and contradictory. I demonstrated how his making serious errors in speaking or in sex relations could hardly make him a totally worthless individual—that this conclusion was a non sequitur. I explained how his conclusion that he experienced horrible pain from risk taking and that he had therefore better not take risks consisted of circular thinking, since his pain did not follow from the risk taking itself but from the definitional statement that he could not stand failing at risk-taking experiences and that if he changed this definition, this "pain" would no longer exist and would not "cause" him to avoid future risk taking. I showed him that if he gave up taking any speaking, sexual, writing, or other risks he might, indeed, lead a safer but hardly a happier existence, since he would there-by make his life quite drab and boring.

I also pointed out to this shy client how his philosophic hy-potheses were supported by no empirical referents and how they were invariably invalid or unable to be validated. Thus, there was *no evidence* that he was a worthless *individual* because his public speaking *performances* were inadequate; this is an essentially tautological, magical proposition. There was no reason why he *should* or *must* be perfectly successful in his overtures toward women, though there might be several good reasons why *it would be better* if he were successful in this respect. These, again, are definitional, nonempirically based statements which could never really be proven or disproven factually.

3. I taught this client how to logicoempirically question and challenge his own self-defeating hypotheses about himself, about others, and about the world, and how to employ the scientific method in regard to himself and the solving of his own problems just as a physical or social scientist would employ it in the solving of external problems. I taught him to find his own magical, tautological propositions—his *should, ought,* and *must* statements—and how to vigorously question and challenge them. I showed him how to ask: (a) *"Why* am I a worthless individual if I speak up inadequately before a group of people?" (b) *"Who says* that I should be perfectly successful in any overture I make toward a woman?" (c) *"Where is the evidence* that if I haven't succeeded with a female during the first thirty years of my life, I am therefore probably a homosexual?" (d) *"Why is it necessary, even* though it may be desirable, that I be one of the greatest novelists who ever lived?" (e) "Why *must* I experience terrible trouble and pain if I try risk-taking experiences?" In this manner, I gradually taught the client the scientific method of thinking and experimenting and how to apply this method to his own life.

4. I demonstrated why and how it was possible for the client to significantly change his thoughts, feelings, and performances and thereby create in himself basic personality change. On one occasion, I taught him how to imagine his actually being successful in his overtures toward a girl; during the following week, partly as a result of this kind of imagining, he was able to go further in taking off a girl's clothes than he had ever done before. On another occasion, I showed him that if he thought of failing sexually, he would easily lose an erection he had already achieved; while if he thought of what a great piece of ass this same girl was,

he could quickly achieve an erection when he did not have one. In one of the group therapy sessions I and several other members of his group demonstrated to him that he was specifically convincing himself that it would be awful if he said the wrong thing in group and that therefore he was saying nothing and that when he stopped to convince himself that it would merely be inconvenient, but not in the least awful, if he said the wrong thing, he immediately lost most of his difficulty in speaking and actually began to enjoy speaking up.

5. I and his group members discussed important questions of philosophy, morals, and politics with the client and helped him clarify to himself (a) what some of his ethical views were, (b) what his purposes in living were, (c) what kinds of goals and vital absorbing interests he would like to set for himself, and (d) what kind of a world he would prefer to live in.

During one session he revealed that he did not want to get involved with a girl for fear that he would later reject her and thereby gravely hurt her. The group showed him that as long as he was honest with this girl it was perfectly ethical for him to reject her after first caring for her, just as it would be ethical for her to reject him, since no one could promise to love anyone else forever. As for his hurting this girl terribly, the group showed him that (a) people are continually getting deprived or frustrated in love affairs, but that is their moral prerogative—to risk frustration in order to achieve possible fullfillment; and (b) he could certainly deprive a girl of satisfaction by first loving and then rejecting her; however, if she became terribly upset or hurt in the process, this would not be the result of his frustrating her but of the nonsense she told herself about how horrible, how catastrophic it was for her to be frustrated—she, therefore, would really be unduly and foolishly hurting herself.

On another occasion, I showed this client that he was terribly afraid that he was homosexual not because being homosexual would be unfortunate—which it might well be in his case—but because he erroneously was viewing it as a great moral sin. I convinced him that fixed homosexuals were not depraved or rotten— that at worst they were emotionally disturbed individuals—and that he would hardly be an enormous sinner if he ever did become homosexual. Immediately after the session during which we had this discussion, the client almost entirely lost his fear of becoming a fixed deviant.

6. I and his therapy group gave this client relevant information, not only about psychology but often about sociology, anthropology, law, education, and other relevant fields. Thus, we explained how and why human beings usually become emotionally disturbed, how statistically normal many of his problems were, why he was not likely to harm himself by masturbation, what some of the laws about homosexuality were, and how he could go about acquiring some better study habits. Although this information was not usually designed to help the client solve some of his basic personality problems, it was intended to have a supportive and palliative effect in the process of his therapy, and it often appeared to help him significantly.

7. I used various supplementary aids in teaching this client some of the principles of human behavior in general and of rational-emotive psychotherapy in particular. I gave him several pamphlets to read and also had him read my books, *A Guide to Rational Living*[18] and *Reason and Emotion in Psychotherapy*.[15] He went to several lectures and workshops at the Institute for Rational Living in New York City, and he purchased a couple of the tape recordings that the Institute distributes. Finally, at my suggestion, he brought along his own cassette tape recorder and recorded a few of the individual sessions he had with me and then listened to these sessions a good many times at home. These various supplementary teaching devices were found to be helpful to the client, especially—he thought—the repeated listenings to the recordings of his own sessions and several readings of the two books.

8. On many occasions, both the client's group and I went over with him the ABC's of personality formation and change which are the essence of the theory of rational-emotive therapy. He was specifically shown that whenever he experienced any disordered emotion, behavior, or psychosomatic symptom at point C, this did not stem from the events or conditions that were occurring in his life at point A, but from his irrational beliefs, attitudes, mean-

ings, and philosophies at point B. More specifically, he was taught to distinguish clearly between the rational or appropriate ideas he was telling himself at point B_1 and the irrational or inappropriate ideas he was telling himself at point B_2.

In one instance, for example, the client became very angry at his parents when he remembered how they had overprotected him during his childhood and thereby helped him to become shy and inhibited. He was shown, by me and his group, that his anger at point C did not stem from his parents' overprotection (or from his remembrance of this overprotection) at point A. Rather, it resulted from the sane ideas at point B^1, "What a handicap it was for them to overprotect me like that! I wish to hell they hadn't done so!" and from the insane ideas at point B_2, "They *ought* not to have been so overprotective. I can't stand thinking about what they did to me! They are horrible people for having acted in that way. They deserve to be punished for their awful behavior, and I hope they drop dead!"

We showed the client that these ideas at point B_2 were irrational because (a) there was *no* reason why his parents ought not to have been so overprotective, even though it would have been lovely if they had not been; (b) he *could* very well stand thinking about their overprotectiveness, although he might never like it; (c) they were *not* horrible people for having acted the way they did, but merely poor, fallible human beings, who unfortunately made a mistake in overprotecting him; and (d) even if their behavior was benighted, they hardly deserved to be killed or otherwise severely punished for having been born and raised to act the way that they did. When the client finally accepted the irrationality of his own B^2 ideas, his anger against his parents completely vanished and he began to get along with them remarkably better than he had ever done previously. He also began to accept more and more the basic tenet of rational-emotive therapy, that, as Epictetus stated two thousand years ago, "men are disturbed not by things, but by the views which they take of them." Thereafter, whenever he became upset or acted self-defeatingly at point C, he tended to quickly look for the B_2 statements he kept telling himself to create this reaction and to challenge and question these statements until he stopped foolishly believing in them.

In many ways, such as those just delineated, this shy and sexually backward client was emotively, behavioristically, and cognitively treated in the course of his rational-emotive individual and group therapy sessions. Within less than a year of starting treatment he lost most of his shyness, became adept at speaking up in front of both small and large groups, had sexual affairs with three girls and began to have steady relations with one of them, entirely lost his fear of being a fixed homosexual, and was half way toward completing his first novel. At times he was still anxious and guilty, especially when stressful situations arose, but his feelings of self-acceptance appreciably increased and his hostility toward his parents and other individuals was minimal. All the members of his therapy group agreed that he was quite able to quit treatment and get along by himself. That was about a year ago. I have had two letters from him since and have spoken to him briefly when he attended some of our workshops at the Institute for Rational Living, and he appears to be holding his gains and even strengthening himself further in some areas.

This, of course, does not always happen. Even though rational-emotive therapy is a comprehensive form of treatment which includes several important cognitive, emotive, and behavioristic approaches to basic personality change, it is hardly a miracle cure and does require a considerable amount of effort and practice on the part of the client. Hence, it is hardly the therapy of choice for individuals who want to be coddled, who think they require immediate gratification within the therapy sessions, who believe that they will magically be cured by some kind of sudden insight, or who refuse to work at helping themselves. It is also not exactly the cup of tea of the kind of therapist who wants primarily to gratify himself during therapy, who is in dire need of his clients' approval, who prefers to be passive during most of the therapeutic process, and who is enamored of discovering many fine details of the events of his clients' past or present existence.

RET, however, can be used with a large variety of clients, including individuals who are severely neurotic, borderline psychotic, and overtly psychotic, those who are bright and somewhat retarded, those who are from high-level socioeconomic and educational backgrounds and from culturally deprived homes, and those who come for many or for only a few sessions. In my very first paper on rational-emotive psychotherapy (which I gave at the American Psychological Association meetings in Chicago on August 31, 1956) I concluded with two challenging hypotheses: " (a) that psychotherapy which includes a high dosage of rational analysis and reconstruction, as briefly outlined in this paper, will prove to be more effective with more types of clients than any of the non-rational or semi-rational therapies now being widely employed; and (b) that a considerable amount of—or at least, proportion of—rational psychotherapy will prove to be virtually the only type of treatment that helps to undermine the basic neuroses (as distinguished from the superficial neurotic symptoms) of many clients, and particularly of many with whom other types of therapy have already been shown to be ineffective."

On the basis of a great deal of clinical evidence that has accumulated since I stated these hypotheses some thirteen years ago, I think that there is now some data to support them. However, controlled studies still have to be done to supply much more definitive data. In any event, the active-directive, cognitive-oriented, homework-assigning methods that have been vigorously espoused by me and my associates during the last decade have now begun to be increasingly incorporated into other, originally more monistic systems of psychotherapy, so that a comprehensive system of therapy is slowly—but I think surely—evolving.

REFERENCES

1. Adler, A.: *Understanding Human Nature.* New York, Greenberg, 1927.
2. Adler, A.: *What Life Should Mean to You.* New York, Blue Ribbon Books, 1931.
3. Bach, G. R., and Wyden, P.: *The Intimate Enemy.* New York, Morrow, 1969.
4. Berne, E.: *Games People Play.* New York, Grove Press, 1964.
5. Cautela, J.: Treatment of compulsive behavior by covert sensitization. *Psychol. Rec., 16:*33-41, 1966.
6. Davison, G. S.: Systematic desensitization as a counterconditioning process. *J. Abnorm. Psychol., 73:*91-99, 1968.

7. Dunlap, K.: *Personal Adjustment*. New York, McGraw-Hill, 1946.
8. Ellis, A.: The emerging counselor. In *Canadian Counsellor,* 1969.
9. Ellis, A.: Helping people get better rather than merely feel better. In Blau, T. (Chmn.) : *The Necessary and Sufficient Conditions for Change in Psychotherapy.* Conference sponsored by the Division of Psychotherapy of the American Psychological Association and the University of South Florida, Tampa, January 10, 1969.
10. Ellis, A.: *How to Live with a Neurotic*. New York, Crown, 1957.
11. Ellis, A.: *If This Be Sexual Heresy. . .* New York, Lyle Stuart, Inc., and Tower Publications, 1966.
12. Ellis, A.: *Is Objectivism a Religion?* New York, Lyle Stuart, 1968.
13. Ellis, A.: Rational-emotive therapy. *J. Contemporary Psychotherapy, 1:* 82-90, 1969.
14. Ellis, A.: Rational psychotherapy. *J. Gen. Psychol., 59:*35-49, 1958.
15. Ellis, A.: *Reason and Emotion in Psychotherapy*. New York, Lyle Stuart, 1962.
16. Ellis, A.: A weekend of rational encounter. In Burton, A. (Ed.) : *Encounter.* San Francisco, Jossey-Bass, 1969.
17. Ellis, A.: What *really* causes psychotherapeutic change? *Voices,* 4 (No. 2) : 90-97, 1968.
18. Ellis, A., and Harper, R. A.: *A Guide to Rational Living*. Englewood Cliffs, N. J., Prentice-Hall, and Hollywood, Wilshire Books, 1967.
19. Ellis, A., Wolfe, J. L., and Moseley, S.: *How to Prevent Your Child from Becoming a Neurotic Adult*. New York, Crown, 1966.
20. Gendlin, E.: *Experiencing and the Creation of Meaning*. New York, Free Press of Glencoe, 1962.
21. Homme, L.: Continency management. *Newsletter, 5* (No. 4) , 1966. Section on Clinical Child Psychology, Division of Clinical Psychology, American Psychological Association.
22. Homme, L. C., de Baca, P., Devine, J. V., Steinhorst, R., and Rickert, E. J.: Use of the Premack principle in controlling the behavior of nursery school children. *J. Exp. Anal. Behav., 6:*544, 1963.
23. Kelly, G.: *The Psychology of Personal Constructs*. New York, Norton, 1955.
24. May, R.: *Psychology and the Human Dilemma*. Princeton, Van Nostrand, 1967.
25. McGill, V. K.: *Emotions and Reason*. Springfield, Thomas, 1954.
26. Otto, H.: *Group Methods Designed to Actualize Human Potential: A Handbook*. Chicago, Achievement Motivation Systems, 1968.
27. Perls, F., Hefferline, R., and Goodman, P.: *Gestalt Therapy*. New York, Julian Press, 1951.
28. Phillips, E. L.: *Psychotherapy*. Englewood Cliffs, N. J., Prentice-Hall, 1956.

29. Phillips, E. L., and Wiener, D. N.: *Short-Term Psychotherapy and Structured Behavior Change.* New York, McGraw-Hill, 1966.

30. Potash, R. R., and Taylor, J. E.: Discussion of Albert Ellis, Phobia treated with rational-emotive psychotherapy. *Voices, 3* (No. 3): 39-40, 1967.

31. Premack, D.: Reinforcement theory. In Levine, D. (Ed.): *Nebraska Symposium on Motivation, 1965.* Lincoln, University of Nebraska Press, 1965.

32. Rogers, C. R.: *Client-Centered Therapy.* Boston, Houghton Mifflin, 1951.

33. Rogers, C. R.: A conversation with Carl Rogers, by Mary Harrington Hall. *Psychology Today, 1:*19-21, 62-66, December, 1967.

34. Rogers, C. R.: *On Becoming a Person.* Boston, Houghton Mifflin, 1961.

35. Schutz, W.: *Joy.* New York, Grove Press, 1967.

36. Stoller, F.: The long weekend. *Psychology Today, 1:*28-33, December, 1967.

37. Whitaker, C., and Malone, T. A.: *Roots of Psychotherapy.* New York, McGraw-Hill, 1953.

38. Wiener, D. W., and Stieper, D. R.: *Dimensions of Psychotherapy.* Chicago, Aldine, 1965.

39. Wolpe, J.: *Psychotherapy of Reciprocal Inhibition.* Stanford, Stanford University Press, 1958.

40. Wolpe, J., and Lazarus, A. A.: *Behavior Therapy Techniques: A Guide to the Treatment of Neuroses.* Oxford, Pergamon Press, 1966.

In RECENT years developments stemming primarily from academic psychology have had an increasingly significant influence on psychotherapeutic practice. The impetus has been seen primarily in the area of psychotherapy called behavior modification, where it received its initial germination from learning theory and attempts by therapists to apply some of the techniques and concepts also emerging from this theoretical structure. Dr. Michael Merbaum, in his paper, describes the developments within this new sector and reviews some of the arguments for and against behavioral modification. He develops some cogent arguments, indicating that the proximity of practice to both learning theory and the experimental laboratory are not quite as close as some proponents of this system believe. Dr. Merbaum does not, however, state that the practice cannot be anchored in learning theory nor that the model does not include the experimental paradigm as part of its core. In fact the research base to behavior modification plus the flexibility in utilizing this aspect of our therapeutic armamentarium seem central to the advantages that he envisions within this approach.

Dr. Merbaum's discussion of psychotherapeutic issues is characterized by an eclectic and critical approach to both behavior modification and other techniques as well. He assesses the limitations and advantages in behavioral modification and indicates what the moot questions are that still need to be answered. Thus, he is very clear about what are assumptions, what are hypotheses, and what are the beginning answers in the different methods of psychotherapy. The base he provides for understanding behavior therapy and criticism of existent notions is both broad and specific. Additionally he details both the theoretical and technical aspects of the many different approaches that are subsumed under this general rubric of behavior modification. His paper, therefore, is an excellent representative of the theory and practice of behavior modification as espoused by Dr. Merbaum, for it is both experimental—in the best sense of the word—and flexible.

G.D.G.
D.S.M.

Chapter 11

BEHAVIOR THERAPY APPROACHES
TO PSYCHOTHERAPY

MICHAEL MERBAUM

N OT SO VERY long ago Robert Harper[8] published a little book entitled *Psychoanalysis and Psychotherapy: 36 Systems.* Since then I am sure this list has grown impressively and the variations on each theme expanded almost geometrically. Nowadays almost anyone worth his salt has a new methodological twist to offer, and the list of such personalized techniques is incredibly long. Unfortunately, while there is no dearth of ideas about therapy, there is precious little data to lend credibility to most of them. One is reminded of Ramey's cynical remark a number of years ago at a conference dealing with the therapeutic training of clinical psychologists: "Psychotherapy is an undefined technique applied to unspecified cases with unpredictable results. For this technique, rigorous training is required." While it is tempting to lament the current state of our psychotherapeutic progress and knowledge, there are indeed some developments that warrant close attention.

In recent years the application of principles of learning to the understanding and treatment of psychopathology has been vigorous and widespread. The foundations of this approach rest to a large extent on an extensive body of experimental research and theory associated with the work of Pavlov, Skinner, Hull, and other learning theorists. In 1958, Arnold Lazarus coined the term "behavior therapy" to describe the broad spectrum of clinical techniques that owe a good part of their origin to the findings and methods of experimental psychology.

As a therapeutic movement, behavior therapy identifies the treatment of psychopathology as an objective scientific discipline that depends upon empirical data to verify the economy and utility of different treatment methods. Basic to behavior therapy is its reliance on research generated in both laboratory and natural environment settings and the generalization of such findings to the actual therapeutic situation. The role of research is thus central to behavior therapy and is seen as the most productive direction for the evolution of a second generation of clinical techniques that will effectively influence, condition, or manipulate behavior toward some therapeutically desired goals.

It goes without saying that a commitment to research also implies an equivalent commitment to ideas. As in all clinical disciplines, however, there are numerous theoretical positions that seem to complement, compete with, or even contradict one another. For this reason it is unrealistic to talk about a single behavior therapy approach that can be neatly arranged into a consistent theoretical or methodological system. Rather, at this stage of the game, there is a multiplicity of methods derived from various sources, ingeniously modified to fit the individual client and artistically woven into the fabric of the therapeutic encounter.

Before I discuss a number of specific theories and methods involved in behavior therapy, I would first like to outline some common presuppositions. First of all it is assumed that most persistent pathological behavior has been acquired through the process of learning. Hilgard's (1956) definition of learning as "the process by which new or altered behavior comes about as a result of prior response, provided the changes cannot be attributed to temporary changes in the state of the organism (as in fatigue or under drugs)" is directly relevant to the behavior therapy position. Thus, current behavior is, by definition, more or less continuous with its historical antecedents. However, this assumption does not require that the disturbance necessarily originate in the remote past. Rather, it assumes that at any point in the course of human development, critical experiences have powerfully instigated the patterns of response currently in effect.

Although some developmental sequence is largely shared by most therapeutic schools, this conceptual similarity, while compatible insofar as etiology is concerned, is irrelevant to the conduct of behavior therapy. Therapeutic intervention almost exclusively deals with the present life of the individual. Therefore, most crucial in the behavioral model is the identification and systematic analysis of specific target responses to be modified, with a major focus on how and under what conditions they are now being maintained in the behavioral repertoire. The origins of this behavior are viewed as only peripherally related to the contemporary scene. Consequently, the hypothesis that a substantial portion of the variance in therapeutic change can be attributed to the release of unconscious emotion due to the restructuring of early childhood events is plainly rejected.

The core of behavior therapy is behavior itself. The conviction that "symptoms" are in reality a manifestation of an inferred underlying conflict or motive state has little appeal because of the casual and even flippant way these terms are often used. Unless there is some way of defining the functional bond between the motive and the parallel or consequent effects on behavior, the inference has no practical applications whatsoever.

A charge often leveled at behavior therapy is that successful "symptom" relief brings about something equally catastrophic in its place. The research offers no support for this idea, though a crucial variable is the theoretical definition of the term "symptom." It is quite true that patterns of behavior are tied together in highly idiosyncratic ways and thus more than one "symptom" is the usual target in behavior therapy. However, the notion of "symptom substitution," which implies the automatic replacement of one behavior by another, has not found verification in the clinical or experimental literature.[20]

While there has been a tendency on the part of behaviorists to deal with response parameters that are physically visible and in so doing to neglect the reality of internal psychological factors, there is a noticeable shift toward the analysis of unshared, implicit, covert internal processes. Thus, mental events such as fantasy, thoughts, dreams, and other mediating internal states are not automatically excluded from investigation because of their private nature. Recent research by Kanfer and Marston,[11] Bandura and Walters,[3] and Mischel and Staub[18] on patterns of self-regulation and self-reinforcement has opened up enormous research possibilities to the role of internal mechanisms in the exercise of personal and environmental control. Clinically, the therapeutic positions of Wolpe,[24] Homme,[9] Cautela,[4] Ellis,[6] and Stampfl[22] tend to emphasize the instrumental importance of images, logical and illogical thought cues, and other personal reflections in bringing about therapeutic movement.

However, whether the behavior be publicly demonstrable or privately subtle, the behavior therapist will deal with it both as a means and end in itself. A person suffering from the discomfort of a phobia, for example, may be thought to do so because in his conditioning history certain fortuitous connections have been established between neutral objects in the presence of heightened emotional arousal. The phobic behavior is treated quite literally as a product of faulty relationships that need to be counterconditioned or "cognitively" rearranged. Therapeutic cure is achieved directly by treating the phobic "symptom" itself.

It follows logically from this attitude that almost exclusive responsibility for change is placed on the therapist and his methods. If the client "resists" (i.e. does not respond or experience benefit from the therapeutic program), it is because the therapist has been unable to arrange the necessary conditions to produce modifications in behavior. Under these circumstances it is then incumbent upon the therapist to discard unproductive methods and try something else. From this vantage point the client is always right. His behavior is determined by the complex set of variables that maintain it, and as long as these conditions remain as they are, his behavior will be emitted in consonance with them. The therapist's role is thus geared to interfere directly and actively with this preestablished order and introduce internal (cognitive) and or external (environmental) conditions that will modify existing patterns of behavior that are contrary to the well-being of the client.

It should be noted that the goals of behavior therapy are quite straightforward and appear more limited in scope than those of many of the traditional schools of therapy. It is quite sufficient, for example, to relieve a specific area of suffering without tampering with other aspects of a person's behavior found through assessment to be unrelated to the target behaviors. In fact, whether or not personality change has occurred in the process is basically irrelevant to the goals of behavior therapy. If the undesirable behavior has been eliminated so that the life of the individual can proceed without the excess baggage of emotional distress, the treatment program has been effective.

Turning to the therapeutic situation itself, there are many behavior therapy techniques currently being used. Among these are negative practice, extinction procedures, aversive conditioning, behavior shaping techniques, implosive therapy, and systematic desensitization, to name just a few. The types of patient populations to which these methods have been applied covers the entire psychopathological spectrum, and include all forms of neuroses, psychoses, child behavior disorders, mental deficiency, and so forth. Many of the reports indicating clinical success are of the case history variety, but the experimental literature (using better controls) is growing.

I might comment at this point on the use of case study data in the substantiation of treatment effects. There is a large difference between anecdotal case history material and data acquired on an individual client through use of detailed analytical techniques. As long as adequate premeasures are obtained, with a thorough review of the therapeutic activities presumably instrumental in producing change as well as process and outcome measures tied to the therapeutic operations, these data would seem to qualify as relevant additions to the experimental literature. The systematic study of the single case has many advantages in increasing our therapeutic understanding as long as the procedural variables at all levels of inference are clearly explicated. Unfortunately, the usual case reports stemming from the dynamic literature do not meet these criteria since almost all of the evidence presented is in anecdotal form. Thus, replication is virtually impossible.

Current clinical practice in behavior modification tends to revolve around two major theoretical systems. The first is Joseph Wolpe's theory of reciprocal inhibition[24] and the second, B. F. Skinner's operant conditioning paradigm. Wolpe's theory, which is very much an outgrowth of classical conditioning and Hullian learning theory, is focused on the disastrous effects of anxiety in eliciting neurotic behavior patterns. Since neuroses are usually characterized by persistent habits of anxiety response to situations in which there is often no objective danger, therapy, according to Wolpe, must be directed toward the suppression of anxiety. He believes that all human neuroses are produced as a consequence of the association between high intensities of anxiety and neutral stimulus events which have occurred in close temporal relationship. Wolpe reasons that the successful treatment of neurosis would depend upon the counterconditioning of the neurotic anxiety responses through the creation of behavior that is physiologically antagonistic to it.

Therefore, in systematic desensitization therapy, the client is trained in relaxation and eventually exposed to a succession of anxiety-arousing stimuli that are presented in imagination while the person is in a relaxed state. Relaxation, once instilled in the client's repertoire of behavior, serves the purpose of reciprocally inhibiting anxiety. An important feature of Wolpe's system, however, is that any response with an anxiety-inhibiting quality can be used to countercondition the anxiety state. These include assertive responses, sexual arousal, humor, and so on, all of which have the capacity to dissipate the intensity of anxiety-arousing cues. Wolpe reports very high rates of success using this method and Lazarus[15] has published data supporting to a somewhat lesser degree his extraordinary claims.

The method of systematic desensitization has generated a group of research papers designed to compare its efficiency with other treatment approaches and appropriate controls. Lang and Lazovik[14] found that snake fears could be substantially reduced with desensitization and that the gains were durable over time. Paul[19] studied the use of desensitization, brief insight-oriented psychotherapy, a drug-placebo control, and a no-treatment control in the treatment of intense public-speaking anxiety. The assessments before and after treatment were extensive and included tests, ratings, behavior observations, and physiological recordings. Systematic desensitization was discovered to be the superior method of treatment.

If desensitization works, and there is ample evidence to suggest that it does a good part of the time, the reasons why are of particular interest to the clinician. Wolpe's interpretation is clear. Intense anxiety is an aberrant physiological state and relaxation acts as a parasympathetic suppressor to heightened autonomic arousal. However, for relaxation to be a significant counterconditioning agent, it must be joined to anxiety-arousing cues in a stepwise fashion or its potency will be diluted. The process for Wolpe can be succinctly described as physiological conditioning.

A number of research studies have critically examined the process of desensitization and its components of relaxation and presentations of graded aversive stimuli. Davison,[5] for example, investigated whether the contiguity between relaxation and the anxiety hierarchy was necessary for effective outcome with Ss experiencing snake fears. In his design he compared the usual systematic desensitization procedure with a simple-relaxation group who visualized neutral scenes, an anxiety group without relaxation, and a no-treatment control. Only the genuine desensitization group significantly reduced their fears.

Although Davison supported Wolpe's counterconditioning hypothesis, other explanations are perhaps equally plausible. For instance, Folkins, Lawson, Opton, and Lazarus[7] found that desensitization was not as effective as a cognitive rehearsal procedure in lowering anxiety reactions to a stress-inducing movie. In fact, desensitization fared no better than a plain relaxation treatment. The authors' interpretation of these data highlights the role of "cognitive processes" in instituting better "self-control" under stress-producing experiences.

Despite the fact that desensitization was discovered to be less effective than other treatments, a disconcerting finding for its advocates, the role attributed to cognitive variables in desensitization-like treatment methods is temptingly close to notions expressed in the dynamic literature. In a critique of the Folkins *et al.* experiment[7] and in defense of the efficacy of desensitization, Davison[5] also conjectures that during the visualization of aversive material a "cognitive" reappraisal of these same events might result. London[16] similarly suspects that if the aversive cues in the desensitization hierarchy fail to evoke the anticipated anxiety reaction, the expectancy of such disastrous consequences in real life may be sharply reduced.

Valins and Ray,[23] from their research, believe that desensitization is equivalent to training in self-control. Success in this venture provides a recognition that "I" have been the instrument for change. The cognition of "helplessness" is replaced by one of positive self-control.

While reference to "cognitive processes" has great appeal, other data indicate that the reinforcing properties of the social interaction in desensitization must be added to the equation. Leitenberg *et al.* compared desensitization without positive feedback to desensitization with therapeutic instructions and verbal praise following the successful completion of an anxiety item. The positive-reinforcement desensitization group was significantly more successful than the desensitization group without reinforcement and a no-treatment control. The latter two groups did not differ from each other in the criterion task, approaching a snake. It would appear that positive reinforcement is an important variable enhancing the desensitization effect.

Although the implication that a therapist's effectiveness in desensitization is optimized when he responds positively to the interpersonal quality of the relationship, other studies eliminating the therapist from the therapy situation are also intriguing. Lang[14] has devised an intricate automated desensitization machine in which a computer system provides immediate feedback to the relaxed subject. Kahn and Quinlan[10] studied the question of how much therapist contact is necessary for desensitization therapy. In one condition they saw clients in a single orientation interview in which an anxiety hierarchy was constructed and then supplied them with a do-it-yourself desensitization kit to work on at home. Telephone contact was maintained with the clinic on a once-a-week basis. A control group received conventional desensitization over a six-week, twelve-session period. The results favored neither group although the home group did slightly better than the control group that had more therapist contact. The authors suggest that these data support Wolpe's prediction that if significant learning opportunities are given to the client, regardless of the form in which they are presented, the presence of the therapist may be superfluous.

To dismiss Wolpe's notion of conditioning through reciprocal inhibition would be premature at this stage. Nonetheless, the classical conditioning interpretation is certainly vulnerable to alternative explanation. It is evident that desensitization is a complex multidimensional process with a variety of interacting ingredients. My view is that the most powerful consequence of this method is the creation of a cognitive alternative to the habitual and compulsive anxiety-avoidance responses that have become so firmly entrenched. The strategy in desensitization is designed to interrupt this rigid behavioral pattern by carefully training the client to discriminate the anxiety cues presumably responsible for releasing the anxiety response. In so doing, the strange and mysterious quality of feelings typically experienced by people struggling with intense anxiety are directly retranslated into terms more concretely tied to specifiable events. Once this attitude has been strengthened, the environment inevitably becomes less terrifying and the individual's potential to better regulate his emotional state is greatly enhanced.

In the course of his training in desensitization the client has acquired a number of controls in containing the effects of anxiety. For example, he has learned to relax in the presence of disruptive experiences or say to himself certain cue words such as "calm" or "relax" that have been associated in the desensitization procedure with relaxation, thus minimizing the impact of anxiety. With a therapeutic cure, however, the client will simply not respond with anxiety to the stimulus contexts which previously elicited anxiety because these cues are no longer relevant to his immediate affective experience.

Behavior therapy's close affiliation with experimental research is hardly better illustrated than in the application of operant conditioning methods to produce behavior change. In broad terms the emphasis in operant conditioning is on the consequences of behavior or, put concisely, on the relationship between the organism and its environment. Behavior is viewed as lawful, predictable, and thus potentially controllable once the relevant reinforcing variables have been determined. In order for these techniques to be used with precision, the target behavior must be observable, measurable, and reproducible. If the response measures fail to satisfy these criteria, operant procedures are not feasible.

For this reason, aside from the philosophical and metapsychological issues involved, there is no room in the operant paradigm for the scientific acknowledgment of inferred internal states. This does not mean that internal states are completely excluded from analysis, since Homme[9] and others do attempt to treat thoughts and ideas as identifiable responses that can be overtly manipulated. However, constructs such as anxiety, aggression, hunger, dependency, and so forth are in the main considered as merely imprecise descriptions of behavior.

This is particularly evident when the notion of causality is attached to these constructs by various personality theorists. For example, anxiety, as a behavioral phenomenon, does not cause a person to tremble, sweat, or experience general distress in living. Rather, anxiety is the response of trembling, sweating, and general distress. The construct, then, is simply a descriptive device for subsuming various behaviors under its umbrella. It is consistent with the operant position that the theoretical explanations of Freud and Wolpe both suffer from similar misconceptions in that they erroneously attribute the causes of behavior to inferential states that do not materially exist except as vague theoretical rhetoric.

Operant conditioning research and treatment in the area of psychopathology has, for the most part, been carried out in settings where strict environmental control is possible. Hospitals, schools, and various types of remedial institutions are prime examples. The usual one-to-one psychotherapeutic relationship is less often the focus of systematic study, though some interesting innovations have been created to make this situation amenable to operant analysis. Nonetheless, within the former situations, the dispensing or withholding of reinforcement variables can be practically arranged in a more comprehensive manner. In addition, the operant therapist in institutions with a confined population has authority over a wider range of environmental variables than one usually has in the conventional psychotherapeutic relationship. Thus greater engineering possibilities are available.

My treatment of an autistic child who had spent the better part of five years violently abusing himself illustrates some therapeutic uses of operant conditioning techniques. After discovering that this boy had been exposed to an endless progression of unsuccessful treatments it was finally decided to use aversive conditioning procedures to effect behavior change. An operant program was designed in which a brief but painful electric shock was made the immediate consequence of self-punishment. Prior to the introduction of the shock contingencies, extensive behavioral observations were made to determine the frequency of the target behavior, under what circumstances it appeared, and its duration. It was discovered, for example, that his rate of beating his face, within a series of ten-minute samples, varied between three and four hundred overt acts, and overall, many thousands of these acts occurred each day.

The program yielded dramatic results almost immediately. Following a few presentations of the shock contingencies, the abusive behavior dropped to zero. There was nothing spontaneous about his reaction since, when the shock apparatus was not visible, he continued to beat himself with great tenacity. Eventually the parents were trained in the same operant program, and the behavior began to be extinguished both at home and in a broader range of situations.

What is most interesting is that once this behavior was reduced in frequency and intensity, other behaviors were drastically affected as well. His general mood was brighter, he became more intensively involved in social interaction, and he started to use his hands in more constructive play.

It should be noted that in any comprehensive program of behavior change many target responses are potentially involved. In this case the major goal was not only the control of self-punishment but the concomitant replacement of self-abuse with other more socially adaptive behavior. During this aspect of the program positive reinforcers such as food, affection, and general selective attention as well as punishment are being used, hopefully to extend his level of speech and other complex behavior.

Kushner[13] has presented extensive data on the use of aversive conditioning procedures with both children and adults. For the most part, however, the operant conditioning literature on animal and human subjects has emphasized the effectiveness of positive reinforcers in altering response probabilities. Nonetheless, various schedules of reinforcement which provide for the avoidance of an undesirable response under threat of punishment, combined with positive reinforcement for a constructive response alternative, have been found to be of therapeutic value.

An innovative application of operant conditioning in hospital settings can be seen in the development of token economy programs. An extensive though preliminary study by Atthowe and Krasner[2] is typical of the procedures initiated. Consistent with the principles of behavioral engineering, it was assumed that behavior is functionally dependent upon its consequences. Therefore, if "sick" behavior is ignored and "nonsick" behavior reinforced, there should be significant changes in the reinforced behavior.

In the first stage of the research project selected behaviors were carefully observed in order to gather reliable base rates prior to the onset of the experimental treatments. Following this phase, the patients were informed of the radical changes that were about to occur in their usual ward routine. The instructions were explicit in outlining the consequences of various kinds of behavior. For the responsible enactment of certain predetermined behaviors, tokens were given which could be turned in for consumable items such as candy, cigarettes, and the like as well as being used as passes for many desirable social privileges. The ultimate in reinforcement was a card which allowed its holder to buy himself out of the system. This "Carte Blanche" authorized reinforcements without any tokens required.

The results of the study were encouraging. Very substantial increases were observed in the quality and quantity of social interaction, following of ward rules, and control of aggressive behavior. Furthermore, during the token program almost double the number of men were discharged in comparison with previous rates of discharge. However, one-half of this number returned within the next nine months. In many ways this pioneering study is less sophisticated than ones currently in progress in which there is a greater effort to tailor the reinforcement contingencies to the unique needs of each individual participant.

The translation of the therapeutic process into the language of reinforcement theory is becoming more acceptable even in the traditional psychotherapies. There is currently an awareness that social reinforcers such as attention, praise, and other minimal verbal and nonverbal gestures of therapist interest are powerful influences on behavior, thoughts, and feelings, included. The anachronistic notion that the therapist can be conceived as a blank screen, even in the most socially detached therapeutic relationship, is pretty much obsolete. The facts are plain that reinforcement has a substantial role in the movement of the client toward the condition most desired by his therapist and that behavioral manipulation, intentional or unintentional, is a natural consequence of all psychotherapeutic relationships. In his paper, "Psychoanalysis as an Educational Process," Jud Marmor[17] has highlighted some of the compelling features of this process:

> In face to face transactions the expressions on the therapist's face, a questioning glance, a lift of the eyebrows, a barely perceptible shake of the head or shrug of the shoulder all act as significant cues to the patient. But even behind our couches, our 'uh-huh' as well as our silences, the interest or the disinterest reflected in our tone of voice or our shifting of postures all act like subtle radio signals influencing patients' responses, reinforcing some responses and discouraging others.

At this juncture it would be useful to reflect briefly on the behavioral model with special attention to the directions in which behavior therapy is apt to move. My own feeling is that behavior therapy can be best thought of as a general attitude toward therapeutic practice. The cardinal assumption underlying this attitude is that behavior is lawful in the sense that it follows predictable patterns and is thus potentially alterable once the specific variables that control it have been clearly illuminated.

The practical extension of this thinking is that the behavior therapist can, without committing theoretical heresy, apply any scientific principles and social engineering designs currently available to effect behavior change. This framework does not require a rigid commitment to stimulus-response conceptions of behavior or even that conditioning methods should comprise the entire repertoire of useful therapeutic interventions. Rather, one of the most powerful and compelling features of the practice of behavior therapy is its flexibility. The behavioral clinician is to a large extent freed from an orthodoxy of rules that are rarely based upon anything more than vague guidelines passed down from one therapist generation to another. Thus, there is no hesitation to concentrate on the interpersonal facets of a relationship as a vehicle for change or to be intimately concerned with questions of value, attitude, and belief.

Depending upon the problem, the therapist should be versatile enough to use any clinical technique which in his moral and ethical judgment could be of therapeutic benefit. These strategies might include systematic desensitization, operant conditioning, modeling procedures, covert sensitization, and implosive therapy, as well as interpretations, rational persuasion, role playing, and so on. The point is that behavior therapy is largely empirical, oriented toward action, and atheoretical, except where the experimental data supports a special theoretical formulation.

While it is true that learning theory provides a takeoff point for many of the behavior therapy techniques, it is not only premature but illusory to infer that there is a comprehensive theory of human learning that covers the entire range of human experience. In fact, many of the preconditions for the application of behavior therapy methods are little more than intelligent hunches. For example, the opinion that maladaptive behavior is principally an outgrowth of defective patterns of learning is a speculation tenuously deduced from animal research. An extrapolation of this sort to relationships dealing with complex human functions produces an anthropomorphism that may eventually interfere with more effective theorization. In addition, the mere fact that a remediation procedure rooted in conditioning methodology can be therapeutically helpful has no direct bearing on the etiology of a behavior disturbance.

Gaps in our knowledge are also particularly evident in the areas of self-control or self-regulation. How individuals initiate, maintain, and alter their perceptions and feelings is central to all forms of psychotherapy; behavior therapy is no exception. Research along these lines is yielding some interesting and useful insights.

Lang[14] has reported experiments in which Ss learned to achieve control over their cardiac rate after receiving both accurate and inaccurate feedback of their own physiological state. Schachter and Singer[21] highlight the relevance of verbal labels in the control of emotional behavior as a function of Ss' interpretation of external events. Bandura and Walters[3] report extensive data on imitation and modeling. The effectiveness of vicarious reinforcement and self-reinforcement in maintaining complicated chains of behavior has direct clinical relevance. Adelson and Goldfried[1] have adapted some of Bandura's modeling techniques in eliminating dental phobias of children by having them observe a child who was an excellent dental patient.

Kanfer and Phillips[12] utilized evidence from their studies in self-regulation to devise a procedure called instigation therapy. This method focuses on training the client in self-observation, evaluation, categorizing behavior, and environmental planning on the basis of learning procedures. Techniques for self-reinforcement are stressed in this program.

Homme[9] has created interesting clinical techniques to modify what he refers to as coverants—the operant responses of the mind. Using ingenious tricks, the client is trained in methods of self-control by varying the amount of reinforcement he is willing to allow himself contingent upon the successful performance of certain acts of self-improvement. The whole area of self-regulation, however, is probably the most critical yet theoretically under-developed aspect of the behavior therapies.

In conclusion, there are many controversial issues surrounding behavior therapy not directly touched in this paper. Critics of behavior therapy have raised the specter of mechanization, antihumanism, and symptom substitution, while behavior therapists have countered with their own nasty rejoinders. More positively, however, polemical disagreements often stimulate inquiry and sharpen the tools of science. But despite the many real and imagined differences in psychotherapeutic schools, the common ground is a vital concern for the well-being of the individual, and after all, this is what the whole thing is about.

REFERENCES

1. Adelson, R., and Goldfried, M.: Handling the Fearful Child in the Dental Situation. Unpublished paper, 1968.
2. Atthowe, J. M., and Krasner, L.: A preliminary report of the application of contingent reinforcement procedures (token economy) on a 'chronic' psychiatric ward. *J. Abnorm. Psychol., 73:*37-43, 1968.
3. Bandura, A., and Walters, R. H.: *Social Learning and Personality Development.* New York, Holt, 1963.
4. Cautela, J. R.: Treatment of compulsive behavior by covert sensitization. *Psychol. Rec., 16:*33-41, 1966.
5. Davison, G. C.: A procedural critique of 'desensitization and the experimental reduction of threat.' *J. Abnorm. Psychol., 74:*86-87, 1969.
6. Ellis, A.: *Reason and Emotion in Psychotherapy.* New York, Lyle Stuart, 1962.
7. Folkins, C. H., Lawson, K. D., Opton, E. M., Jr., and Lazarus, R. S.: Desensitization and the experimental reduction of threat. *J. Abnorm. Psychol., 73:*100-113.
8. Harper, R. A.: *Psychoanalysis and Psychotherapy: 36 Systems.* Englewood Cliffs, N. J., Prentice-Hall, 1959.
9. Homme, L. E.: Control of coverants, the operants of the mind. *Psychol. Rec., 15:*501-511, 1965.
10. Kahn, M., and Quinlan, P.: Desensitization with Varying Degrees of Therapist Contact. Paper presented at APA Convention, Washington, D. C., 1967.
11. Kanfer, F. H., and Marston, A. R.: Conditioning of self-reinforcing responses: An analogue to self-confidence training. *Psychol. Rep., 13:*63-70, 1963.
12. Kanfer, F. H., and Phillips, Jeanne S.: Behavior therapy: A panacea for all ills or a passing fancy? *Arch. Gen. Psychiat., 15:*114-128, 1966.
13. Kushner, M.: Faradic Aversive Controls in Clinical Practice. Paper presented at Ninth Annual Institute for Research in Clinical Psychology at University of Kansas, 1967.
14. Lang, P. J., and Lazovik, A. D.: Experimental desensitization of a phobia. *J. Abnorm. Soc. Psychol., 66:*519-525, 1963.

15. Lazarus, A. A.: The results of behavior therapy in 126 cases of severe neurosis. *Behav. Res. Ther., 1:*69-75, 1963.

16. London, P.: *The Modes and Morals of Psychotherapy.* New York, Holt, 1964.

17. Marmor, J.: *Psychoanalytic Therapy as an Educational Process from Science and Psychoanalysis.* New York, Grune & Stratton, 1962.

18. Mischel, W., and Staub, E.: Effects of expectancy on working and waiting for larger rewards. *J. Personality Soc. Psychol., 2:*625-633, 1965.

19. Paul, G. L.: *Insight vs. Desensitization in Anxiety Reduction.* Stanford, Stanford University Press, 1966.

20. Rachman, S.: Spontaneous remission and latent learning. *Behav. Res. Ther., 1:*133-137, 1963.

21. Schachter, S., and Singer, J. E.: Cognitive, social and physiological determinants of emotional state. *Psychol. Rev., 69:*379-399, 1962.

22. Stampfl, T. G., and Levis, D. J.: Essentials of implosive therapy: A learning-theory-based psychodynamic behavioral therapy. *J. Abnorm. Psychol., 72:*496-503, 1967.

23. Valins, S., and Ray, A. A.: Effects of cognitive desensitization on avoidance behavior. *J. Personality Soc. Psychol., 7:*345-350, 1967.

24. Wolpe, J.: *Psychotherapy by Reciprocal Inhibition.* Stanford, Stanford University Press, 1958.

D R. ERNEST KRAMER brings to this paper an extensive knowledge of the clinical use of hypnosis. He is widely published in the area and his expertise shines through in this easygoing account of his clinical utilization of hypnosis.

In a clear, easy-to-read style, interlaced with a dry sense of humor, Dr. Kramer, former Director of Psychological Services at Adelphi University, gives his perspective on the use of hypnosis in therapy. Initially he warns us against our grandiosity and specifies the limits and areas of application of hypnosis. Tracing in case-history fashion his experiences with hypnotism, he outlines the characteristics of its use with schizophrenic patients, where he found, contrary to many published reports, that his patients were normally hypnotizable. The next series of cases interestingly unfold, each with a new and different experience which helps alert the experienced as well as the inexperienced therapists to problems they might possibly have in clinical work. He provides a general frame of reference of the where, when, and how of hypnosis, emphasizing that hypnosis is only one tool of the many to help the experienced psychotherapist. He feels that "hypnosis is not and cannot be a therapeutic technique in itself," and this message is abundantly clear to us by the end of this very straightforward and concise paper.

Dr. Kramer's many years of teaching serve him well in his presentation of this material. We learn bibliographic sources, advantages and disadvantages of hypnosis, and even suggestions on training as a hypnotist. All in all it is a comprehensive presentation, scholarly and at the same time one that holds your interest throughout.

G.D.G.
D.S.M.

Chapter 12

SOME USES OF HYPNOSIS IN PSYCHOTHERAPY

Ernest Kramer

THIS CHAPTER is a sampling of some of the uses I have made of hypnosis in psychotherapy. I assume in it some general familiarity with hypnosis. (For those who lack that, I recommend Hilgard's excellent book[5] as an introduction.) Here then are some ideas about hypnosis and some case histories in which the patient and I have learned something and from which I hope the reader will as well.

Let me tell you first about a phone call. It came one evening during final exam period at the University. A nervous-sounding young lady at the other end introduced herself as a University student and said that she had learned from a fellow student that I did work with hypnosis. She said that she hoped that I would be able to help her with the extreme anxiety she felt over final examinations. I asked her in an exploratory way if she had had such intense anxiety during other exam periods. She said this was the worst she had ever had. I asked rather tentatively whether this might be related to her state of preparation for the exams. She said she had, in fact, studied less this year than ever before— apparently for social rather than for psychopathological reasons. It began to sound like something a bit out of my line, but I suggested she drop by my office the next day and we would talk about it further. "Oh!" she exclaimed, "I have my exam tomorrow morning at 8:30. I guess I thought maybe you could just help me with it on the telephone."

Even hypnosis is limited in its applications. I did not accept the case. However, I did, in addition to feeling a little annoyance, have a brief fantasy of how nice it would be if my magic powers did extend to her telephone needs. That brings me to my first subject here.

FANTASIES OF THE PSYCHOTHERAPIST

Anyone who has read any of the literature on hypnotherapy knows that hypnosis is often used for encouraging fantasies in patients. I have also noticed, though the published literature neglects to mention this, that the very idea of using hypnosis in therapy produces fantasies in the psychotherapist. Occasionally, one does find a printed reference to "countertransference" problems in hypnotherapy. But transference and countertransference have more exact meanings that do not necessarily include the two therapist fantasies I want to mention here.

The first fantasy is that all patients can be hypnotized if the therapist learns the proper skills thoroughly enough. Freud himself stumbled painfully through this fantasy. When he first found that he could not hypnotize all those who came to him for help, he laid the blame on his own inability. Perhaps he was thinking of his days in Paris when he watched Charcot successfully demonstrate hypnotic procedures with one patient after another. However, Charcot was not picking his patients at random. They had been chosen and prepared by his assistants.

Approximately one out of ten of your patients will remain steadfastly unhypnotizable regardless of your best efforts. A considerably larger percentage will show only mild or moderate signs of involvement. A few years ago I knew a psychiatrist who used hypnosis in therapy and who could not stand the frustrations of the hard-core unhypnotizable. He would give every patient a small dose of a sedative shortly before beginning the hypnotic induction procedure. "Then at least," he explained to me, "they cannot tell me they are not sleepy at all unless they are absolutely lying."

The role of the hypnotist's personality and skill in determining the hypnotizability of the patient is somewhat unclear. This much is clear: How the hypnotist is perceived and what he does makes some difference,[9] but it makes much less difference than the folklore of the subject would suggest.[5] It makes much less difference than the patient's aptitude for being hypnotized.

A second major fantasy of the therapist is that hypnotherapy is an almost totally different business from psychotherapy without hypnosis. For the skilled clinician, this fantasy is a fearful one. It suggests that he will have whole new worlds of skill and knowledge to master before he can use hypnosis with his patients. For the unskilled and inadequately trained clinician—the legitimate beginner or the untrained black marketeer of therapy—the fantasy is a hopeful one. If he can learn this special hypnotic bag of tricks, he will not have to master the extensive training and discipline of the fully qualified psychotherapist.

One of the clearest statements of how things really stand here is by Lewis Wolberg.[17] He has written, ". . . hypnosis is not psychotherapy. It is a catalyst which sometimes enables certain things to take place in psychotherapy." In other words, hypnosis by itself cannot guarantee that anything useful will happen. Perhaps we need to get rid of the term "hypnotherapy." It presumes to name something new, whereas what is more usefully done is something older. What is usefully done is the psychotherapy we have been trained in, with the occasional addition of limited hypnotic techniques.

THE VARIETIES OF "HYPNOTHERAPY"

A corollary of that is that psychotherapy using hypnosis is as varied as psychotherapy itself. There is, for example, "hypnoanalysis," marked by the traditional hallmarks of psychoanalysis—couch, frequent sessions, many hours, and free association. There is "sensory hypnoplasty," in which the hypnotized patient plays with colored and smell-impregnated clay.[7] There are hypnotic adjuncts to the behavior therapies, those learning-theory–based treatments which Dr. Merbaum has written of elsewhere in this volume.

Fortunately, Milton Kline[6] has assembled a good summary chapter on hypnotherapy techniques, which appears in the *Handbook of Clinical Psychology*. That summary is about six years old now, but it is still a reliable overview of the most common uses of hypnosis in psychotherapy.

I want to note, however, my sense of dissatisfaction as I read through that summary and also the full texts of many recent articles on the psychotherapeutic uses of hypnosis. First, there was the striking paucity of experimental studies. While there were some experiments on aspects of hypnosis potentially relevant to therapy, in the treatment literature itself there were few studies that had anything like decent control groups. Hans Eysenck's famous claim that there are no controlled studies providing support for the efficacy of psychotherapy is now demonstrably untrue. Unfortunately, however, that is how things seem to stand with hypnotic techniques in therapy. The crucial studies remain to be done. The added value of hypnosis in various forms of therapy stands neither established as surely helpful nor condemned as guilty of uselessness; the Scottish court verdict "Not Proven" states the case.

Still, there are many promising and thought-provoking clinical studies published; some of them are single case histories and others describe fair-sized groups of patients. In reading these I experienced a disappointment of a different sort. There was simply not enough detail. It was extremely rare to find even a description of the induction procedure used. The ensuing therapy techniques themselves were described in the briefest outline. Now I have been guilty of this kind of super-brevity myself, and I know perfectly well that it is partly the result of journal demands to save space. But one of the consequences of it is that it is hard to judge the quality and reliability of the work reported in an article.

I got some feeling for this problem a few years ago when I did some work on the hypnotic susceptibility of schizophrenic patients. I was working at a California state hospital then. I vaguely remembered having read that schizophrenics could not be hypnotized. I am going to tell you about the research project that showed that was wrong,[11] and then I will go on to talk more about some of my clinical uses of hypnosis.

HYPNOSIS AND SCHIZOPHRENIA

On one of the wards which formed part of my assignment at the state hospital was an 18-year-old girl who allegedly showed some signs of multiple personality. Partly out of genuine therapeutic interest, but partly out of a desire to find a "Three Faces of Eve" sort of case history for myself, I decided to try treating her.

Hypnosis had a history of association with cases of multiple personality, so I carefully approached the psychiatrist in charge of the ward to sound out his attitude about hypnotic procedures. (Part of what I remembered from the Stanton and Schwartz study[13] of mental hospitals was that whenever administrative and treatment staff disagree, it is the patients who suffer.)

I had just about managed to say, "How do you feel about hypnosis?" when he bounced back enthusiastically with, "Wonderful, let's do a study on it! I've always wanted to do some research with hypnosis, and I never got to finish the one I started during my residency." So while I began treatment of my patient (to whom I shall return, and who did not turn out to have a multiple personality), we began to plan an investigation of the hypnotic susceptibility of schizophrenic patients. A thorough study of the existing literature provided some ground for pessimism and a great deal of ground for confusion.

Persons diagnosed as "schizophrenic" had generally been considered far less susceptible to hypnosis than either "normals" or "neurotics." Copeland and Kitching[1] went so far as to declare hypnosis to be of value for differential diagnosis—"without exception, cases which presented as true psychoses could not be hypnotized; if susceptibility to hypnosis developed, we were compelled to revise the diagnosis."

Most other clinical studies, while less extreme, tended in the same direction. Turning to controlled, experimental studies, when those dealing with only waking suggestibility of schizophrenics had been eliminated, only four investigations of hypnotic susceptibility of schizophrenics remained. Two of these[2,16] reported considerable success, with well over half the subjects entering at least a light stage of hypnosis. The other two[3,4] reported a considerably smaller percentage of successful inductions, although some schizophrenic patients were found to be susceptible in all studies.

Most of the previous work had varied the hypnotic induction technique with each patient. In our work we used the Stanford Hypnotic Susceptibility Scale (SHSS) Form A[15] with all subjects. The SHSS includes both a standard induction procedure, read verbatim from the manual, and a standard set of twelve tasks on which the hypnotic susceptibility of the subject is rated. The scale measures the number of times the subject acts like a hypnotized person when hypnosis is induced by a standard procedure and when the opportunities to react are presented in a standard manner. Norms are available for the distribution of scores which result from its use with a nonpsychiatric population.

The subjects were twenty-five patients from a female admission and acute treatment ward of the large state hospital where we worked. Anytime our clinical schedules gave us forty-five free minutes, one of us would approach the nearest patient about participating in the study while the other of us made a quick look for her chart to see if she had been diagnosed "schizophrenic." Thirty-one patients, unselected by any conscious bias on our part, were originally approached about participating in "some research involving hypnosis." Six of these firmly refused. This would seem to introduce a relatively small amount of volunteer bias into the study.

The subjects were generally told that they would be of help to the doctor, rather than that the doctor would be helping them. The introduction to the induction session followed the outline given in the SHSS manual, and the performance was scored according to the explicit criteria of the scale. We flipped a coin for who would try hypnotizing our first subject. I lost, so I had to try. I began reading the excellent and detailed induction which is part of the Stanford scale, when the patient interrupted to say, "But, Doctor, if you'd only say 'one, two, three, sleep,' I would!"

The possible range of scores on the Stanford scale goes from a bottom of zero to a top of twelve. Our very first subject—who I did insist listen to the entire induction—hit the top score. For all twenty-five patients, the range of scores went from five to twelve.

By and large the data resembled that for "normal" subjects. The fact that six of the prospective subjects originally approached were allowed to decline probably helps account for the absence of bottom-range scores. Another factor may be that, although subjects were informed that this was not a part of the hospital treatment procedure, the hypnotists were hospital staff members with the potential power to reward or at least punish the subjects.

Much of the previous work in which hypnosis was attempted with schizophrenics used special techniques of induction: not informing the subject he was to be hypnotized and varying the procedure for each subject. The rationale had been that schizophrenics require special handling. To this extent the experimental conditions may have reinforced one of the general messages which a hospital setting may convey to the individual: "You are not a normal person." The varying induction techniques also would seem to provide an opportunity for the investigators' possible doubts about the hypnotizability of the subjects to be conveyed to them.

The subjects in our study were given, verbatim, the induction technique used with the normal standardization group. They were treated like helpful and welcome subjects rather than patients; for example, they were told that they were helping the investigator with his research. One meaning of the difference between the results here and those found frequently elsewhere may be that, at least in the area of hypnotic behavior, if you treat a schizophrenic patient like a normal person he will respond in an essentially normal manner.

None of the patients in that research study or the two that followed in the hospital[8,14] showed any adverse effects from hypnosis. No psychotic patient appeared to become worse; no borderline patient became blatantly psychotic.

Leakage in the Subconscious

This was not quite the case, it seemed, with the 18-year-old girl who had indirectly started the research. I first tried using hypnosis to uncover her "alternate personality," which immediately vanished. I continued to use hypnosis as a kind of relaxing technique for her while we worked mainly in more traditional modes of psychotherapy. However, I began getting reports from her hospital ward that she had begun showing periods of distraction and not responding to people since work with hypnosis had begun. In retrospect, it seems highly significant to me that she showed these "symptoms" when she was given some sort of restriction she did not want to follow. I was too anxious about my hypnotic technique with hospital patients, however, to focus on the highly adaptable use she made of her reported "distraction."

I talked with her about the reports from the ward. Being a college-educated young lady—a Berkeley student—and very well read, she carefully explained to me that her present symptoms were due to the fact that material from her "subconscious" was erupting into her conscious due to the weakening of defenses through hypnosis. Well, if that is how she saw it, that is how we would work. I hypnotized her with a signal we had used before, and I asked her to slowly move from her conscious down into her subconscious and report to me what she saw.

I believe it is Dr. Martin Orne who has described the hypnotic interaction as a *folie à deux*—a highly special one, but still a kind of shared madness. So it was here. She told me she saw a yellow layer, and her subconscious lay beneath it. But the yellow layer looked different than it used to—not as thick as it once was. Down we went, though, through the yellow layer. (Remembering it now, scenes from the Beatles' "Yellow Submarine" film flicker in my mind.) Then I suggested that we turn and rise back up through it. But I stressed, too, that it would harden behind us as we rose. Sure enough, she described how the yellow layer hardened, and the unconscious was sealed off. I looked down with her and commented on the hardness and also on the fact that I had left a door in it. The door in this hard and safely sealed yellow layer was securely locked and needed two keys, one of them in my possession and one in hers. I awoke her. There were no more symptoms of distraction and vagueness on the ward after this. Our joint psychosis had accomplished its aim.

In this situation I responded partly to my own anxieties rather than to a cool appraisal of the situation. I think, looking back, that the reported symptoms were not dangerous ones and that their acting-out component could have been explored fairly readily without hypnosis. I do think, though, this is a fair example of a kind of thinking which is useful in controlling possible bad effects of hypnosis. Hypnosis, as Sarbin[12] had stressed, is a kind of metaphor. It is also a source of metaphors. If you can understand the popular conception of hypnosis plus catch the individual shades of meaning which hypnosis stands for for your patient, you can get inside the metaphor. You can operate creatively within it.

WHEN TO HYPNOTIZE

My typical use of hypnosis in clinical practice is as a temporary intervention into the intense talking and listening relationship of nonhypnotic psychotherapy. The idea of using hypnotic techniques with a particular patient may come from any of three different sources. I may think of it first myself. I may say to myself that this person seems to need some kind of relaxation training or some kind of dream imagery or some kind of loosening-up practice which hypnosis *might* help provide. Or the referral source which sent the patient to me may suggest it, as in the cases where another therapist has sent a patient to me specifically because I use hypnosis. Third, the patient himself may suggest it. If so, I am often willing to give it a try. I listen very carefully to patients partly because I regard them as experts on themselves. Not all their ideas and suggestions pan out successfully, but that is true for my ideas, too.

Sometimes it becomes clear fairly rapidly that hypnosis is not the most useful way to proceed. While I was working with inpatients at a state hospital, one of the psychiatrists sent me a patient for therapy. He told me that this young man had been tentatively diagnosed as hysteric, and therefore I should try hypnotherapy with him. The reasoning offered was that hysteria was an indication for hypnotherapy because Freud used hypnosis with hysterics before he gave up using hypnosis. Well, the reasoning was wrong at a few points, but state hospital work is often desperately hard and may impair anybody's logic.

I saw the young man a couple of times and then hypnotized him and continued our interview while he was hypnotized. Later, after awakening him, I asked about his feelings concerning it. He said he found it an interesting experience, but he did not know if he really liked it. The trouble with it, he explained, was that he had so many things he wanted to talk with me about and, since he talked more slowly under hypnosis, he was afraid he might not get as many of them said. I got the message. We skipped hypnosis and worked together profitably in other ways.

Insight into a Stiff Neck

Another patient (whom I have written about elsewhere[10]) was sent from the same ward with rather similar reasons for referral. I did use hypnosis with him in a way that was most helpful, although it accounted for only a small percentage of our sessions together. This is, as I have suggested, typical of my clinical use of hypnotic techniques. In this case, hypnosis was important in mobilizing the motivation and hope that led to psychotherapeutic change.

He was a 46-year-old man suffering from severe torticollis. Besides this extremely severe stiff neck, he had an odd and awkward way of walking that seemed to go with it. He was a salesman, and his disfiguring ailment put him completely out of work. No organic basis for his symptoms had been found, but I felt it would not be a good notion to try to attempt direct symptom removal through hypnosis. He had shown a variety of other symptoms over the past three years—hot and cold flashes, heart palpitations, and so on—which seemed to me to suggest the possibility that he could easily find a new symptom if the present one were taken away without other changes accompanying its disappearance. Psychological testing done by another psychologist at the hospital had suggested that his psychophysiological reaction was probably part of an underlying psychotic process. I decided to try some hypnotic techniques with him in the hope of establishing some relaxation techniques that might give him partial relief from the painful discomfort of his stiff neck.

As is often my practice, I began with the Stanford Hypnotic Susceptibility Scale on which he obtained a score of eight out of a possible twelve. Even during that initial hypnotic experience, his neck relaxed somewhat. He saw this as a certain amount of evidence of the psychological nature of his discomfort, but he still had reservations about it. Despite some previous experience with psychotherapy, he found it hard to accept the notion that his torticollis could be an emotional, tension-induced symptom rather than primarily a physiological one. At our second session together he also expressed doubts about whether he was really hypnotized. I induced trance by a hand levitation method like that described by Wolberg,[17] and I suggested a simple posthypnotic signal which would induce trance in the future. I awoke him and immediately rehypnotized him as we had arranged by tapping the desk with my pencil and saying, "I want you to be asleep now." As had happened before, his neck noticeably relaxed and straightened during trance.

In the hope of convincing him that the hypnotic state really was something he was experiencing and able to experience, I decided to repeat an item from the Stanford scale to which he had given strong response. I suggested that his arm would be rigid, "stiff and rigid as a bar of iron," and I then challenged him strongly to try to bend it. He showed signs of great effort, but his arm did not bend. As he struggled to bend it, his neck restiffened to the awkward and painful posture it showed in his waking state. I instructed him to let his arm relax, which he was able to do. I then awakened him, and he made the following comments to me, speaking first in a low and dull tone of voice:

> One thing that does disturb me, that I was aware of. When you asked me to hold my arm, uh, rigid, and I did, it became so rigid I felt like it was an iron bar and I couldn't move it. But I was also aware of the fact that it increased tension in my neck at the same time, and my head did not remain as straight as it was. This was disturbing to me. This made me feel that. . . . [here his voice suddenly took on a very marked increase in volume and brightness of tone.] Well, then again, it *shouldn't* be disturbing, because, uh, when. . . . In other words, when there is tenseness in some part of my body, the symptom is going to show up in my neck. So that if I could be a relaxed person, I could get rid of the tension in my neck.

This seemed to be his first emotional, his first truly experienced acceptance of the notion that his symptom had a psychological origin. At our next session together his motivation for psychotherapy was still running high, and as we worked together in further sessions we soon stopped using hypnosis. The sometimes flat, sometimes obsessively intellectual quality which had marked our first couple of conversations together now appeared only rarely and never lasted anywhere near a full therapy hour.

The patient and I both felt that the course of psychotherapy was crucially helped by the insight achieved during the hypnosis-aided hour that I have quoted from. Approximately three and one half months after our first session he was discharged from the hospital. His clumsy, twisting walk had disappeared and his neck was almost totally improved. The remaining signs of the torticollis disappeared during the first week out of the hospital. When I last saw him, a few months following his discharge, he was still symptom-free.

A Stumbling Teenage

Hypnosis has uses in diagnosis as well as in therapy. These are well beyond the scope of this paper, but one example of them occurs with the next patient I shall describe. This was a 17-year-old girl whom I saw as an inpatient in a psychiatric ward. She had been transferred there from a medical ward in the hospital. She had great difficulty in walking, moving with an extremely awkward gait and frequently losing her balance entirely. The medical service had been unable to find a satisfactory source for her problems and therefore transferred her to our psychiatric ward. My first use of hypnosis with her was primarily a diagnostic one. Psychological test material and interview had left me unsatisfied about the hypothesized hysterical nature of her illness. Clearly, she did have some marked emotional difficulties, but the test material did not show any clear relationship between these and her presenting symptom.

As is my usual custom, I first hypnotized her with the standardized Stanford Hypnotic Susceptibility Scale to get a notion how good a subject she was. She obtained a score of eleven out of a possible twelve, marking her as an extremely susceptible subject. She also showed a clear ability to experience age regression in hypnosis. When asked to imagine herself in second grade, her handwriting changed to a childish style of printing and her voice altered in style and quality. I tried to obtain as realistic and vivid a hypnotic regression as I could for a period of a few years before the actual time we were in. She seemed able to experience this well and to keep her eyes open without altering the hypnotic state. Despite this, her stumbling gait and frequent falling in no way changed. This argued strongly against the diagnosis of hysterical disorder.

On the basis of this and my other impressions of her I pleaded strongly, against the initial protests of the psychiatrist in charge, for a more thorough and detailed medical and neurological examination. It was some weeks before this could be obtained. During that time most of the ward staff continued to treat her as a seriously disturbed psychiatric patient with marked hysterical symptoms. I shall describe some of the results of this shortly. When a more thorough examination was finally done, a small neurological tumor was discovered. Although I was not able to follow the final disposition of the case, it was apparently considered to be something that would respond to treatment.

During the girl's stay on the psychiatric ward, between my initial evaluation and the eventual disposition back to medicine, the ward staff became very concerned about new symptoms she was showing. It was suggested by some of them that she was becoming schizophrenic. They commented on her patterns of withdrawal, seeming disinterest in her visitors, and her lack of affect. I was again called into the treatment program to try to determine whether or not this was indeed the onset of schizophrenia. I discussed with her the symptoms which had concerned the hospital staff and asked her what she made of them. She seemed puzzled and had difficulty responding. I then suggested that we might be able to understand the meanings of these changes better with the help of hypnosis. She agreed, and we proceeded with this approach. I hypnotized her and asked her to have a dream about the meaning of her symptoms. I told her:

> I want you to have a dream which will stand for what these things mean to you. The meaning of the dream may be very clear and plain or it may be in the kind of symbolic language that dreams sometimes use. It will be a dream, like the dreams you have at night, so neither you nor I know exactly what that dream is going to be. In a few moments I shall be quiet and ask you to have this dream about what these changes in your behavior, which we have been

talking about, mean to you. If I speak to you again before the dream has ended, the dream will stop at that point. If you should stop dreaming before I speak to you, you'll stay in the comfortable, relaxed state you are in now and wait for me to speak to you again. In any case, you will have this dream, and you will remember every detail of it even after you awaken.

She had her dream. In this dream various members of her family and her boyfriend came into her hospital room. They stood around her bed, but at a distance from it. She kept thinking to herself, over and over again, "I want them to stay away. I don't want them to come any closer to me." She felt as if they could not yet see that it was she in the bed, and she felt that if they did come closer and see her in this bed, they would know that she was crazy.

The pattern of withdrawal was not one of schizophrenia. It was the terror of a girl who had absorbed the common social image of psychiatric illness as bad and stigmatizing and who was being taught by her psychiatric hospitalization to make this frightening picture a part of her self-image. Through her withdrawal, she hoped to hide from herself and others the stigma and self-hated that was growing in her. I shared my interpretation of this very clear dream with her. In a few therapy sessions following, during which hypnosis was not used, I think I was able to help her in a quite direct fashion to retard and work against this impairment in her picture of herself. I think that my findings, when I shared them with the rest of the ward staff, finally helped to hasten the additional medical diagnostic work which resulted in an organic case being found for her presenting symptoms.

A Patient Finds It Safe to Remember

I shall conclude my small sampling of case histories here with an outpatient example in which hypnosis played a different role in therapy from those I have described so far. I do not usually press for dreams in psychotherapy, but this young woman frequently commented on the fact that she rarely dreamed. She also commented on her inability to remember childhood experiences. At her request, I tried suggesting under hypnosis that she remember some incidents from her childhood. I suggested that she look for pleasant memories, figuring this would get us into the least trouble to begin with. Following the single session in which I did this, she began reporting dreams and memories of childhood. These were often sad and frightening ones as well as pleasant memories. At first I tried interpreting the dreams, and we worked together at relating the childhood memories to her present ways of behaving.

She had originally come to see me partly because of periods of severe depression. The dreams and memories of childhood continued in future sessions. Our attempts to interpret them and relate them to the present got virtually nowhere, but her depression ended. It took about four sessions for both of us to come to the realization that for her the "interpretations" were interesting but unnecessary. It was the ability to remember more about herself that counted. The dreams belonged here, too, as we both knew that she must have dreamed before but that these dreams had been buried from memory.

Now she experienced herself as existing in time. She was in touch with her past and with the sleeping hours of her present. It seemed—though I must offer this tentatively—as if she had been afraid of this part of herself, afraid that she would find something so unacceptable that she would hate herself all the more and her depression would deepen. The hypnotic relationship had provided a safe-feeling way for her to begin this remembering. When the first steps in remembering proved safe, in fact, she could continue it. She was able to experience herself and her life more fully, and what she found in that experience was not so bad after all.

LEARNING TO USE HYPNOSIS IN PSYCHOTHERAPY

It must be clear that learning to use hypnosis in psychotherapy means learning first to do psychotherapy. Hypnosis is not and cannot be a therapeutic technique in itself. But assuming that one does have some grounding and experience in traditional therapy, what next? Some of the books and papers I have noted in this chapter are helpful, but they are plainly not enough. It seems to me that learning to use hypnotic techniques in a helping way requires good supervision from an experienced "hypnotherapist" plus, ideally, a kind of apprenticeship. That is, I think you not only need to learn about it indirectly, but ideally you should watch your consultant use hypnosis and have him watch you. And I do not mean merely watch special demonstration subjects; I mean watch each other with actual patients. This is, of course, somewhat anxiety-producing for both you and your consultant, but it is an important and vivid way to learn. The need for it comes, as I noted earlier, partly because the published literature on hypnosis and psychotherapy is fascinating but never tells as much as you want and need to know.

REFERENCES

1. Copeland, C. L., and Kitching, H. E.: Hypnosis in mental hospital practice. *J. Ment. Sci., 83*:328-352, 1937.
2. Friedman, J. J., and Keup, W. K.: Hypnotizability of newly admitted psychotic patients. *Psychosomatics, 4*:95-98, 1963.
3. Gale, C., and Herman, M.: Hypnosis and the psychotic patient. *Psychiat. Quart., 30*:417-424, 1956.
4. Heath, E. S., Hoaken, P. C. S., and Sainz, A. A.: Hypnotizability in state-hospitalized schizophrenics. *Psychiat. Quart., 34*:65-68, 1960.
5. Hilgard, E. R.: *Hypnotic Susceptibility.* New York, Harcourt Brace, 1967.
6. Kline, M. V.: Hypnotherapy. In Wolman, B. B. (Ed.) : *Handbook of Clinical Psychology.* New York, McGraw-Hill, 1965.
7. Kline, M. V.: Sensory hypnoplasty. *Intern. J. Clin. Exper. Hypn., 16*:85-100, 1968.
8. Kramer, E.: Group induction of hypnosis with institutionalized patients. *Intern. J. Clin. Exper. Hypn., 14*:243-246, 1966.
9. Kramer, E.: Hypnotic susceptibility and previous acquaintance with the hypnotist. *Amer. J. Clin. Hypn., 11*:175-177, 1969.
10. Kramer, E.: Motivating insight for psychotherapy achieved through hypnosis. *Amer. J. Psychiat., 120*:117, 1964.
11. Kramer, E., and Brennan, E. P.: Hypnotic susceptibility of schizophrenic patients. *J. Abnorm. Soc. Psychol., 69*:659, 1964.
12. Sarbin, T. R.: Contributions to role-taking theory: I. Hypnotic behavior. *Psychol. Rev., 57*:255-270, 1950.
13. Stanton, A. H., and Schwartz, M. S.: *The Mental Hospital.* New York, Basic Books, 1954.
14. Vingoe, F. J., and Kramer, E.: Hypnotic susceptibility of psychotic patients: A pilot study. *Intern. J. Clin. Exper. Hypn., 14*:47-54, 1966.

15. Weitzenhoffer, A. M., and Hilgard, E. R.: *Stanford Hypnotic Scale: Forms A and B.* Palo Alto, Consulting Psychologists, 1959.
16. Wilson, C. P., Cormen, H. H., and Cole, A. A.: A preliminary study of the hypnotizability of psychotic patients. *Psychiat. Quart.,* 23:657-666, 1949.
17. Wolberg, L. R.: *Medical Hypnosis.* New York, Grune & Stratton, 1948.

D<small>R.</small> P<small>ETER</small> H<small>OGAN</small>, one of the pioneers in the use of videotape playback in group psychotherapy, presents in this paper a comprehensive overview to all those interested in learning more about this new technique in treatment. He begins his paper with a brief history of the technique, then relates how he uses it, and illustrates this with examples from his clinical experience. For the sake of clarity in presentation he has divided his paper into seven sections, each on one aspect of videotape playback technique that he finds valuable.

The first section relates to the separation of the participating and observing functions in therapy for both patient and therapist. Following this he indicates the value to the participants in enabling them to compare their external behavior with their inner experience. The third section indicates how the patient can see aspects of himself that he was previously unaware of or not in touch with at the time the videotape incident was recorded. The fourth section deals with the observer of the videotape and the sensitivity to aspects of other people that develop. The fifth section leads into a discussion of the complexities and subtleties of the viewer's interaction with others. Then he describes the value of a consistent utilization of video playback and its ability to delineate long-range behavior and change over a period of time in both therapist and patient. The last portion of the paper focuses on its capacity to educate the person involved in the group as well as others who had not participated in the group in nonverbal behavior and communication.

These seven sections certainly cover the vast majority of the uses that video playback techniques could be put to. Additionally, he could have stressed the potential of it for teaching psychotherapy as well as doing supervision of psychotherapy. The research potential of this approach in providing an objective record of what actually transpired would be of considerable assistance in the development of psychotherapy research. He does not particularly emphasize the disadvantages of this technique. To name one that immediately comes to mind is possible loss of contact with the therapist in the context of the therapy session while he is operating the machine. The minor areas that are omitted are so minimal that they do not detract from the impact of this comprehensive, clearly written, and very personal paper.

G.D.G.

D.S.M.

Chapter 13

THE USE OF VIDEOTAPE PLAYBACK AS A TECHNIQUE IN PSYCHOTHERAPY

PETER HOGAN

IN THIS PAPER I would like to present some of the values I have found in using videotape playback as a technique in ongoing psychotherapy. This technique has been used by Ian Alger and myself[1,2] in outpatient private practice since 1965 and even earlier with hospitalized private patients by Moore *et al*. Previously, videotape had been used as a supervisory aid by Kagan *et al*.[4] at the University of Michigan in the training of counselors. Scheflen, at Bronx State Hospital, has used videotape playback in addition to 16 mm film in the elucidation of nonverbal components of behavior of therapists and patients during the therapy interview[6] and has also used it in the investigation of family dynamics with videotapes taken within the home.[7]

In my use of videotape, the camera is left in the open without disguise. My experience is that, after a brief initial self-consciousness, the equipment is forgotten by the participants. I use the playback in two ways. The first way is with a beginning or experienced individual patient, marital couple, family, or group that is not familiar with the videotape playback technique. In this method, the first ten to fifteen minutes of the session is recorded and then immediately played back for the participants' examination. The playback can be stopped at any point for examination and review by either therapist or patient. This method stimulates rapid emotional involvement, permits beginning patients to begin expressing their feelings, and sensitizes the participants to nonverbal communication.

The second method consists of recording the session without interruption until some incident occurs which requires clarification. This method is used with participants who are familiar with the videotape technique. While I use the videotape playback initially with all new patients, I do not continue to use it in every session. After an initial period of several weeks' regular use of the videotape, I reduce the use to once a month on a regular basis, unless an impasse develops in therapy. When an impasse develops, I again use videotape playback on a regular basis until the impasse has cleared.

An important aspect of videotape playback is that it provides an objective record of the behavior of the participants without depending upon their memory. While the record is objective, it is limited unless all participants are recorded at all times. This can easily be done during individual, marital, and family therapy but is not feasible with groups.

A further limitation comes with the use of the zoom lens, although I prefer it for group therapy. The advantage of the zoom lens is that it allows a selective focus on a face, gesture, and so on while excluding all other elements of the interaction. This selective focus is valuable for developing emotional involvement of the person selected as well as the other participants. Objective understanding of the total interaction is, of course, sacrificed in this use.

This objective though limited record can then be used in an outgoing way during the therapy session itself (as noted above), and this allows examination not only of the patient's behavior but also of the therapist's behavior as a part of the interpersonal process. Therapist and patient are on a more equal collaborative level in this examination, since both can refer equally to the videotape, and since either can stop the tape for questioning, associating, and so forth.

Immediate reexamination of the therapeutic incident as many times as is necessary for understanding is another value of videotape. In addition, the playback often stimulates historical recall on the part of both patient and therapist. When videotape playback is used over a period of time, the participant can see the range of his behavior and develop a more accurate self-image.

This technique is ideally suited for the examination of the many levels of communication present in any interaction. It particularly allows the comparison of inner experience with outer behavior and therefore leads to a better understanding of the discrepancy between one's inner experience of oneself and the reactions of others. A therapist-participant in a recent demonstration group, for example, could understand my apparent lack of reaction to her anger towards me when she looked at the playback of her angry statements. Although she said that she was angry, she was smiling and speaking in a soft tone of voice, with a relaxed body. While she had been told of this discrepancy before, she had been unable to really experience it until she saw and heard it.

Following these introductory remarks, I wish to go into more detail about aspects of the videotape playback technique that I have found valuable. I will discuss these aspects in seven sections.

SECTION I

The use of videotape playback allows a separation of the participating and observing function in therapy for both patient and therapist. A clinical example that illustrates this point concerns a man who deliberately manipulated people to evoke a desired response. In his job as a salesman this was sometimes an asset, but he was aware that his "phony" behavior alienated his intimates and occasionally interfered with his business relationships. In playing back a videotape of an interview which focused on his facial expressions, he became aware that his "phoniness" was transparent to an observer. In a short while he began pointing out his phony expressions and verifying that they corresponded with his internal intent. Following this interview, he began catching himself with the inner feeling that accompanied his phony facial expressions and took the responsibility for attempting to be authentic in his communications.

The separation of functions is also important for the therapist. In one very intense group situation, for example, I was quite taken up with the interaction of my cotherapist and a member of the group. I was so involved that I did not look around the group as I usually do. On playback of the videotape of this segment of the group process, I saw that the man next to me had tears in his eyes at the time when I was not related to the group. I was then able to respond to the man's feelings, which I had previously missed.

Separation of observing and participating function can be quite valuable for the therapist in individual treatment as well. Early in my use of videotape I became aware that if there was no interaction between the patient and myself—that is, if the patient talked on uninterruptedly for a period of several minutes—I reacted by appearing frozen on the screen, and I frequently felt mildly bored inside. I found that actively breaking through the monologue frequently enlivened the session both for the patient and myself. I was so enthusiastic about this discovery when I first made it that I used it at every available opportunity. With one young woman I broke into her monologue and shortly thereafter commented on how much more alive she appeared to be. When we replayed the videotape, however, it became quite clear that she had not changed. It was I who was more alive and animated and interested. The use of videotape playback brings objectivity into the session, not through the therapist's detachment from the situation, but by providing a neutral recording of the event which can be viewed by therapist and patient together in a collaborative enterprise.

SECTION II

The objective recording made available by the videotape allows all participants to compare their outside behavior with their inner experience. It also allows all the participants a second chance to reevaluate or to clarify and communicate their inner experience more clearly.

An amusing example of this occurred in the practice of my former associate, Dr. Ian Alger. He was leading a group wherein one of the participants was chronically depressed and looked it. In the first session involving use of videotape playback with this group, this depressed man, seeing himself, stated that he felt upset about his appearance. Dr. Alger sought to reassure him by noting that since he was chronically depressed his appearance would reflect this. "That's what I'm upset about, Ian," said the man, "today I'm not depressed."

The comparison of the outside appearance and the inner experience allows the participants a second chance, as noted above, to work through the original interaction. With one married couple using videotape for the first time, the husband was able to modify his behavior to an important degree. In this episode his wife had become quite upset and tearful about a previous individual session with her therapist. Her husband intervened in a courtly, gentlemanly manner, talking to both cotherapists, explaining how his wife was really quite a strong person. On the playback, he was able to say that he felt quite moved and touched by her tears. His own background and upbringing had emphasized a nondisplay of feeling, and so the only way that he could express his concern for his wife in the original episode was to talk to the therapists in her behalf rather than respond to her directly. After revealing this, he reached out and held his wife's hand, with tears in his own eyes, saying directly how important she was to him.

The ability to compare inner experience and outside behavior gives each person an area of objective data that he has not previously had in his life. Looking into a mirror is quite quickly adapted to early in life and does not have the same self-confronting effect as viewing oneself on the video screen. Cornelison[2] has found that self-confrontation of hospitalized schizophrenic patients by means of photographs, movies, and videotapes resulted in attracting the interest and attention of quite withdrawn and regressed patients who otherwise have not responded to therapeutic contacts. Cornelison feels that a basic narcissistic investment is responsible for the attention-getting aspect of self-confrontation with the aforementioned modalities.

Since I have an outpatient practice, I do not have such seriously disturbed patients. However, I have noted a pronounced interest in their appearance by borderline patients, both in individual therapy and in group. In particular, borderline patients with a fragmented sense of self and lacking a sense of continuity have gotten definite relief from viewing themselves. They are able to compare their appearance and behavior with that of other people and are thus able to see that their behavior, at least, is not that different from the behavior of others. This narcissistic involvement is so pronounced that the lack of such response is quite rare. I was able to pick up a well-disguised depression in one patient I saw in consultation because of his total lack of interest in his image on the screen.

Group or individual interactions involving the therapist and the patient can be clarified with the use of videotape playback so that either may communicate inner experience more clearly. During one group I felt quite touched by a woman's tears and wanted to help her reach and express her emotion more openly. I asked, "Did that conversation affect you personally?" (referring to her discussion with another group member). "Of course it did," she replied in an irritated tone. "Don't say 'of course,' " I replied with controlled irritation. I could see that we were at an impasse; upon replay of the incident, I was able to say to the patient that I did not express my concern directly. I then did express my concern directly. and clarified my initial good intent. The patient was able to accept this clarification, responded to my concern warmly, and we were then able to move through the impasse.

Finally, comparison of inner experience and observed behavior is helpful in confirming the decision to terminate therapy. People who are ending therapy, even if viewing themselves for the first time on videotape, consistently report a congruence between their inner sense of themselves and what they see on the screen.

SECTION III

The use of videotape playback enables the viewer to see aspects of himself that he was previously unaware of or that he was not in touch with at the time that the incident was recorded.

In an individual session, a male patient was describing in humorous terms his refusal to allow his mother into his apartment with chicken soup while he was ill with measles as an adult. He laughed uproariously at the end of the story. There was something about his laughter that seemed exaggerated to both of us when we viewed the tape, and when he repeated the motions he saw on the screen, he immediately recalled being physically beaten by his father. First his head went back and then it went from side to side, as though he were being hit. This "funny" story then led to an examination of his fear and rage toward both of his parents.

In another session, with a married couple, I commented casually before replaying the tape that the husband was quite angry with me in this session. He denied this vigorously, and I could not recall what there was in his behavior that led to my impression. As we replayed the tape, however, we came to a section of about thirty frames' duration (approximately one second) where his face (turned towards me) was contorted with rage. On seeing this, the husband accepted that he must be angry and worked toward getting in touch with his anger towards me.

Another incident involving a married couple revealed their private versus their social behavior. This revelation came about by accident. I left the room to answer a phone call I was expecting but did not stop the videotape. When I returned and we played back the section where I had left the room, we saw that the wife's behavior had changed completely. Whereas before she had been quite alert and cheery, when I left the room she sagged, assumed a depressed air, and began complaining to her husband. The husband responded with patient weariness. They both cooperated to resume the image of gaiety when I returned to the room. Both were not aware of the change in behavior during my absence.

Another incident concerns myself, again in a group session. In this incident, one woman crossed the room to embrace another woman seated next to me. My impression of myself was that I felt quite pleased that these particular women were able to make a feeling contact with each other. When I viewed the incident back on the TV screen, however, I saw an actual physical retreat on my part when the two women embraced. In reviewing my reactions internally, I was able to be aware that on one level I felt that this was a very private moment between the two women and that by sitting as close as I was to the embrace I was intruding into their privacy. I was also able to be aware, however, that on a deeper level I was retreating from my own need for intimate personal contact, which was awakened when the women embraced. I shared both of these reactions with the group.

Another incident again concerns a married couple. Fairly early in the interview, the wife said to her husband that what she did not like about him was that he did not try to reach her emotionally and he gave up very easily. He accepted this criticism and became depressed. As we reviewed the tape, however, we saw many attempts on the husband's part to reach out and contact his wife in an emotional way, in spite of her discouraging behavior. As a result of this experience he was able to begin trusting his own perception of his intent and behavior rather than accepting his wife's definition completely.

A final incident illustrating this point follows. In individual therapy with a male homosexual, I had frequently mentioned his boyish adolescent appearance following any reported improvement in his symptoms or any assertive moves towards women. During our first TV interview, such a change in his appearance took place. Instead of it being a theoretical construct which he was taking on my say-so, he was able to see for himself the immediate change in his behavior following his report that he had dated an attractive woman and had some sexual contact with her. This experience became an ongoing part of his awareness of his behavior towards me and other people. He was then able to get in touch with his competitive anxiety toward other men. The continued use of videotape aided this process. In this regard, I have noted that insight following such self-observation has the impact of a well-timed interpretation tying several themes together. The image remains in awareness as a focal point for continued working through.

SECTION IV

The use of videotape playback allows the participant to see aspects of other people in an interpersonal situation which he had not seen before. For example, in an interview with a married couple who were estranged, I focused the camera on the husband's face. He was struck by a certain sadness in his face and associated to early childhood situations where he felt isolated from his mother. His wife was both able to see his sadness in his face and relate to the incidents he described. Her image of her husband was always one of hardness and strength, so that this experience brought up a side of his personality which had not been a part of their previous relationship.

This awareness of others also extends to the therapist, as the following example will illustrate. This incident took place with a patient who always took the role of a country bumpkin. At the end of a five-minute segment, I turned my back to the patient to stop the tape and rewind it. Since this was his first TV experience, the patient was not aware that the recording was continuing while my back was turned. When we came to the section of the replay where my back was turned, the patient gave a knowing smile, then lowered his head. The smile was a giveaway to us both that his usual appearance was at least a semiconscious act. While I had confronted this patient previously with my hunch that his country bumpkin appearance was a disguise, the anxiety about success which underlay this disguise was not apparent to the patient until he saw his "giveaway" smile. This insight was not quite as simple as I have presented it, however. The patient's anxiety about his smile resulted in such denial that we had to review the smile eight times before he could admit it.

SECTION V

Videotape playback allows the viewer to see his own role in a complex interaction between himself and others. For example, a new member in a group was attempting to be friendly and responsive but was actually quite reserved and guarded with others. Finally, one member of the group asked if she could shake his hand. He said "sure" and extended his hand but crossed his legs at the same time as the woman moved towards him. She stopped, felt hurt, and retreated. The new member could not understand what had happened until he saw his nonverbal behavior in playback, when he realized that he was giving a receiving message verbally but a rejecting message nonverbally.

Similarly, in an interview with a married couple, the husband was quite deferential and submissive in his relationship with his wife. He had been told this frequently by his individual therapist, but he had never realized the degree to which this was true until he saw his behavior on the TV screen. The impact of it was so great that sweat burst out on his brow when he saw his obsequious behavior. This image of his obsequious behavior remained with him and was a focus for his individual therapy for several months thereafter. He was also able to understand that some of his wife's contemptuous and rejecting behavior was related to his own obsequiousness.

A further episode involves myself. My theoretical orientation in analysis and therapy is that the therapist both participates and observes. Therefore, the patient's behavior in an interview is related to the analyst's behavior as well as the patient's own internal projections. The episode I am about to describe occurred with a new patient shortly after I began working with videotape for the first time. In my memory of the incident, I had asked the patient to try to be aware of his feelings when a friend did not invite him to a party. The patient seemed to avoid the question, and I quickly turned to the videotape to demonstrate his difficulty in reaching and expressing feeling. What we saw when we viewed the tape was that, when I asked the patient about his feeling, I looked at my fingernails. When I asked the patient how he responded to my looking at my nails, he said that he felt that I was not really interested in his feelings and that I was asking in a perfunctory manner. Then he became aware of a mild depression.

I knew that as a part of my social personality I tended to disguise or hide or to direct attention away from the fact that I was really interested in a particular area, but I did not realize that I did this in a therapeutic session. My original understanding of the incident completely ignored my own behavior in the patient's response. The behavior was so minimal, the patient himself was not able to confront me with my apparent disinterest. This is the kind of episode which could not be accurately reported in either a case presentation or a control session because the therapist himself, myself in this instance, was not aware of his own relevant behavior. As an additional bonus for the therapist, then, videotape playback including the therapist as part of the session has the virtue of an ongoing continuing supervision.

SECTION VI

The use of consistent videotape playback shows both the range of behavior and a change over a period of time in the therapist and the patient. For example, a patient and I reviewed a five-minute section on videotape taken eighteen months previously and compared it with a five minute section taken at the time of the review. We were both surprised by the extent of change shown. A good deal of the change had not been noticed by the patient himself. I had kept track of all the changes but what surprised me was that I was not aware of the degree to which the patient changed. Switching to the therapist alone, again, viewing myself almost daily over a period of time showed me a wide range of behavioral modes depending in part upon my mood of the day, in part upon the particular patient I was seeing, and in part upon what the particular patient was dealing with at the time of the interview. To see this range was quite important to me since I tend to have a somewhat static self-image. I found that I was more outgoing and exuberant on the one hand and more frozen on the other than I was consciously aware of. In fact, the first time I saw myself on playback, I looked so frozen that I was startled. I had an immediate fantasy of running out of the office, grabbing passersby, and shouting that I really was not dead the way I appeared on the TV screen. To see that I could also be lively or quiet, but clearly interested and alive, was a welcome relief.

SECTION VII

For myself the videotape playback presented an opportunity not only to be more sensitive to myself and my patients in the conventional ways that I had learned, but I was able to first note and change my relative insensitivity to nonverbal communication. I found that I tended to deal with and remember interviews in terms of the verbal content of the interview. Constant use of the videotape resulted in a sensitization to nonverbal behavior in both the patient and myself, and especially to nonverbal cues which contradicted the verbal behavior. For example, with one patient I first noticed a large physical pullback on the TV screen which accompanied talking about topics which she felt were unpleasant, although she had not communicated a feeling of unpleasantness to me. After seeing this on the TV screen, I was able to see it during interviews without using the videotape, to the advantage of both of us.

CONCLUSION

Videotape recordings played back to patients as a part of ongoing psychotherapy have a number of values for both patients and therapists. In addition, it is an objective record of the therapeutic event that becomes a concrete experience and not an abstract interpretation. The recordings themselves, when preserved, can be used to review the range of behavior as well as behavioral change in both patients and therapists. They have the additional value of being available for review by other professionals. This latter use can lead to an eventual consensus on what happens in therapy and what constitutes therapeutic change.

REFERENCES

1. Alger, I., and Hogan, P.: The use of videotape recordings in conjoint marital therapy. *Amer. J. Psychiat., 123*:1425-1430, 1967.
2. Cornelison, F. S., and Arsenian, J.: A study of the response of psychotic patients to photographic self-image experience. *Psychiat. Quart., 341*:1-8, 1960.
3. Hogan, P., and Alger, I.: The impact of videotape recording on insight in group psychotherapy. *Int. J. Group Psychother., 19*:158-164, April, 1969.
4. Kagan, N., Krathwohl, *et al.:* Studies in Human Interaction—Interpersonal Process Recall Stimulated by Videotape (monograph). East Lansing, Michigan State University, December, 1967.
5. Moore, F. J., Chernell, E., and West, M. J.: Television as a therapeutic tool. *Arch. Gen. Psychiat., 12*:217-220, 1965.
6. Scheflen, A.: Stream and Structure of Communicational Behavior (monograph). Philadelphia, Eastern Pennsylvania Psychiatric Institute, Temple University, 1965.
7. Scheflen, A.: Personal communication.

D̲ʀ. D̲ᴀᴠɪᴅ J. V̲ᴀɪʟ once again brings to one of our volumes the breadth and perspective gained through his years of experience as an analytically trained psychiatrist and as the administrator of mental health facilities for the State of Minnesota. The title of his paper, "Milieu Therapy and Psychoanalytic Psychotherapy Processes Compared," provides a key to understanding both the paper and the man. The paper is characterized by Dr. Vail's honesty, directness, and personal openness in his very well organized comparison of the areas of milieu therapy and psychoanalytic psychotherapy.

His approach to his paper was a very systematic one. He began with the concept that the best way to compare these two areas was in terms of the processes that he thought best characterized each. Using this frame of reference on the processes as the basic structure of the paper, the content of the paper became the comparison between the quality and quantity of the caseloads and the setting within which each kind of therapy is performed. To explain his characterization of the processes, he compared and delineated the characteristics of verbalization, self-understanding, confrontation, covenanting, and goal setting. Through these comparisons he quite succinctly explicated these concepts in an understandable and meaningful fashion.

Dr. Vail's discussion of the quality and quantity of caseloads is imaginative and informative. It provides a new perspective on old information that could only come from an experienced professional viewing the issues with honesty and directness. Again when he approaches the area of comparing the setting of each, his ability to provide a fresh approach to old ideas is evidenced as he goes beyond the discussion of physical surroundings to defining the psychological aspects of the physical setting.

In a very well organized and easy-to-read style, Dr. Vail has completed the task he set for himself. After reading this carefully constructed and personally documented paper, with its excellent definitions and thorough bibliography, each of us not only will have been part of Dave Vail's struggle to understand all this for himself but will have the benefits of his pragmatic thinking and equally direct writing style to help us understand the similarities and dissimilarities between these two forms of psychotherapy, milieu therapy and psychoanalytic therapy. His humanness shines through and illuminates a major area of concern to us, the area of milieu therapy.

G.D.G.
D.S.M.

Chapter 14

MILIEU THERAPY AND PSYCHOANALYTIC PSYCHOTHERAPY PROCESSES COMPARED

DAVID J. VAIL

I AM QUITE pleased to be able to appear in this symposium on innovations in psychotherapy and honored to be among such distinguished company. I am especially pleased and honored to have been invited back for the second year in a row; my visit here last year was, for me, one of the high points of 1968.

I chose the theme of milieu therapy for this is the field I have operated in for the past seventeen years. I will try to compare, relate, and to some extent contrast it with psychoanalytic psychotherapy.

I have found this a very difficult paper to get organized for a variety of reasons. First, the topic of milieu therapy is terribly large, multifaceted, and elusive, like a great many-sided crystal that is slippery and hard to lift; when after a struggle one gets it in position to look therein, it is found to be clouded. There is much that is self-evident in the contrast between milieu therapy and psychotherapy, and it is hard to work out lines of thought that can avoid the obvious.

I suffer from two personal disabilities. One that I must honestly confess is that I am not deeply versed in the literature on the subject and do not consider myself a scholar of the caliber that an assemblage of this sort would normally expect. I offer in compensation direct experience going back to my days in the early 1950's working with young adult retardates in a state hospital in Maryland. Of at least equal and in some ways greater value than my direct experience with milieu therapy has been the chance I have had over the past ten years to observe a wide variety of milieu programs going on in the Minnesota state hospital system.

My other main disability is that I learned about psychoanalysis

215

and psychoanalytic psychotherapy long ago and far away in the
Baltimore Psychoanalytic Institute in the early 1950's. Whether
it was because that school was quite narrowly orthodox in its
approach, or because my career took me increasingly away from
settings in which psychoanalytic psychotherapy was of direct value,
or because of some change in my personality, or for whatever reasons, I no longer use—or am at any rate aware of deliberately using
—psychoanalytic concepts. You will, no doubt, find my views of
psychoanalysis and psychoanalytic psychotherapy to be quaint
and old-fashioned, though possibly of antiquarian value. In these
days of ecumenism and liturgical change, my image of the analyst
still turns his back to the congregation and sings in Latin.

For all these reasons, I decided to "cool it" pretty much as
regards psychoanalytic psychotherapy and to some extent let the
paper write itself. In this way, I was led into curious and unexpected pathways off to the side of the main theme. So for me, at
least, the experience has been original and rewarding.

May I please indulge myself in one other personal comment.
This is that I should identify myself not only as a psychiatrist but
also as an administrator in public employment for the State of
Minnesota. My position includes, but is not limited to, the management of the state hospital system of Minnesota. This is a big
and important experience that has taken up almost one fourth of
my life so far and so it would be a gross understatement to say
that the experience has "colored" my views on milieu therapy.
Rather the experience and the views are part of the same life-
educative—indeed, existential—process.

As the paper is about process, let us start with that. In addition,
one would have to talk about quantity and quality of caseloads
and one would have to talk about the setting. Indeed when it
comes to milieu therapy it is, of course, the setting itself that is
the focus of the discussion.

For clarification and for didactic purposes let us define two
contrasting modes. By psychoanalytic psychotherapy I refer to the
type of classical one-to-one interaction described most satisfactori-
ly in my day by Franz Alexander.[2] By milieu therapy I mean the
deliberate structuring, use, and (I hesitate to use the term be-

cause of its pejorative connotations) manipulation of the environment or surroundings of a particular place—including most importantly the field of interpersonal relationships—to bring about desired behavioral changes on the part of some or all of a group of persons residing therein or subject to its influences. The interpersonal field will normally include a group phenomenon: *esprit de corps,* morale, the climate of feelings and attitudes, the attitudinal atmosphere, or what you may call it.

For the sake of simplicity I will not attempt to deal with the enormous array of therapies that lie between these poles. Especially troublesome for one who would write a clean and simple paper are the many existing forms of group psychotherapy, psychoanalytically oriented or otherwise, and milieu approaches based on psychoanalytic precepts or relying heavily on psychoanalytic techniques. Other complicating dimensions are the variety of family therapies and special approaches, like psychodrama and sociodrama.

PROCESS

Process is difficult semantically. For example, in my view *verbalization* is a *sine qua non* for psychoanalytic psychotherapy. I cannot conceive of any transaction taking place in this modality without spoken words on both sides. Yet in the context of milieu therapy one can conceive of effective programs on behalf of nonverbal persons, e.g. retardates. Whether verbalization is a process or a means or a technique by which a process occurs is a fine point over which we could quibble.

Self-understanding or insight is to me basic in the model of psychoanalytic psychotherapy but again is not necessary in the milieu therapy process. Furthermore, Reiff[41] has pointed out the importance of *self-actualization,* the idea of becoming a better person, in the entire "mental health ideology," which would include psychoanalytic psychotherapy as this is usually understood; self-actualization is again not a necessary component or aim of the milieu therapy process.

Confrontation is necessary to all psychotherapy though it will, of course, take vastly different forms. In classical psychoanalysis the interpretation of the transference is a form of confrontation, though of course, it is a muted echo in the French horns, pretty sissy stuff compared to the kind of blaring and percussive outbreaks that can occur in group and milieu therapy. In fact confrontation is a basic process in milieu therapy, and the judicious handling of confrontation is one of the critical responsibilities of the therapist.

So far then we can list verbalizing, self-understanding, self-actualizing, and confronting as parts of the psychoanalytic psychotherapy process, provided we do not get hung up semantically over verbalization as a mode, confrontation as a technique, and self-understanding and self-actualization as goals. Two other major items to look at under process—again using the word loosely—are covenanting, or making the contract, and goal-determining.

Covenanting in the practice of psychoanalytic psychotherapy is ordinarily voluntary on both sides. Here we find a marked contrast to milieu therapy. While I think it is safe to say, "No contract, no therapy," still in many milieu therapy programs there may be no contract at first and the contract may take a long time to develop. The most striking example of this that I can recall is the work of George Stürup[48] at the Psychiatric Detention Center in Herstedvester, Denmark. To this place are remanded a variety of sexual deviates and antisocial personalities who are usually in no frame of mind to make a contact. Stürup waits, for years if necessary, for the men are under an indeterminate sentence. Milieu factors are extremely powerful and very skillfully used. Stürup's specific technique, once the contract is joined, is something akin to transactional analysis and it has been very effective. An analogous situation to the delayed contract could arise in the practice of psychoanalytic psychotherapy, such as the case where Daddy is paying for the therapy to keep his son out of jail. However, I should think these would be relatively isolated instances.

Goal determining is, strictly speaking, part of the contract, to be worked out by the two parties. But the applicant (client, patient, analysand, or whatever you call him) in psychoanalytic psychotherapy usually comes with some goals in mind, with an intent to achieve certain purposes for which he seeks and pays for the services of the therapist. As every therapist knows, the goals may be vague, deceptive, and many-layered. They may change or evolve during the therapy process itself. Ordinarily the goals have to do with obtaining relief from some subjective state of anguish or pain. The important point is that the problem is individually defined, and the goals as to what to do about the problem are worked out directly between individual parties.

Contrastingly, in many situations in which milieu therapy is appropriate—or at any rate is taking place—the basic contracting and goal-determining processes are different from this dyadic relationship, especially as one must often account for a third party among those present: the state or the body politic. In the kind of setting in which a great deal of milieu therapy takes place, the goals themselves may differ very much in quality from those of psychoanalytic psychotherapy. They tend to be more elementary and, in the usage of Reiff, aimed at self-determination rather than self-actualization. A goal such as getting out of a hospital and being able to hold a job is of a far more basic order than a goal such as feeling greater fulfillment in interpersonal relationships or finding a meaning in life. The state's interest in the goals may be formulable in entirely negative terms: to stop bothering people, for example, or to stop being a burden on the taxpayers. A frequent goal in psychotherapy as stated by the applicant is gratification in sex, but this would be of no interest to the state except insofar as nongratification would lead to or in some way connect up with offensive sexual behavior.

In summary, then, I have listed six items under the heading of process and compared their use in psychoanalytic psychotherapy with their use in milieu therapy (Table 14-I).

Before getting into the critical matters of caseloads and settings, it is important to address myself to a point that is potentially troublesome. This is, I should make it very clear, that I am not equating psychoanalytic psychotherapy exclusively with private practive on the one hand nor milieu therapy exclusively with public practice on the other. There is no doubt that individual psychotherapy in rather pure form could occur in the most restricted of public settings, and there is equally no doubt that milieu therapy could be organized in a private setting. One could find ample factual evidence for both postulates.

TABLE 14-I

Process	Psychoanalytic Psychotherapy	Milieu Therapy
Verbalizing	Yes	No
Self-understanding	Yes	No
Self-actualizing	Yes	No
Confronting	Yes	Yes, yes
Covenanting	Yes	Yes, but. . . .
Goalsetting	Yes	Yes, but. . . .

Note. In this oversimplified model, "yes" means that the process usually takes place or is important or necessary; "no", the opposite. "Yes, yes" is obvious. "Yes, but. . . ." refers to the highly involved processes or contracting and goalsetting as they may be found in certain milieu therapy situations.

Still the chances are, on the average, that circumstances will dictate a relationship between private practice and psychotherapy on the one hand and milieu therapy and public practice on the other. Minnesota is a state with average resources (though with probably an above-average payoff from those resources), and the foregoing proposition certainly holds true for us. Whether one could extrapolate from our 2 percent of the national population is conjectural, but I would be willing to bet money on it.

It should also be said that the foregoing simplistic construct entirely leaves out group psychotherapy. This is in a sense deliberate; trying to include group psychotherapy in a short paper becomes impossibly tedious. For example: A therapist might use psychoanalytically based techniques in his private office where a group might come together, let us say, two or three times a week. The group will in time develop a kind of culture or "personality" or solidarity, but I doubt if one could truly refer to such an enterprise as milieu therapy as that term is usually understood. But one could argue this at some length. Moreover, in order to be complete one would have to deal with group therapy that takes place *within* and, so to speak, added to the milieu processes.

QUANTITY OF CASELOAD

In the dimension of group size the contrast between individual psychotherapy and milieu therapy may be too vivid. The way I learned it, the ideal caseload for individual psychotherapy is, of course, one person, and for group therapy it is around eight. But in milieu therapy the groupings may be larger in number. Indeed the possibilities are infinite. In one setting in Minnesota, for example, there is a distinct milieu identity for a total group of over two hundred mentally retarded adult persons, but programming and living arrangements break this number down into subgroups and sub-subgroups to the point at which the real action occurs in units of around a dozen or fewer residents working with a staff person.

This point is in a way obvious, and yet it is interesting to speculate about numbers. Goffman[19] talks about "a large number of like-situated individuals" in the total institution, and the nursery rhyme talks of the old woman who "had so many children she didn't know what to do"; neither states precisely how many persons are involved. The *process* of group interaction will affect the numbers question; i.e. a well-managed milieu program including sixty to seventy clients could be more effective than a poorly managed group of eight or, for that matter, a botched-up single case of individual therapy. This goes to the question of *impact,* which it seems to me is a vital consideration in the evaluation of program results.

QUALITY OF CASELOAD

Now we are getting into a very critical and indeed sensitive area. For the target group most involved in psychotherapy (especially psychoanalytic psychotherapy and, in particular, individual psychoanalytic psychotherapy) is what Schofield[44] has called YAVIS—an acronym for young, attractive, verbal, intelligent, and successful. The process factors previously listed, especially verbalizing, self-understanding, and self-actualizing, all are to be found in association with this case profile.

When things get interesting is when we look at persons who

are along one or more dimensions *non-YAVIS,* who are no longer young and/or are unattractive and/or are nonverbal and/or unintelligent and/or unsuccessful. What do we do then?

First let us find the non-YAVIS. Well of course that is easy, for they are everywhere: they are in the bars, living in tenements and run-down frame houses, standing around down by Perkins' Drug Store on Main Street, out on little no-account farms and nonfarms in the country; you can hear them any time calling in on open-mike radio stations. But you will find the greatest concentration of them in the public institutions scattered across the face of this great land, in places where they go or have been sent for various reasons having to do with their behavior.

Now it would be interesting to examine the entire history of milieu therapy taken in the broadest sense to include all milieus* that consciously and deliberately undertake to raise the human estate of individuals according to a plan and a clear set of values and a constitution. Taken this broadly, the study would then have to go back at least as far as the Essenes; it would have to include the many created utopias established on this continent within the past one hundred and fifty years; it would have to include special schools like Summerhill and its progeny, or the community of the Green Valley School in Florida, and special settings like Outward Bound and even offbeat experiments like that depicted fictionally in *The Dirty Dozen.*[35] One could go on and on: lamaseries and other religious communities, hippie colonies, special summer camps, and so forth. There is no point in speculating about the quantitative aspects of the matter, except to say that in many cases—possibly in most cases if we take in a big enough sample—the milieu has been founded, created, established, constituted in some planful way by an individual or group with a thing they wanted to do.

Not so with the non-YAVIS losers in the public institutions. There the reverse process has taken place. There is at the onset no real plan except to get them off the streets or out of the bars or out of their houses and into a place according to some alleged

---

*In purist usage the plural of the French word *milieu* is *milieux*. The English form is more comfortable.

rationale, notably "treatment" (or "care," "protection," "super-vision," "safekeeping," etc.) or "correction" (or "reform," "train-ing," etc.). The rationale is usually violated or it might be fairer to say not effectuated by performance for the most part; that is, the treatment or correction is either not undertaken or it does not produce results. It is against this background of planlessness that much of milieu therapy was sought for and produced by desperate do-gooders who wanted to see what they might be able to do with extremely limited resources including a virtual absence not only of contracts but of contractability.

The point is that in process terms we have something quite opposite from the founding of a religious community where the leadership proclaims its idea and recruits. The milieu therapy process I am talking about starts with a group of non-YAVIS losers who are already there; the therapist finds them, he inherits them, they are remanded to him. Something like the religious com-munity process may occur in public institutional settings where a staff person with a particular approach he would like to try finds an available bit of space and then selects or recruits individual clients for his unit from among the large mass of residents. The milieu therapy approach arises after the fact, one might say as a coping effort. Some reported results are excellent. What is amazing in the circumstances is that there could be any results at all.

Now at this point, as I was composing this paper in my mind a few weeks ago, a funny thing happened. Under the slow-acting influence of Szasz,[49] Albee,[1] and, I suppose, Karl Menninger[33] and possibly others, and arising from the more immediate impact of an article by Livermore, Malmquist, and Meehl[31] in the *Pennsyl-vania Law Review* and a speech by Judge David Bazelon, and during a working tour of duty in a hospital after ten years in the fastnesses of the state central office—for whatever reason, I have undergone a conversion or something of the sort.

Looking at the process of milieu formation as it relates to the non-YAVIS losers in our public institutions I began to ask, Why? What is this all about? How crazy it is to have to create a special remedial setting for those poor souls who are there, without examining the question, What in the hell are they doing there in the first place? I was reinforced, if one wants to call it that, in this thought by recalling that my project in Maryland from 1953 to 1955 or so, which was highly successful, was really a matter of returning to the general community a group of young, mildly mentally retarded men and women who never should have been in a state institution to start with.

How weird and monstrous it is for a person to be committed, placed under the custody of a total stranger (the superintendent), and kept by him in a strange place called a mental hospital or a prison (for "superintendent," read "warden"). At best, such a place can be a kind of home, as that word is used in Robert Frost's poem, "The Death of the Hired Man": "Home is the place where, when you have to go there,/ They have to take you in." At worst it is what William Blake called a "dark, satanic mill."

It is time for society to try to come up with new models. If we admit that there are certain forms of losing that are so destructive to society's interests that some intervention is required, what might we try other than to remand to institutions?

There are, if we look for them, infinite possibilities. But three that occur to me are (1) commitment to the individual guardianship of an interested person who is known to one, (2) direct placement under mandate to family care, and (3) direct placement under mandate to a small group setting where the group size would be no larger than that which would comfortably fit into an ordinary dwelling place. One could, of course, combine these three options in a variety of ways.

Now it is not appropriate to debate or explore this complex matter at the moment. However, we can look at the prospect of family and small-group placement in the context of *milieu;* for, of course, there would be a setting involved, both in the physical sense of cleanliness, safety, and so on and in the more important sense of an interpersonal field. Judgments would have to be made as to the suitability of the milieu; hopefully, the client, prisoner, patient, or whatever you would call him would also be a party to the judgment and would have some freedom of choice.

It should come as no surprise to you to know that there are already judgments being made on milieus in the child welfare field. Three main relevant areas of assessment are (1) adoptive parents, (2) foster parents, and (3) small-group residential facilities for children. In Minnesota these functions are legally ascribed to the Department of Public Welfare and in professionalistic terms are under the overwhelming, almost exclusive, dominance of social workers.

Now it is obviously important and in the public interest that the infant or child removed in some way from his natural parents should be in "an environment that contributes to healthful individual and family living" (P.L. 89-749). The public laws creating mental hospitals, prisons, and other such places have not explicitly laid down criteria for the quality of the environment. This has been up to the program people to derive long after the fact. It is small wonder that in many cases the best that could be said is that they are, in the words of the late President John F. Kennedy in his message to Congress in February of 1963, places of "cold mercy." The infant or child should be in a "good home." It is obviously important to David Copperfield, the child, and to the state—if the state has become concerned over his destiny— whether he will stay with competent but cruel Murdstone, foolish but kind Micawber, or some other person.

Who is to judge what is a "good home," a "good milieu," and by what standards? In Minnesota and presumably elsewhere there have been official responses to these questions. The Minnesota responses are significant in their value assumptions. Among other things one marvels at the enormous *power* that is displayed here, in the sense of an imposition of values—as anyone who has tried to adopt a child through a public agency can attest to.

I believe that the criteria of the "good parents" or the "healthy family environment" for public purposes should be fully explored scientifically, broadly debated, and (distasteful as it may be) thrashed out in the legislative assemblies of the world. For the day will come when couples will have to apply to the state for permission to bear and rear children; the decisions as to who will be qualified are much too important to be left to the professional specialists.

I would like to return to milieu therapy in a brief discussion of setting and then to two final points under process.

SETTING

I use "setting" in this section to refer to the physical surroundings of the activity. To repeat, one cannot dispense with the psychological or emotional climate that is part of the setting, especially the matrix of interpersonal relationships and attitudes among the residents and staff. In fact, this is essential and part of that which is deliberately worked with and adapted in milieu therapy, but the physical surroundings are also important.

Many years ago someone passed along to me the saying that in order to carry out individual psychotherapy all you need is two chairs, a table, and a box of Kleenex; in a jam you can do without the table. This is of course an oversimplification, but it is an interesting postulate nonetheless. It is at least as valid as the human experience that intimate and meaningful conversations that have deep impact may occur in unforeseen and even absurd circumstances. John Donne wrote in "The Good Morrow":

> And now good morrow to our waking soules,
> Which watch not one another out of fear;
> For love, all love of other sights controules,
> And makes one little room an everywhere.

For the group, the setting assumes considerable importance, as we can readily understand from personal experience and simple observation if we consider the dimension of available space per person, i.e. the question of crowding. The work of Hall,[21] Sommer,[45] Spivack,[46] and others has enlarged the therapeutic horizons of environment to an extraordinary degree. Though the work is of long standing, one gets the impression that the impact of proxemics is relatively recent. It cannot help but contribute to improvement of group and milieu programs, especially where a residential-care component is involved. I call your attention to a remarkable paper by Wolfensberger[54] showing how expectations or models of the retarded person led historically in this country to very specific design features.

MORE ON PROCESS

There are two items of cardinal importance under milieu therapy process that must be mentioned. These are what could be designated as "primary grouping" and "behavior modeling."

Primary Grouping

I use "primary grouping" in the sense that there occurs both direct and face-to-face verbal and nonverbal interaction among residents and staff and also some degree of declassing—that is, a dedifferentiation of status and indeed professional roles. A total declassing is not necessary and is probably neither entirely helpful nor appropriate. Furthermore it is phony. I can think of high-level staff, for example, who do menial chores in the unit as "one of the gang," insist on being called by their first names, insist that their human skills and qualities are no better than those of any other joe; yet, on payday, they are professional staff and make no mistake about it.

I think that dedifferentiation of status is essential in the milieu therapy process and may be one key to its success. In the process the group itself develops a distinct identity and a great strength which can support or sometimes destroy group members. Depending on the quality and quantity of membership, its sources, the leadership, the techniques employed, and to some extent the setting, the primary group experience may have an extraordinary impact on the individuals. Numerous experiences are available to us from our school days, military duty, and so forth, not to mention specific and constructed phenomena such as sensitivity training. Milieu therapy banks very heavily on primary grouping. In his therapeutic community concept, Maxwell Jones[25] made a great contribution in this area; no doubt others have also.

In a 1968 review of results in adolescent units in three of our Minnesota state hospitals for the mentally ill, I was struck with the diversity of structure and rationale of the three units. One was run by a psychiatrist, for example, the second by a special teacher, and the third by a social worker. Though the caseloads were roughly similar, the rationales, key personalities, staffing patterns, and techniques were quite different. The results were uniformly good. Whether it was causative in the good outcomes or not would be speculative, but the most impressive finding in the report was the quality of primary grouping—the ethos of all for one and one for all—that was readily detectable in each of the three units.

Primary grouping, such as one can observe in milieu therapy settings and to some extent in outpatient group therapy, is an impressive and, if one has been lucky enough to have been through it, powerful and indeed beautiful experience. It is part of the strength and the effectiveness of milieu therapy. I cannot find it, indeed cannot conceive of it, in psychoanalytic psychotherapy, though it may arise in some therapy groups. On our chart, therefore, I will enter a "no" for this item under psychoanalytic psychotherapy and a "yes" under milieu therapy (see Table 14-I).

Behavior Modeling

One would have to make the same entries under "behavior modeling." I use this term to denote the process whereby one individual serves as an example or model of behavior to another person. This process, of course, occurs throughout life, based in males (at least supposedly) on the resolution of the Oedipus complex, with the result that we are constantly modeling our attitudes and behavior on a succession of upperclassmen, teachers, bosses, and revered leaders. Whatever the derivation, this is a well-known and powerful force that not only makes for much good or, as it may be, evil in the world but also is absolutely vital in the process of socialization and even civilization. Even very sophisticated, worldly, and callous or jaded persons cannot fail to be dismayed at the prospect of high national officials, such as Supreme Court Justices, on the take, for though we know them to be human, we look to them as examples of desirable behavior.

A very clear and complete account on the effects and effectiveness of behavior modeling is to be found in the monograph *Ward H* by Speigel and Signorelli. The idea of that project is that the staff persons who have the most contact with the hospital residents (that is, the attendants or psychiatric aides), participate in daily decision making (e.g. going off the ward or making weekend visits at home) traditionally and fictitiously ascribed to the physicians. More importantly, through their regular and close contact with the residents, the basic personnel serve as models for more effective human behavior than the residents are currently given to. We have applied this model in Minnesota quite explicitly at the Fergus Falls State Hospital, and, of course, the process is taking place wherever a dependent or underdeveloped group looks up to leaders, guides, or older and/or wiser friends.

This process is supposedly absent in psychoanalytic psychotherapy; in fact, I was taught that the therapist is supposed to keep his jerkball personality out of things. I say *supposedly* for of course there is behavior modeling going on, but I think it is, as a rule, neither sought for nor honestly acknowledged.

The comparative chart, when complete, for purposes of this paper will appear as in Table 14-II.

TABLE 14-II

Process	Psychoanalytic Psychotherapy	Milieu Therapy
Verbalizing	Yes	No
Self-understanding	Yes	No
Self-actualizing	Yes	No
Confronting	Yes	Yes, yes
Covenanting	Yes	Yes, but....
Goalsetting	Yes	Yes, but....
Primary grouping	No	Yes
Behavior modeling	No, but....	Yes

EXAMPLES

Here I will simply list some examples of milieu therapy projects that either have been reported in the literature or are currently in process and could be visited or otherwise inquired about. These are directed at non-YAVIS groups.

SUMMARY

Aspects of milieu therapy processes have been postulate, described, and compared to those of psychoanalytic psychotherapy. Operationally, in the psychiatric and related behavioral fields, it appears today that milieu therapy tends to arise out of the need to cope with or to help in some way a population of institutionalized persons with severe biopsychosocial dysfunctions. Other models for dealing with such groups are proposed; analogies are

TABLE 14-III

Place	Target Group	Therapist/Author
A. Outside of Minnesota*		
Herstedvester, Denmark	Sexual deviates, antisocial personalities	G. Stürup[48]
Green Valley School, Florida	Severely disturbed adolescents	G. von Hilsheimer[52]
Rosewood State Training School, Maryland (Experimental Training Unit)	Mildly-moderately retarded young adults	D. Vail[51]
B. Within Minnesota**		
Anoka State Hospital	Adolescents	R. Kyllonen[29]
Willmar State Hospital	Adolescents	R. Hallvorson[22]
Fergus Falls State Hospital	Adolescents	H. Grey[20]
Minnesota Valley Social Adaptation Center***	Severely mentally retarded adults	C. Turnbull

*Also, at the 1969 annual meeting of the Americal Psychiatric Association, Moises Grimberg invited people to view an exhibit on a special program, as follows:

A new concept in the rehabilitation of the mentally ill has been used with great success in the Talbot Rehabilitation Center at Westboro State Hospital in Westboro, Massachusetts.

Our creation of 'A Surrogate Society' within a state hospital has brought about the return to society and the community of countless chronic mental patients.

**For Minnesota readers it should be clear that this is a partial listing only and there is no intent to slight other efforts not mentioned, including those such as the structuring of a closed observation ward or a unit for alcoholics at the Anoka State Hospital that are as of May, 1969, still in formative stages.

***This program borrows heavily at the conceptual level from the work of Polsky.[39]

made to milieu processes and judgments thereon as they may be found in the child welfare field in relation to adoptions, foster home placements, and small-group home placements.

REFERENCES

1. Albee, G.: We have been warned! In *Distress in the City: Essays on the Design and Administration of Urban Mental Health Services.* Cleveland, Case Western Reserve University Press, 1969, pp. 213-222.
2. Alexander, F.: *Psychoanalysis and Psychotherapy.* New York, Norton, 1956.
3. Appleby, L., Proanao, A., and Perry, R.: Theoretical vs. empirical treatment models: An exploratory investigation. In Appleby, L., Scher, J. M., and Cumming, J. (Eds.) : *Chronic Schizophrenia.* Glencoe, Free Press, 1960.
4. Aronson, H., and Weintraub, W.: Patient changes during classical psychoanalysis as a function of initial status and duration of treatment. *Psychiatry, 31:*369-379, 1968.
5. Artiss, K. L.: *Milieu Therapy in Schizophrenia.* New York, Grune & Stratton, 1962.
6. Ayllon, T., and Haughton, E.: Modification of symptomatic verbal behavior of mental patients. *Behav. Res. Ther.,* 2:87-97, 1964.
7. Bockoven, J. S.: *Moral Treatment in American Psychiatry.* New York, Springer, 1963.
8. Caudill, W. :*The Psychiatric Hospital as a Small Society.* Cambridge, Harvard University Press, 1958.
9. Clark, D. H.: The ward therapeutic community and its effects on the hospital. In Freeman, H. (Ed.) : *Psychiatric Hospital Care.* London, Bailliere, 1965.
10. Clark, D. H., and Oram, E. G.: Reform in the mental hospital. An eight year follow-up. *Int. J. Soc. Psychiat., 12:*98-108, 1966.
11. Cumming, J., and Cumming, E.: *Ego and Milieu: The Theory and Practice of Environmental Therapy.* New York, Altherton Press, 1962.
12. Dunham, H. W., and Weinberg, S. K.: *The Culture of the State Mental Hospital.* Detroit, Wayne State University Press, 1960.
13. Edelson, M.: *Ego Psychology, Group Dynamics and the Therapeutic Community.* New York, Grune & Stratton, 1964.
14. Fairweather, G. W.: *Social Psychology in Treating Mental Illness.* New York, Wiley, 1964.
15. Fairweather, G. W., Sanders, D. H., Maynard, H., and Cressler, D. L.: *Community Life for the Mentally Ill: An Alternative to Institutional Care.* New York, Aldine, in press.
16. Fairweather, G. W., and Simon, R. A.: A further follow-up of psychotherapeutic programs. *J. Consult. Psychol.,* 27:186, 1963.
17. Fairweather, G. W., Simon, R., Geband, M. E., Weingarten, F., Holland, J. L., Sanders, R., Stone, G. B., and Reahl, J. E.: Relative effective-

ness of psychotherapeutic programs: A multicriteria comparison of four programs for three different patient groups. *Psychol. Monogr., 74,* 1960.

18. Frank, J. D.: Common features account for effectiveness. *Int. J. Psychiat.,* 122-127, July, 1969.

19. Goffman, E.: *Asylums: Essays on the Social Situations of Mental Patients and Other Inmates.* Garden City, New York, Doubleday, 1961.

20. Grey, H.: *Goals Seminar Conference.* Fergus Falls, Minnesota, June 7, 1968.

21. Hall, E. T.: *Silent Language.* New York, Doubleday, 1959.

22. Hallvorson, R.: *Goals Seminar Conference.* Fergus Falls, Minnesota, June 7, 1968.

23. Hofling, C. K.: A current problem in milieu therapy. *Hospital and Community Psychiatry, 20:*78-81.

24. Jackson, J.: Factors of the treatment environment. *Arch. Gen. Psychiat., 21:*39-45, 1969.

25. Jones, M.: *The Therapeutic Community.* New York, Basic Books, 1953.

26. Kraft, A. M.: The therapeutic community. In Arieti, S. (Ed.) : *American Handbook of Psychiatry.* New York, Basic Books, 1966, vol. 3.

27. Kraft, A. M., Binner, P. R., and Dickey, B. A.: The community mental health program and the longer-stay patient. *Arch. Gen. Psychiat., 16:* 64-70, 1967.

28. Korczak, J.: *Selected Works.* Warsaw, Poland, Central Institute for Scientific, Technical and Economic Information, 1967.

29. Kyllonen, R.: *Goals Seminar Conference.* Fergus Falls, Minnesota, June 7, 1968.

30. Linn, E. L.: Drug therapy, milieu change, and release from a mental hospital. *AMA Archives of Neurology and Psychiatry, 81:*785-794, June, 1959.

31. Livermore, J. M., Malmquist, C. P., and Meehl, P .E.: On the justifications for civil commitment. *University of Pennsylvania Law Review, 117:*75-96, November, 1968.

32. Martin, M.: A practical treatment program for a mental hospital 'back' ward. *Amer. J. Psychiat., 10:*758-760, 1950.

33. Menninger, K.: *Crime of Punishment.* New York, Viking Press, 1968.

34. Menninger, K.: *Vital Balance.* New York, Viking Press, 1963.

35. Nathanson, E. M.: *Dirty Dozen.* New York, Random House, 1965.

36. Parsons, T.: The mental hospital as a type of organization. In Greenblatt, M., Levinson, D. J., and Williams, R. H. (Eds.) : *The Patient and the Mental Hospital.* Glencoe, Free Press, 1957.

37. Pine, F., and Levinson, D. J.: A sociopsychological conception of patienthood. *Int. J. Soc. Psychiat., 7,* 1961.

38. Polley, G. W., McAllister, L. W., Olson, T. W., and Wilson, K. P.: Mental Health Training for County Welfare Social Work Personnel:

An Exercise in Education and Community Organization. Unpublished paper, 1969.

39. Polsky, H. W.: *Cottage Six—The Social System of Delinquent Boys in Residential Treatment.* New York, Wiley, 1962.
40. Potsubay, R.: Therapeutic community behind bars. *Sk & F Psychiatric Reporter, 43:*13-16, Spring, 1969.
41. Reiff, R.: *Child Welfare Retreat.* Hill City, Minnesota, February 2-4, 1966.
42. Rosengren, W. R.: Communication, organization, and conduct in the therapeutic milieu. *Administrative Science Quarterly, 9:*70-90, 1964.
43. Scheff, T. J.: *Being Mentally Ill: A Sociological Theory.* Chicago, Aldine, 1966.
44. Schofield, W.: The YAVIS Syndrome and Training for Psychotherapy. Unpublished paper, 1964.
45. Sommer, R.: *Personal Space—The Behavioral Basis of Design.* Englewood Cliffs, New Jersey, Prentice-Hall, 1969.
46. Spivack, M., MCP: Sensory distortions in tunnels and corridors. *Hospital and Community Psychiatry,* January, 1967.
47. Stanton, A. H., and Schwartz, M. S.: *The Mental Hospital.* New York, Basic Books, 1954.
48. Stürup, G. K.: *Treating the Untreatable.* Baltimore, Johns Hopkins University Press, 1968.
49. Szasz, T. S.: *Law, Liberty, and Psychiatry.* New York, Macmillan, 1963.
50. Towbin, A. P.: Self-care unit: Some lessons in institutional power. *J. Consult. Clini. Psychol., 33:*561-570, 1969.
51. Vail, D. J.: Mental deficiency: Response to milieu therapy. *Amer. J. Psychiat., 113:*170-173, August, 1956.
52. von Hilsheimer, G.: Is there a science of behavior? In *Humanities Curriculum.* Orange City, Florida, 1967.
53. Wilmer, H. A.: *Social Psychiatry in Action: A Therapeutic Community.* Springfield, Thomas, 1958.
54. Wolfensberger, W.: The origin and nature of our institutional models. In *Changing Patterns in Residential Services for the Mentally Retarded.* Washington, D. C., President's Committee on Mental Retardation, January 10, 1969.

THE HISTORY of psychoanalytic psychotherapy is punctuated by many intense conflicts surrounding orthodoxy and deviations from the accepted mode and technique. In many instances these struggles have hindered the even development of a theory of treatment. For the battles, particularly within the field of psychoanalysis, have most frequently split off from the mainstream of psychoanalytic thinking those contributors who were most brilliant and original. These developments have been both fruitful and harmful in the search for ultimate truth and knowledge. Eissler's focus on parameters of psychoanalytic technique was a major force in maintaining the integration of newer conceptions within the general framework of psychoanalytic theory. Dr. Bernard F. Riess' paper is similarly an original contribution to the continuing evolution of technique and theory within the constellation of psychoanalysis.

Dr. Riess outlines in the beginning of his paper those principles and theoretical conceptions of psychoanalysis that he feels are the essential guiding principles. This thorough reevaluation of these conceptions is fundamental to an understanding of the proposed modifications that he presents subsequently. Drawing on his experiences in intensive, marathon consultation to industrial firms he elucidates some of the positive effects of modification in technique within these settings. He clearly explicates the techniques and theoretical underpinnings of these innovations and the reasons for their effectiveness. From those experiences he extrapolates to individual practice and indicates how the fruits of his labors in a different setting can be appropriately applied to the usual practice of psychotherapy. His exposition is clear in his presentation of the rationale for introducing some of the techniques of massed-time psychotherapy into his work with individual patients, some of the resistances of therapists to adopting these procedures, and the limitations of the techniques as well.

G.D.G.
D.S.M.

234

Chapter 15

IS ANALYSIS INTERMINABLE?

BERNARD F. RIESS

M Y TITLE CONTAINS a certain connotation which requires explanation because I am devoted to an old non-Parkinsonian tradition. One of my definitions of psychoanalytic therapy, stolen in part from Dr. E. K. Schwartz, is that individual treatment is an interaction between two people, one of whom knows what he is talking about—and hopefully that person is the therapist.

I am also convinced that traditional psychoanalysis is neither dead nor outmoded. Neither, however, is it a social salvation nor an answer to the many unmet needs of what we are now calling community mental health. The theory, etiology, and treatment of syphilis did not attempt to solve the problem of its social causation. Psychoanalytic psychotherapy still remains what is started as—a theory of the origin and development of personality and a search for methods of altering self-harmful individual behavior. Whatever innovations I shall suggest in this talk will have to do with revisions of theory and methodology rather than with the goals or applicability of psychotherapy to the social problems of today. I believe that we clinicians must wear two hats: the first, that of the agent of change for multiply generated individual problems; the second, but no less important, that of social-psychological revolutionary. However, we must not mix roles nor confuse goals.

Next, in order only of complexity, is a conviction that therapy without theory is of little validity. To know what one is doing with a patient, client, or person—however one describes the "other" in the therapeutic situation—demands a concern with some underlying principles of action and intervention. Thus I reject any simple-minded concept of psychotherapy such as that which states that emoting, experiencing closeness, or nudity is therapy. Many experiences are therapeutic, but that does not make a therapy out of experiencing.

The straw man usually constructed as a model of the psychoanalyst shows him as an authoritarian, detached, cold, and noninteractive observer, unfeeling in his attitudes to the patient. How false this is we can see, for instance, from Freud's own behavior toward Gustave Mahler, whom he cured of impotence in one session during which they walked and talked together for several hours. Please keep that last phrase, "for several hours," in mind, for Freud did not work by the clock.

Alexander Wolf has written that "while a warm regard for the patient is important, it is of as much use as compassionate tears for a person suffering from appendicitis. Just as a surgical case needs the application of surgical skill, the mentally disturbed patient requires psychoanalytic expertness. Insights are not cold, detached, unrelated dirty words. If the patient experiences the analyst as nonaffectively abstract, it may or may not be so. If the therapist is, in fact, a cold, detached, unfeeling person, the patient would be well-advised to seek help elesewhere."

From this point of view (with which I heartily agree) comes the idea that one of the best ways in which to innovate in psychotherapy is to think and to ponder on what the individual sufferer is like and what his behavior means in the context of any given consistent theory of human nature. "Relevance" is a catchword of today's students and black power innovators. It should also be an important concern of the therapist. What is relevant to the individual person who comes seeking help?

To answer that question involves both finding out what kind of difficulty the person has and what kind of person the trouble has. Diagnosis must be carefully done, and then the relevant techniques of treatment can be applied. This selection involves thought, a concept remote from the armamentarium of many emotive and relationship practitioners.

It is obvious that the overall purpose of treatment is to produce, stimulate, or facilitate change. The latter ranges from symptom removal to fundamental alterations in outlook, values, relationships, and self-perception. The capacity to change, to learn, and to grow is inherent in the nature of the living organism. We deal, therefore, with two problems; one is the understanding of resistance to change and the other is how to bring about the condition for change.

Freud dealt with the former, the blocks to change, only late in his life. In 1937 he described three conditions which limit change: first, the quantitative relationship between the severity of the trauma and the illness—the greater the focal trauma, the greater the potential for change; second, the strength of drives or instincts in relationship to the potential of the ego was seen as inversely tied to change—the greater the force of the instinct, the more difficult the change; and finally, the intactness and integrity of the ego was postulated as positively associated with change—the more distorted the ego, the greater the resistance to modification. These conditions for and against adaptive flexibility underly the traditional repression, transference, superego, and id resistances.

It is then appropriate to ask what kinds of change are looked for in psychoanalytic therapy. Love and work, the capacity to enjoy, and the capacity to achieve are the basic areas of modification. Expressed in other terms, the individual will change in the direction of more compromise with reality, external and internal, and will find enjoyment in attachment to real persons and objects rather than fantasied attachments. Mastery and a feeling of achievement will find a place in the arena of work, and finally the individual will be more aware of his unconscious motivations; i.e. "Where id was, there shall ego be."

It is also important to very briefly summarize the means whereby change is supposed to be produced in psychoanalysis. First, anxiety must be elevated to the point where it mobilizes defenses. This is essential since no understanding of unconscious processes is possible without the pinpointing of defenses. Second, the backward tracing of the feelings associated with both anxiety and defenses provides the historical antecedents of ongoing neurotic processes. Third, the vicissitudes of the defenses as they are aroused, reactivated, altered, and fixed by the varying perceptions of the therapist in the development of transference and transference neurosis are worked through by the insight of the therapist and the working relationship established with the patient. If this all sounds hopelessly old-hat and old-fashioned, its perpetrator should be pardoned since he has become a charter member of the new APA Division of Senescent Psychology.

With this introduction and orientation to what I see as the task and the basic technique of psychoanalytic therapy, I shall now turn to the question posed by my title: Is analysis necessarily interminable and how can technique be altered to expedite change without the popular desertion of good individual therapeutic behavior?

The precipitating element in the new direction came from experiences over the last six years in working with a team of industrial consultants in a program of self-evaluation and executive innovation in top industrial executives. The program developed by Jerome Barnum Associates combines individual and group therapy with role playing, simulation of industrial decision making, marathon sessions, and goldfish bowl living. The subjects were all volunteer, top-echelon business executives, either in a single industrial complex or in a multihouse group. Their motivation for the involvement in a full week of eighteen to twenty hours per day was the recognition that interpersonal relationships in top management teams depend on self-evaluation and self-knowledge.

Let me describe briefly both the setting and procedure. The participants, fifteen to twenty-one in number, meet in a hotel whose living rooms are transformed each morning into executive offices with a live secretary and in- and out-baskets of mail. In each room there is a closed circuit TV camera, the monitors for which are in the control or monitor room. All action is therefore seen, heard, and taped for playback. On the first afternoon, each participant is given a complete history of the fictitious corporation of which he will be an officer during the week. The fifteen to twenty-one people are divided into three teams which parallel each other and within which each member rotates roles each day, assuming the person of a different corporate executive each time. In addition to the general corporate history, for each role-palying exercise, each executive gets a confidential briefing containing material, gossip, business information, and so on with which he might normally have contact in his assumed role.

Each morning and afternoon session starts with a crucial day in the life of the corporation. These crucial periods are selected to maximize problems and decision-making situations relevant to human factors in management teams. The situations are challenges to innovative business practices and are open-ended in that there are no prescribed or predetermined correct outcomes. In addition to the crucial situations, the monitoring staff can introduce "triggers" to pinpoint, bring out, or force defensive reactions.

When the teams have had time to work out their idiosyncratic solutions, they meet with the monitors (psychologists) to engage in small-group self-evaluation sessions. Once a day, the whole group meets together in a "grinder" session to evaluate each other and to dig into and to expose individual behavior patterns. As a result of this exposure, there arise questions of personal involvement and pathology which require individual, in-depth investigations of personality. It is here that the clinical psychologist functions as a psychoanalyst. What differentiates our sessions from those customarily found is the length of the confrontation. Some of the sessions have lasted from six to ten hours and are repeated several times over the course of the week's work.

After some fifteen experiences in this setting, I came to realize that changes in the individual participants took place with rapidity and intensity such as I had not seen in my regular practice with my patients. Furthermore, over a period of years, I had feedback from wives and children about the visibility and permanence of the alterations. These observations caused me to reflect upon and question the reasons for the changes as well as to wonder whether some of the techniques might not be adapted to my usual practice.

Three factors seemed to be related to the rapid change in the participants. These were, first, the heightened anxiety brought about by the critical observations made possible by the TV tapes and monitoring, second, the improvement in efficiency resulting from the impossibility of time-wasting descriptions of daily life experiences and the sharpening of focus on the why's of behavior, and finally, the protracted therapeutic sessions, which centralized the defensive maneuvers of the participants.

What seemed to be of special value to the participants was the long session with the psychologist. Most of our subjects rated this as the outstanding contributing feature of the whole experience-compression engagement. This finding was congruent with the reports of marathon therapy patients but with the difference that the protracted time was built upon a history of knowledge of the patient and observation of his or her former behavior.

The M.I.T. and Harvard studies of the creative and innovative process have isolated four significant parameters or conditions: first, the recognition that there is a problem, second, disgust or revulsion toward the inefficient present mode of dealing with the problem, third, a free-ranging, exploratory experience not necessarily limited to the specific problem under study, and finally, the solution and the loss of tension resulting from the solution.

I have described the industrial situation above mainly because it coincided with increasing dissatisfaction with my usual office practice. It pointed up the slowness of the change. The exploratory, nontunnel-vision aspect was made possible by my involvement with the varying types of interaction in experience compression. When I observed the participants finally reflecting stereotyped or customary points of departure, I suddenly found myself wondering what aspects of traditional analysis I could throw away and thus free myself to work with the patient.

It also occurred to me that some of the most dissatisfying moments in therapy were brought about by my mental time-set. I experienced the oncoming end of the session as a frustration or as a relief. I also found myself wondering how often the patient could come in with the same story. At the same time I recalled Freud's success with Gustave Mahler not because it was so startling but because it involved throwing away two of our cherished traditions, the sessile position of the therapist and the time limitations of his sessions. However, not having the Wiener Wald in which to wander, I decided to try out extended sessions. There is no claim here to pioneering. It is certain that for practical reasons, some patients have double-length sessions in many settings.

There is need, however, to spell out the kinds of patients and the types of problems for which extension of ordinary time limits is theoretically advisable and how it can be made practically possible. I should like first to postulate what are the analytic considerations which justify the departure from tradition. In a recent paper in *Psychotherapy,* Roth, Berenbaum, and S. J. Garfield present the rationale for a one-session, ten-hour therapeutic experience. Their procedure is based on what they call developmental psychotherapy. This theory postulates that

> . . . the key of psychotherapy lies in the assumption that people grow as a result of significant human interaction; i.e., people seek to create relationships which will be significant to them, and thus produce growth. Patients seek psychotherapy because of fixations below their chronological age (which defines immaturity). They can be helped by a relationship which recognizes their level of fixation and the consequent need for a given kind of interaction. Only this interaction will produce growth.
>
> The therapeutic agent in this relationship is called interactional flow, which refers to a depth of experience shared by two people in whom barriers (in the form of resistance and defense) are lifted and an aura of intense interaction is obtained. This concept may sound mystical, but an adequate description is difficult to communicate to those who have not experienced it, while being quite obvious to those who have. If this concept is accepted, however, one can view therapeutic technique as designed to alter interferences in communication so that the interactional flow can be experienced. The famous therapists developed their theories out of experiences with specific categories of patients, e.g., Sullivan and Arieti with schizophrenics, Freud with hysterical neurotics, and Rogers with adolescent reactions. Each developed a conceptual schema that applied to their patients, and each developed techniques which effected changes in resistance and defense, leading to a depth of relationship. Today, the complete therapist deals with many kinds of patients, but tends to identify with one set of techniques and conceptual systems. These are his tools. It is proposed here that a therapist must be armed with many conceptual schemas for many different kinds of patients.
>
> Developmental Psychotherapy offers each patient a relationship appropriate to his stage of development. The purpose is to achieve interactional flow.

In summarizing their experiences, the authors point to several factors: the opportunity to get a total view of the patient-therapist interaction, the increasingly clear relevance of defenses to personality, the rapid increase of intensity in the interaction, and the dilution of the warming-up and end-anticipation periods.

While somewhat different from my orientation, there are similarities. The deviation or innovation I am suggesting is used in conjunction with more orthodox procedures and more often when the therapist and patient feel stymied by lack of progress and by the repetition of analytic work without resulting changes. It thus becomes a prominent mode of attack on the working-through phase of therapy.

Classically this period is that in which ego resistances are maximized—often expressed by patients who say that they *know* what is wrong, they have insight, but still continue with their neurotic defenses. As is so often stated, direct attack on the defense simply solidifies it. There is not sufficient anxiety mobilized to enable the patient to face his defense. The hour ends just as the patient has successfully resisted getting beneath the defense.

As he now faces two, three, or ten hours of continued interaction, the defensive use of description and denial is no longer effective. He must talk about something and has already exhausted the obvious. Fear of the unconscious rises in the form of anxiety-fear seeking an object; the defenses used to allay the anxiety first become very obvious and then useless, since they do not exhaust either time or the therapist. The introjected bad parent whom the therapist represents then becomes focal. Negative transference and hostility break through and can quickly be analyzed.

Here the therapist can make rapid and forceful interpretations—interpretations, not mere reflections or rewording of the patient's productions. The therapist quickly has an accumulation of observations which can be used and brought to focus on the defenses. The most common defenses of intellectualizing, denying, and projection are difficult to maintain, and the primary-process feelings and thoughts are given an opportunity to emerge. Finally the benevolent, ego-enhancing aspects of the patient-therapist relationship emerge as the patient eventually feels that he is being listened to at a tremendous cost to the therapist. In my experience (as in that of Roth *et al.*), the gains in putting insight into practice are tremendous, and months of shilly-shallying in the mess of working-through can be short-circuited.

There are other reasons for the use of massed time therapy. It is a frequent experience that it takes a long time for a patient to see that he is being defensive when he has other alternatives. In describing events in the world outside the office, there are always extenuating circumstances and happenstances that disguise the defensive maneuvers. Bosses, spouses, and parents can be blamed for the so-called neurotic behavior. However, within the nonreality of the office, the frustration of almost unlimited time enhances the need for defenses and strips the patient of excuses for not seeing them. Only the transference qualities of the therapist are available and can be quickly seen and interpreted by the observant therapist.

Finally, the technique facilitates the focus of the patient on what analysts are now generally emphasizing; namely, the identification processes of the patient. How does he see himself when he is cut off from mere verbal descriptions of life outside?

These remarks do not imply that social events and the realities of love and work are nonexistent. The technique works because it gives the dyadic participants an opportunity to separate reality from self-perception.

Although the method has been used primarily to facilitate the ending of the interminable working-through phase, it has occasionally been used to develop a fast initial phase—one in which the working alliance of patient and therapist is established. Here again the emergence and utilization of anxiety as the fuel for change is the primary factor.

For what kinds of problems and patients do I see this approach as the method of choice? It is relatively ineffective—as indeed are most analytic methods—for the obsessive-compulsive; however, it is no less effective here than are traditional, analytical, or behavioral therapy procedures. It has been particularly useful for patients whose defenses are intellectual, verbal diarrhea, denial. It is probably not to be recommended for a very regressed, infantilized individual. On the other hand, it is helpful where the presenting complaint is anxiety or phobia. The demonstration that there is an economy underlying these symptoms and that anxiety can be tolerated and reduced when understood is consonant both with analytic and desensitizing therapies.

Thus far I have dealt with the process of therapy and with the patient. What of the therapist? Here I find several sensitive areas of resistance to change. The most peripheral, and therefore not the least difficult to overcome, arises from the twin obsessions of time and money. Our daily schedules seem sacrosanct, and our devotion to fixed fee schedules is almost as unshakable. We expect our patients to be flexible and to recognize that Father Time is a parent from whom one can declare relative independence. Community mental health research has indicated the value of variable time limits for various kinds of people and problems. Conditioned response therapists have pointed to the importance of a free reinforcement schedule. Can we not then arrange for massed hours?

Similarly, the problem of how to charge for the four, five, or six-hour session should raise problems no different than the setting of a regular dollar value for forty-five minutes of time. We have already found patients improving in group therapy despite a reduced per-session fee. If we can stop the endless analysis, is not the gain in satisfaction worth the departure from our self-imposed fee barriers? Alternatively, if the sessions are successful, the patient will be willing to pay regular amounts because of the consequent shortening of the analytic expense period. So these resistances are nominal or numerical but not of real significance. That some of us are here today is evidence that we can shift schedules when we so desire.

More basic is the resistance to in-depth involvement in doing analysis. It is easy to listen for forty-five minutes, since much of this period is only heard but not attended to. Longer sessions require more integrative thinking by the therapist, more searching for the emergency of defenses, resistances, slips of tongue, unconscious emergence of repressed ideation and feeling, and more focus on transferential phenomena. Moreover, listening is not enough. The therapist is called upon to interpret faster and more directly than is customary. It may also produce clearer evidence of countertransferences. Thus, therapeutic skills can be sharpened and tested in the long encounter.

I could go on to describe other innovations which come from the industrial psychology arena; i.e. the use of variable reward to enhance progress—that is, lower fees for productive sessions, and so forth. What I have presented here is one technique which has been tried by a few practitioners and found to be effective. If it encourages experimentation and a desire to eliminate the traditional ceremonial aspects of analysis in favor of the relevant elements, my purpose will have been achieved.

Dr. Seymour R. Kaplan, of the Montefiore Hospital Medical Center, combines those rare talents of an administrator, a clinician, and a researcher. This paper reflects his extensive abilities through the clarity and thoroughness of his presentation, well utilizing his outstanding foundation in background material and organization. The Lincoln Hospital, where Dr. Kaplan had been in charge of the residency training program and clinical programs, is in the heart of the Bronx's black and Puerto Rican ghetto. His firsthand knowledge of the population and sensitivity and sophistication about their requirements is obvious throughout the paper.

In a well–thought-through and thorough manner, Dr. Kaplan first delineates the sphere of the disadvantaged, and in this process shows us the breath and scope of this area. He cautions against the tendency to equate poverty with mental illness and illustrates concretely that poverty can occur without mental illness and certainly mental illness can occur without poverty. There are, as Dr. Kaplan shows us, definite connections between social class and specifics of mental health practices that professionals must avail themselves of with these people. The lower one finds oneself on the social class ladder, Dr. Kaplan feels, the more unavailable does effective psychiatric care become. In this fascinating paper Dr. Kaplan traces the meaning of social class considerations for the severely ill and then for the less severely ill patient. He provides us with an understanding of the possible negative attitudes of psychotherapists toward the lower social class patients and indicates the maladaptive characteristics arising in lower-class patients that make therapy with them that much more difficult.

With a comprehensive command of the field based upon his psychoanalytic background and training, an extensive search of the literature, and his practical job experience, Dr. Kaplan gives not only the psychodynamics and innovative treatment approaches but also future directions to handling the maladaptive characteristics of the lower-class patient. This chapter may be a particularly unique reading experience for it provides us with an educational experience in an area with which most of us have limited familiarity.

G.D.G.
D.S.M.

Chapter 16

PSYCHOTHERAPEUTIC APPROACHES IN WORKING WITH THE DISADVANTAGED

SEYMOUR R. KAPLAN

INTRODUCTION

THE "WAR ON POVERTY" has brought the mental health legions to the bastions and has stirred to action still larger numbers of social scientists. However, when the psychotherapist arrives at the front, he finds that the battle lines are not clearly drawn and the enemy difficult to identify. This is to be expected if one uses as a guide generalizations about social class and culture and depends upon the metaphor for transportation. Therefore, before proceeding on the ambitious journey which I—perhaps immodestly—have agreed to undertake (that is, to map out innovative psychotherapeutic approaches in working with the disadvantaged), I should like first to bring to your attention the complexities of the task. While I do think that for heuristic reasons it is useful to draw upon generalizations about the disadvantaged, the limitations of this approach should be kept in mind.

Taxonomic Considerations of Social Classes

I assume that by the term "disadvantaged" we are referring to the economic situation of populations whose annual income falls below a certain level (about $3,000 for a family of four is a frequently used base line) and who therefore suffer the effects of poverty. While even this assumption can be challenged on economic grounds, one cannot proceed much further without encountering difficulties about specific social class and/or cultural determinants in attempting to describe the effects of poverty.

To begin with, the term "disadvantaged" is often used synonymously with "lower social class" or "working class" or to refer to deprivations that result from being a member of a minority

248

ethnic group. The taxonomic and conceptual problems in researching these terms are very complex. Indices utilized may vary from specific factors like level of education, income, and type of employment to less tangible entities like "style of life."[76,115]

Lewis[65] talks about the inadequate attention given to localities in thinking about the poor and points out that even when referring to the more circumscribed "urban poverty" we are not talking about a single condition. This "under-recognition of the heterogeneity among the poor"[75] and the need for a "more differentiated definition of who the population is" has been hampered, according to Srole,[115] by tendencies to focus on gross socioeconomic categories which make crosscultural comparability impossible or to apply huge monolithic titles to huge segments of the population (e.g. "the culture of poverty"), perhaps in the hope of elevating the thinking about these populations by such description.

A variety of recent studies have in fact recognized major differences within the universe of poverty.[64,74,88] In the following sections, therefore, I at no time mean to underestimate the breadth and diversity of the low-income or "disadvantaged" populations by subsuming them, for purposes of exposition, under one head. Furthermore, I will not attempt to distinguish them from cultural factors.

Social Class Considerations of the Epidemiology of Mental Illness

Another important point to clarify is the misconception that has begun to emerge recently—that being economically disadvantaged is synonymous with being emotionally disadvantaged. The converse, as Townsend[122] notes, is "the misconception that in a relatively prosperous society most individuals have the capacity to meet any contingency in life."

The classic Hollingshead and Redlich study[43] did reveal a greater prevalence of mental illness, specifically schizophrenic reactions, in the lower socioeconomic classes than in the higher class. In addition, there seemed to be some basis for concluding a greater incidence (i.e. greater production of new cases) in the lower class as well. Other studies appear to have corroborated these basic findings.[35,49,116] However, it should also be made clear that living under reduced economic circumstances does not necessarily produce greater proportions of mentally ill.

Some investigators are questioning the implicit assumption that it is poverty that causes the higher incidence and prevalence of mental illness. In referring to the inverse relationship between social class and psychiatric disorder, Dohrenwend[19] noted that "these results can be explained with equal plausibility on the one hand as evidence of social causation, with the pressures of low status producing psychopathology; and on the other hand as evidence of social selection, with the disability of preexisting disorder leading to low social status." Dunham[21] reviews the social causation versus social selection issues from the epidemiological point of view.

Relating to the issue of social class causation in mental illness, Srole[115] has pointed out that the American Indians have been found to be by far the most impoverished group in the nation. Yet, the Winnebago tribe in Wisconsin—socioeconomically comparable to other Indian tribes—with an unemployment rate throughout most of the year of about 50 percent to 60 percent, little or no schooling for children or adults, shack homes reminiscent of slum areas in rural parts of the country, death rates three to four times higher than that of the general population, and so on, did not reveal (according to Srole) "any unusual prevalence of gross psychopathology."

Leighton,[62] after comparable observations regarding a Navajo community of two hundred families, made the further point that not only can poverty occur without (what he called) "sociocultural disintegration"—e.g. the community despite poverty maintained "their social structure . . . and their sense of worth"—but "sociocultural disintegration" can occur without poverty. To wit, the effects upon that same community of increased prosperity was found to be child abuse (formerly rare among the Navajos), beating of spouses, deterioration of homes, broken families, and so forth.

Aside from fostering some of the more specific myths mentioned above, the "poverty/mental illness" equation in general seems in danger of having the poor reinherit old attitudes of rejection which got foisted onto the mentally ill at a time in the 1800's when mental hospitals were singled out for the "poor and indigent mentally ill," and endowing to each, in effect, the worst of both possible worlds.

Aside from being subject to similar stigmas and struggling to get free from prevalent stereotypes, Gruenberg[39] notes that, especially of late in our society, the task of reducing psychotic disorders tends to get confused with the problem of reducing the amount of poverty. For example, Gruenberg noted the findings of the Dutchess County study of the severe social deterioration associated with chronic psychotic disorders. In reference to the success in reducing the frequency of this condition in poor patients, he observed that "although nothing had been done to alleviate their poverty, the services had apparently been successful in minimizing the damage associated with psychotic illness." He went on to add that it seemed to him that "there is much progress to be made in this direction without any direct attack on community poverty." As always in our zeal to bring about innovative changes, we must guard against the danger of a simplistic point of view.

SOCIAL CLASS AND MENTAL HEALTH PRACTICES

Social Class Considerations in Current Patterns of Mental Health Services

Lewis[65] said, "The poor are defined by what they do as well as by what is done to or for them." Studies have indicated that the nature of the delivery of mental health services or more aptly the discrepancies in whole "patterns of patient care"[32] makes for the "under-utilization of mental health services by the poor."[36] Furthermore, social class factors appear to influence the type of psychiatric treatment received by the different social classes or segments of the population. The studies by Redlich and Hollingshead[43,96] established the fact that patients of higher classes (Classes I and II) more frequently received psychotherapy, particularly insight therapy, than lower classes (Classes IV and V) and that the latter were more likely to receive supportive therapy, organic treatment, or no therapy.

Initially, cost of treatment seemed an easy explanation. But even when ability to pay was not an issue, social class was still found to be related to acceptance of patients for therapy, length of therapy, duration of therapy sessions, and, in some instances, experience level of therapist.[11,83] As McMahon[72] summed up the situation: "The lower one finds oneself on the social class ladder, the more unavailable does effective psychiatric care become."

Apart from the issue of availability of resources, one of the social class determinants in the utilization and type of treatment offered may be the result of the tendency for the disadvantaged patients to seek out psychiatric treatment only when there is severe distress. This would influence the higher percentage of psychotic compared to nonpsychotic conditions among patients seen in mental hygiene clinics in disadvantaged areas compared to clinics in areas of higher social class composition. For example, over 40 percent of the patients seen at the psychiatric clinic at Lincoln Hospital, which is located in a severely economically disadvantaged area, are diagnosed as psychotic. The staff at Lincoln is familiar with the cultural influences upon symptom formation (for example, "cultural paranoia" among black patients[38] or socially sanctioned hallucinatory experiences and dissociated hyperactive states, or "ataques," among Puerto Rican patients[24,64,69,73]) and, as often does occur, would tend not to misdiagnose them as psychotic patients on the basis of these symptoms alone.

The higher proportion of psychosis in a patient population at any given treatment facility would then tend to influence the statistics of treatment choice in the direction noted above. However, I think it would be a mistake to assume the converse—that is, that chronic psychotic patients from the higher social classes are likely to receive effective treatment. As Greenblatt and Sharaf[36] have noted, there is "a kind of therapeutic nihilism toward patients with chronic schizophrenia," and this is true regardless of social class.

However, even if corrections are made so that similar diagnostic groups are studied, it is likely that social class factors would influence the treatment situation. The Hollingshead and Redlich studies[43,96] and Brill and Storrow[11] found that therapists more frequently reacted less positively to lower-class patients than to their upper-class counterparts or more frequently "disliked" Class V patients, by which it was meant that the therapists "did not understand their values and often had difficulties understanding them as persons." Willie's study[128] of social class preferences of public health nurses (that is, whom they chose to serve) corroborated the kind of picture the above authors present.

Gruenberg[39] has observed, in this regard, that the mental health professional has a "tendency to seek patients in his own image and to reject patients who do not cater to his predilections." Wilder and Coleman[126] found this kind of social class selectivity when they compared their total Walk-In-Clinic sample to the 10 percent who got referred to long-term psychotherapy—specifically that "the long-term therapy patient is likely to be younger, averaging 31 years of age, better educated, and more likely white, Jewish and United States born." It was their impression that the patients referred for long-term psychotherapy were more verbal and introspective, "like the psychiatrists who refer them," and that the social characteristics of those patients "more closely resembled those of the referring psychiatric doctors than they did the characteristics of all the Walk-In-Clinic patients."

Social Class Considerations in the Practice of Psychotherapy for the Less Severely Ill Patient

The epidemiological and social class considerations in the patterns of mental health services described above, to a large measure, refer to the severely ill patient. If one considers specifically the applicability of psychotherapeutic techniques to the less severely ill patient of the lower social classes, many studies refer to the unsuitability or the failure of psychotherapy for this patient population. After an initial diagnostic screening to determine acceptance for psychotherapy, Brill and Storrow[11] regarded a smaller proportion of lower-class patients suitable for continuation in treatment. Hunt[44] concluded that "efforts to impose psychotherapy upon lower-class patients and/or attempts to propagandize them into greater receptivity to such programs may in the long run be creating problems instead of solving them."

However, what is often meant by the "failure of psychotherapy" for lower-class patients is that the lower-class patient tends to terminate treatment early in the process. Because of the preponderance of this finding (i.e. early termination), studies have in fact addressed themselves to this high drop-out rate[28,85] without approaching the more complex issue of improvement in those for whom treatment has ensued. Storrow[120] did suggest that while "the lower-class patient is less likely to seek, accept or continue in treatment, the lower-class neurotic who is treated by psychotherapy in an out-patient clinic does just about as well as a similarly treated middle-class patient." Others,[47,48] on the basis of similar findings, concluded that their criteria for improvement tended to differ for the two classes; that is, there was a tendency to assess the improvement of lower-class patients in terms of symptom relief or capacity to resume work and so on, whereas upper-class patients were evaluated on the basis of some more complex factors, like "developing insight" or "working with one's problems."[36]

Certainly a factor that would influence the failure of psychotherapy is the negative attitude of psychotherapists toward lower social class patients. However, some writers suggest that the choice of patients from a similar social class as the psychotherapist is a requirement for successful psychotherapy. Reusch,[97] whose general point of view was later corroborated by Schaffer and Myers[101] and Hollingshead and Redlich,[43] stated: "The present methods of individual psychotherapy—psychoanalysis included—are methods which were designed for use between people who belong to approximately the same social class and who share in common a large number of assumptions." Following Rapoport's statement[95] of "the impossibility of communication between two people who have not shared common experience," Hunt[44] felt that the therapist comes to deal with patients with whom he shares congruent linguistic conventions and similar conceptual and valuational orientations. Hunt observed, "the therapist selects patients who 'talk his language' " and "express value orientations which are not alien to his own." Kong-Ming New's study[60] of communication patterns between professionals and clients of differing social backgrounds came to a similar conclusion.

While these views concerning the choice of patients by psychotherapists warrant further study, particularly regarding what I would call the need for narcissistic identifications especially by the novice, another relevant and perhaps prior issue is that concerning modification of traditional treatment techniques. While I would not underestimate the difficulties that arise in working with patients of different conceptual and valuational orientations, the problem of technique arises from the fact that modifications of traditional practices are mandatory if the therapist is to establish a working alliance[37] with such patients. Many of the conditions and requirements for traditional psychotherapy (i.e. verbal capacity, psychological-mindedness, acceptance of the therapist in a benign, nonjudgmental sense, a sense of doing for oneself as opposed to being done to, a general delay in gratification, and so forth) are at variance with the attitudes, values, and expectations of the lower social class patient. Apart from such realistic factors as the lack of funds for transportation or babysitters even if treatment is free, an assessment of the suitability of psychotherapy, or of any innovative treatment approaches, should take into consideration the interpersonal and psychodynamic characteristics of the lower social class patient, particularly those characteristics that create problems of adaption.

REFERENCES TO MALADAPTIVE CHARACTERISTICS OF THE LOWER SOCIAL CLASS PATIENT

Keeping in mind the aforementioned cautions about generalizations, there are observations in the literature that suggest shared interpersonal and psychodynamic adaptive and maladaptive characteristics among the disadvantaged. My own experiences corroborate many of the observations, and I would like to briefly summarize some of the views on this subject. The term "maladaptive" is not used as a value judgment nor is it limited to psychopathology. It is used to refer to a range of behaviors, attitudes, and values which are not conducive to the ego interests of the patient within the context of his existing environment, even though the environment originally may have been contributory to the maladaptive behavior.

Interpersonal Maladaptive Characteristics of the Lower Social Class Patient

The disadvantaged patient is described as being nonintrospective, action-oriented, physical in the expression of feelings (particularly angry feelings) , and hostile and suspicious of authority representatives of public institutions. He is described as being present-oriented and geared toward living in the "here and now" and as having a low frustration tolerance and tending toward impulsive actions. He is seen to be lacking in verbal skills and conceptual capacities.

Regarding attitudes toward mental illness, the lower-class patient tends to seek out psychiatric treatment only when he experiences severe distress. Redlich and his associates[96] and Brill and Storrow[11] point out that the lower-class patient tends to consider emotional difficulties as due to somatic causes and to desire symptom relief only. Minuchin[79] notes that the patient seeks suggestion, direct advice, warmth and support, yet he expects the therapist to be authoritative. Besides specific expectations of psychotherapy, Mayer and Timms[71] suggest that a basically "different system" of problem-solving thinking from that of their middle-class therapists operates in working-class clients. They further suggest that the working-class clients are moralistic, unicausal, and suppressive in approach and that they favor repressive more than rehabilitative measures in dealing with behavior.

Malone,[70] in describing acting-out children from disadvantaged areas, comments upon their lack of fantasy and constructive use of play activities, their tendency toward concrete thinking, their poor sense of identity, and marked use of imitation. Deutsch[18] has described a "stimulus deprivation" in lower-class children. He correlates this with their perceptual difficulties in organizing nuances of the environment. The children are described as being inattentive in school, showing memory difficulties, having a poor time orientation, and lacking in expectation of rewards.

This very brief outline primarily reflects observations about social class behavior, and I have made no attempt to distinguish cultural influences. I have also not reviewed the literature on the nature of the family dynamics among disadvantaged populations. References to the disorganized nature of the lower social class family can be found in Pavenstedt,[88] Gans,[31] Malone,[70] Minuchin,[78,79] and Myers.[82] Leighton[62] refers to the impact of poverty upon the families as resulting in a "socio-cultural disintegration," which he sees as a "failing of societal functioning which comes upon many kinds of human 'collectivities' (to use Parson's word)." It is of some interest that the earlier sociological studies of the family, which focused upon such aspects of the child rearing practices as feeding and toilet training, have been less emphasized recently with the shift of attention from psychosexual to psychosocial development and to ego psychology in general.

Psychodynamic Considerations of the Maladaptive Characteristics of the Lower Social Class Patient

Again at the risk of oversimplification, I have singled out three general categories as representative of the underlying psychodynamic factors that characterize the maladaptive behavior of the lower social class patients. This is a necessary exercise if we are to articulate the social class and cultural observations with specific dynamic therapeutic modalities. The categories are (1) ambivalence and problems related to early instinctual fixation or regression, (2) ego functioning and problems related to developmental "lag or delay," and (3) ego identity and problems related to the development of object relationships.

Ambivalence

The existence of unresolved ambivalent feelings of love and hate is more or less explicit in most of the references and is associated with deficiencies in ego functioning and in the formation of object and self representations. I will refer to these latter concomitants below. I am referring here to the problem of ambivalence especially as manifested in authority relationships. The contradictory, coexisting reactions of an intense need for proof that the therapist cares and a hostile rejecting attitude toward the therapist presents the most immediate challenge to the establishment of a working alliance. Whether seen in some instances as a manifestation of early oral and anal instinctual fixation or regression, as described by Scheidlinger,[104] or as a need for affirmation of ego boundaries, as suggested by Minuchin,[78,79] the use of techniques related to the problem of unresolved ambivalent feelings is an important consideration in the treatment modalities to be discussed below.

Ego Functioning

Defective ego functioning in language, cognitive, and attentive skills is frequently described. These factors are noted as explanations for learning problems and general problems of living and are by and large held to be due to a developmental lag or delay as the result of environmental circumstances. When described in terms of ego pathology, attention is focused upon the lack of impulse control, the use of ego mechanisms of defense such as externalization and denial (conducive to the manifestation of "cultural paranoia"), concretistic thinking, and failure of ego integration in organizing internal and external reality. A tendency to motoric rather than verbal expression of feelings, especially feelings of anger, and an inability to conceptualize and to communicate emotional problems is associated with magical expectation of authority figures and a belief in mythological constructs of reality. Whatever the explanation for the nature of the ego functioning, most of the innovative treatment approaches focus upon ego-supportive and/or ego-strengthening objectives.

Ego Identity

Although ego identity is a product of overall ego functioning, I refer to it separately because of the particular importance of the nature of object relationships both in the dynamic factors observed among the disadvantaged and in the treatment approaches recommended. Furthermore, the concept of ego identity carries with it particular developmental considerations that I think have special relevance to the issues being discussed. Besides the need for object constancy and the related separation anxiety, the literature points to a failure of normal superego development with a tendency to the formation of an archaic superego, derived from percepts of good and bad parental object representations, and the existence of good and bad self representations. As a consequence of the unresolved ambivalence, the ego deficiency and the immature self and object relations described, the coalescence of identifications into a normal, age-specific ego identity is impaired.

INNOVATIVE TREATMENT APPROACHES TO THE LOWER SOCIAL CLASS PATIENT

Innovative treatment approaches to the lower social class patient will be discussed in terms of those innovations based upon social class considerations of the patterns of mental health services, those based upon social class considerations of the treatment arrangements, and those based upon psychodynamic considerations. While these considerations overlap or coexist, they each tend to stress the reordering of treatment approaches directed at one or the other components in the spectrum of the biosocial and environmental factors in mental illness.

Treatment Approaches Based upon Social Class Considerations of the Patterns of Mental Health Services

I refer here to the institutional reorganization of services as well as to the programs directed to bringing about the institutional reorganization of services based upon the special needs of the lower social class patients. Because of the concomitant national concerns with the problems of poverty, civil rights issues, as well as overall health care, there has been an unusual investment by federal governmental agencies in both shaping and funding of health services, including mental health services. The latter is most notable in the development of the comprehensive community mental health center concept.[26,33,34,92,127] While not specifically enacted for services in disadvantaged areas, priority of funding has been given to these areas.

The center concept does not refer to treatment approaches as such, but to the organization of services which are to be provided for catchment areas (i.e. delimited populations) and which are to include a comprehensive range of treatment facilities. Addressed to the problem of the fragmentation of services, which has become a serious issue for all health services, the center's objective is to encourage the establishment of community-based mental health facilities. Through such programs as the neighborhood service centers[40] and the utilization of expanded mental health manpower (e.g. the paraprofessional[14,41,66,89]), these programs are attempting to correct the underutilization of services for the disadvantaged. The center programs are encouraged to provide crisis-oriented services in walk-in clinics in which patients can be seen without prior appointments,[84,126] to establish active outreach programs (including home visits when indicated), to develop comprehensive rehabilitation programs,[5,10,61,125] and to provide consultation services to the formal and informal organizations in the community with goals including both immediate service problems and long-range prevention programs.[12,106,107]

Among the controversial aspects of the new programs are those that involve social action and institutional change.[91,92,107] The rationale for these programs under the auspices of a mental health service is based in part upon the concept of the interrelationship between emotional disorders and the sense of powerlessness and helplessness of the disadvantaged patient.[3,14,110,129] Fishman and Solomon[25] report that involvement of minority group adolescents in civil rights protest actions has been associated with a decrease in delinquency. The need for assistance with problems of living around welfare, housing, and employment is an inevitable component of the work with multiproblem families. The involvement of disadvantaged "clients" in welfare rights groups and tenant councils has been an especially prominent form of social action.[40,51,93]

Treatment Approaches Based upon Social Class Considerations of the Treatment Arrangements

I refer here to modifications of the parameters of the treatment arrangements either through broadening of paratherapeutic resources or through changes in the treatment relationship that reflect the social class or cultural characteristics of the disadvantaged patient. The reaching out to patients by geographic arrangements of services and by home visits represents suggested changes from the more typical professional role with patients. In addition, it has been suggested that the professional take a more active participatory and supportive role in the interviewing and early treatment sessions with disadvantaged patients. The emphasis should be less on a probing, uncovering interview than on a problem-centered or crisis-intervention approach. The patient's expectation for intervention, treatment by medication, and a directive role by the therapist should be appropriately extended within the context of the presenting problems and the realistic issues with which the patients are confronted.

The use of paraprofessional staff as adjunct team members to expedite social problems and who can function as "bridge" people helps to diminish the social distance and alienation from large institutions which is characteristic of this patient population. Similarly, the use of family and group approaches helps to diminish the fear and mistrust of authorities. I will discuss below some psychodynamic indications for the use of the extradyadic treatment situation, but I refer here to the use of these settings for paratherapeutic, educational, or supportive purposes.[22,68,90,94,98,99,102,121] The "power of the peer group"[136] has been much discussed recently and for the reasons alluded to has a special relevance for disadvantaged populations.[55,58,112] The concept of the "helper being helped" applies to such diverse uses of group settings as the Alcoholics Anonymous meetings, Synanon-type confrontation groups,[80] as well as the use of the small group in general along the model of the therapeutic community.[46]

Many of the therapeutic approaches to disadvantaged patients are based upon the observations of their tendency to express their feelings through actions. Hence, the suggested use of role-playing techniques.[76] Levine[63] recommends the use of games and card playing during home visits as a medium through which to develop a therapeutic relationship, as well as a source of interactional observations of family pathology. The use of activity groups of adults for this purpose in the outpatient clinic setting is widely utilized in a more imaginative manner than is traditional occupational therapy.[13,102,117] Because of educational deficiencies and related problems about vocational training, it is important to include educational and vocational counseling[5] as a component of the therapeutic plans, either within the treatment facility or at a referral agency.

This latter point highlights the need for a comprehensive treatment approach to the multiproblem family in disadvantaged areas. The coordination of work with as many of the human services as are available in the community may be crucial to the success of any treatment program in these areas. This includes the formal institutions such as the school and the group-serving agencies (i.e. settlement houses, casework agencies, and recreational or "character building" groups) and the informal institutions as well. Particularly important among the latter are the programs provided by so-called home town clubs in the Puerto Rican neighborhoods and the many group activities sponsored by the less affluent religious organizations.[106] There are a number of youth groups under the auspices of churches that provide a valuable referral for younger children who require a more structured social group experience than they have either in their homes or in their neighborhood peer groups.[94] Perhaps somewhat more controversial, but nevertheless worthy of consideration, is the influence of spiritualists who play such an important part in the lives of Puerto Rican patients. Minuchin[79] describes a successful intervention by an "espiritista."

Among the last observations relevant to social class and cultural considerations that I wish to make is the countervailing point of view about the maladaptive characteristics of the disadvantaged patient and his family. Some writers, for example, have pointed to the strengths and advantages of the lower-class way of life. Gans[31] suggests that there are important emotional supports in the community life of the disadvantaged populations. Kohn[59] points to family attitudes and values which he sees as positive in the child rearing practices of the lower class. Davis and Havighurst[17] go further to suggest, "Our own view is that better child-rearing practices can be drawn from both middle and lower-class life and made into a combination which is superior to both of the norms as they emerge in this study." The observations of Srole[115] and Leighton[62] point to the value of extended family relationships as a supportive social framework. Although Parsons[86] has noted the conflict that the extended family presents in the present-day industrial society, Litwak[67] questions the overall inclusiveness of Parsons' assumptions.

From my own experiences, particularly among the Puerto Rican patients, the resources that the family provides in assisting in the social reintegration of the depressed and psychotic patient are not to be underestimated. Minuchin,[79] in particular, comments on the value of including contacts with extended family members in treatment planning. While correlation has been made between migration and increased emotional disorders,[100] I have observed that not infrequently among Puerto Rican patients who came to the Lincoln Hospital psychiatric services in an anxious or depressed state, a trip to their former community in Puerto Rico has a salutary effect on the illness. Mills[77] notes the special circumstances of the Puerto Rican migration, which may have a bearing upon this observation.

Treatment Approaches Based upon Psychodynamic Considerations of the Lower Social Class Patient

I refer here to modification of therapeutic techniques or to the emphasis on particular therapeutic modalities based upon psychodynamic considerations of the special maladaptive characteristics of the disadvantaged patient. The three categories of psychodynamic factors discussed previously (i.e. ambivalence, ego functioning, and ego identity) will be highlighted, particularly in reference to the reasons for the use of extradyadic treatment modalities.

Individual Psychotherapy

For the reasons adumbrated above, the use of intensive long-term individual psychotherapy based upon the evocation through frustration of intrapsychic conflict into a transference neurosis is not indicated. However, this is not to say that the psychoanalytically oriented therapist does not have a great deal to contribute both to clinical research and theory and to innovative treatment approaches to the disadvantaged. Nor am I saying that treatment in the dyadic situation has no place in the therapy of the disadvantaged. Furthermore, psychoanalysis is not contraindicated for middle-class members of minority groups although the therapist must be thoroughly familiar with the psychodynamics of prejudice whether he is of the same or different ethnic or religious group as the patient.[2,9,15,53,54,114] However, for the reasons that will be discussed below, the use of extradyadic treatment modalities—although they are often combined with the use of dyadic therapeutic and paratherapeutic methods—appears to offer the greatest promise at this time.

Extradyadic Treatment Approaches

The use of group therapy and family therapy each have some specific application for the treatment of the disadvantaged patient, based upon the psychodynamic considerations noted above. However, there is considerable overlapping of these treatment approaches because of the similarity of structure and process that evolves from the characteristics of all primary groups. In a later section I will refer to some theoretical implications for future directions that may be derived from research in the process and structure of the primary group and its relationship to larger social organizations and to individual ego functioning.

From the standpoint of individual psychodynamics, in both group therapy and family therapy, a therapeutic alliance[37] can be facilitated by the effect upon unresolved ambivalent feelings. The fears of interpersonal closeness with the therapist that result from the ambivalent reaction to authority are mitigated by the presence of one or more additional persons in the treatment situation. As Slavson[111] has observed, the transference reaction is diluted in the group situation. The presence of others results in multiple transferences so that the unresolved ambivalent feelings do not focus exclusively upon the therapist.

As a more specific therapeutic measure related to the problems of ambivalence in the disadvantaged patient, Steiner and Kaplan[117] recommend the use of an indigenous nonprofessional as an adjunct member of the therapeutic team during group sessions. Described as providing a "bridge" person in interpersonal terms, they suggest that the nonprofessional was perceived as a less ambivalent and less magical transference object compared to the professional. At the same time the nonprofessional served as a surrogate for the professional therapist when he was not present. The treatment groups they described were composed of schizophrenic patients from a disadvantaged area so that the problems of ambivalence and ego pathology were particularly significant.

The group therapy program was combined with the use of activity group meetings, the purpose of which was to limit the regressive aspects of group emotions by establishing task-oriented goals. The use of a presheltered workshop program in which the patients were paid for work they produced, in addition to providing an ego-enhancing experience, also furthered a reality-oriented atmosphere. Many therapists working with the disadvantaged patient, at least in the early treatment relationships, will focus upon problem-solving issues or realistic life crises—not only in response to the expectations of the patient but also as a method of avoiding regressive emotions and the exacerbation of existing unresolved ambivalent feelings and deficiencies of ego functioning.

Another advantage of the extradyadic treatment situation is that the presence of others also mitigates object-directed regression while fostering identification relationships.[50] Positive identification relationships are critical in any treatment situation but are particularly indicated for this patient population. The development of positive identification relationships in group therapy can be fostered by a homogeneous composition of the membership according to age, sex, social class, and ethnic grouping.

An example of the effective use of group composition as well as other specialized group therapeutic techniques for the disadvantaged patient is provided by Scheidlinger.[105] The group he described was composed of adult Negro women from the lower social class who also shared similar family problems; they all had three or more children, experienced difficulties in the mothering role, and were without an effective male member in the household. The specialized techniques required by the therapist were the active initiation of discussion and concrete demonstrations that the therapist cared, which included serving refreshments as well as writing letters for special problems and calling the patients when they were absent. Besides the direct gratification of these oral needs and the specific ego support by the therapist, Scheidlinger attributes the success of the members in weathering the early phases of treatment to the additional ego support of the identification relationship between the group members.

"This kind of banding together of deprived individuals for mutual 'mothering' probably comprises a variety of primitive identifications. A similar phenomenon has been observed to occur by Anna Freud within groups of severely neglected and orphaned children."[29,104] The successful use of the peer group, which has been referred to above, is probably based to a large measure upon the supportive element of this type of identification relationship. If it is a comfort for the beginning therapist to choose patients in his own image, the same needs undoubtedly exist in the patients, who however do not usually have a choice in the selection of the therapist. The presence of other patients of similar background and with similar problems fosters the development of narcissitic identifications which, however, are both group-centered as well as egocentric.

The example provided by Scheidlinger demonstrates one of the differences of focus between group therapy and family therapy. While any therapeutic approach in the extradyadic treatment situation tends to emphasize the interactional and transactional manifestations of individual emotional problems rather than the personal, symbolic expression of the problems, the therapy group of strangers can deal more directly with some of the individual areas of conflict than can family therapy. For example, in both treatment situations problems related to the sexual roles are discussed. However, in the therapy group, members can be more open with one another about the private intimate aspects of their sexual feelings. For example, in the therapy group described by Scheidlinger, even though all were concerned with the problems around being a mother, the personal concerns about the male-female sexual role were discussed in some detail.

In family therapy sessions described by Minuchin,[78,79] the concerns about mothering also were of especial importance, but the woman's functioning as part of a husband-wife parental subgroup was the major focus. This was determined in part by the fact that the primary patient in the Minuchin study was a delinquent child, and the problems around parental control were a predetermined priority issue of the therapeutic goals.

The women in Scheidlinger's group came together for their personal emotional problems even though difficulties within their families were of paramount importance. As Ackerman[1] has demonstrated, intimate sexual details can be discussed with marital partners apart from their parental roles. Minuchin also meets separately with the parents around sexual problems, but there is considerably more restraint, aside from an inherent difference between the group and family therapy approaches. For one thing, Ackerman's work is done primarily with middle-class marital pairs.

There appears to be a decided difference in cultural and social class attitudes concerning the public discussion of private sexual matters; in my experience, there is a particular resistance to this in Puerto Rican families. However, apart from the social class and cultural factors, the ego support of a cohesive group of women who come to know each other in a therapy group but who otherwise are strangers allows for the emergence of individual sexual conflicts and defensive mechanisms that do not occur as readily in family therapy.

As a generalization, I would suggest that the therapy group can address itself more specifically to concerns about the "self" and the related problems of identification and ego functioning. To the extent that individual instinctual determinants of conflict are manifested and can be analyzed in the extradyadic situation, it is more readily accomplished in group therapy than in family therapy. Direct gratification can be given, as Scheidlinger suggests, in the early treatment approaches in group therapy with disadvantaged patients without evoking the degree of rivalry and jealousy from others or the shame or guilt on the part of the recipient that might occur in family therapy. Often a particular problem is encountered in the early treatment stages when the spouse and children are the focus of the blaming process. If this resistance is intense, as is often described to be the case in family members from disadvantaged areas, it can present an insurmountable complication in family therapy.

A somewhat related problem is present in the older adolescent whose blaming of other family members is complicated by a generational response. The ego support of homogeneous group membership has particular value for adolescent patients for whom the peer group plays a major role in the socialization process. This process tends to occur at a somewhat earlier age in disadvantaged areas, and the usefulness of various group approaches for adolescents has been noted. Roman[99] has described the success he achieved by including a patient's natural peer group (i.e. from his neighborhood) in the group treatment process. Here remedial reading was combined with formal group therapy sessions for patients who were delinquent acting-out adolescents referred to a mental hygiene clinic by the courts.

On the other hand, Minuchin and his colleagues[78,79] have also demonstrated successful therapeutic intervention by use of family therapy with delinquent boys referred by the courts to a residential treatment setting. The boys in Roman's study were between the ages of 13 and 15 years, and those in the Minuchin study were under 12 years of age. It is my impression that group therapy approaches tend to be indicated more for the age group seen by Roman, whereas the preadolescent may be more responsive to a family therapy approach. This is not to say that combinations of both would not prove effective, including the use of individual treatment. The effectiveness of activity group therapy has been well documented.[27,103,108] Actually Minuchin and his colleagues manipulated the therapeutic arrangements so that the treatment situation did involve elements of a peer group, family group, and dyadic therapy.

Minuchin's explanations of his treatment objectives were substantially determined by his concepts of family dynamics, particularly the concepts of family roles and structure and of interactional and transactional patterns of communication. His work shows the influence of F. Kluckhohn[57] and Spiegel[113] on cultural and role relationships in families, of Parsons and Bales[87] and Jackson[45] on the interactional aspects of family process, and the clinical style of Ackerman.[1]

Minuchin's clinical focus is upon the children of lower-class families and the manner in which they are influenced by the structure and communication within the family, particularly in relationship to parental behavior regarding control, guidance, and nurturing. Relevant to those families with delinquent acting-out preadolescent boys, he has observed that the parents relinquish the "executive" role, by which he means parental behavior necessary for control, guidance, and protection of the children. He has noted a "rarefication and breakdown of communication between the parents and the children with the latter forming a distinct subsystem which tended toward autonomy and opposition of parental control." He further noted that the sibling subsystem exercises a significant influence on the socialization of the children and that it draws upon the extrafamilial subculture for its values.

Minuchin and his colleagues' major attempt to translate their observations of the family pathology into individual psychodynamics is in terms of the ego development of the children. They suggest a correlation between the lack of differentiation of the ego boundaries of the child and the deficiency in structure and communication of the family as a social system. They attempt to influence this by the manipulation of the treatment situation. Their therapeutic strategy is developed in three stages: "Phase I is the phase of induction," in which the family is seen and related to as a unit and in which the family's therapist and the child's therapist all participate; "Phase II, that of the therapeutic work within the family system," in which the sibling subgroup and the parents are seen separately; and "Phase III, that of disengagement and solidifying the family's autonomy."

In other words, Minuchin and his colleagues, after identifying the divisiveness of the family group as manifested by communication breakdowns and subgroup formations, work separately with the subgroups to enable each to see its operational style. They then attempt to effect a reconsolidation and cohesiveness of the family group through the member's increased understanding of the family interactions and by cultivating more appropriate role behaviors by the family members, particularly the parents. Minuchin and his colleagues pursue this latter goal by translation and interpretation of verbal and nonverbal behavior relevant to specific roles and by such direct influencing methods as inviting individual family members to join the therapists behind the one-way screen. By this process the therapists appear to be encouraging a positive identification by the formation of a coalition with the patient. In this manner they may be able to foster the development of role models based upon the actions, attitudes, and values of the therapist.

Minuchin and his colleagues consider this direct engagement with patients from the lower social class a necessary modification of traditional treatment approaches, particularly with the type of disorganized families they describe. They recognize that through such active intervention they selectively focus on special aspects of the patient's and the family's maladaptive patterns and limit the therapeutic development of other conflict areas. To the extent they are able to assist the family as a whole to develop a greater differentiation of functioning and recognition of individual distinctiveness, an atmosphere for further growth can be carried over beyond the confines of the therapy sessions. In this carry-over effect, the use of family therapy may have a value, at least in short-term treatment, that individual and group therapy do not provide.

FUTURE DIRECTIONS

The Primary Group as a Social System—A Bridge Between the Ego Organization of the Individual and the Larger Social Organizations

In the foregoing sections I have called attention to some social class considerations that have bearing upon both the practice and the theory of psychotherapy. However, my reference to other social science theories has not only been limited by my lack of expertise in these areas but by the fact that there is a wide gap between individual psychology and the other behavioral sciences. The observations of Hollingshead and Redlich[43] remain substantially unchanged from the way they viewed it in the 1950's.

> Psychiatric theories and social science theories, although presumably based upon observation of human behavior, have been developed independently, and few efforts have been made to bridge the gap between the two kinds of theory; even key concepts developed in one discipline are ignored for the most part in the other. This observation is especially cogent because social scientists have been concerned with the concept of social class for more than a century, but psychiatrists until recent years have overlooked it.

The difficulties of integrating key concepts of the various disciplines develops from the fact that the basic assumptions of each discipline are either irrelevant to or inconsistent with the others.

One area that has been fruitful as a locus for the study of divergent theoretical views is the small group, or what Cooley[16] referred to as the "primary group," under which rubric I would include studies of therapy groups, sensitivity or T-groups, and family therapy groups, as well as laboratory and natural social groups. In particular, I would suggest that studies of the structure, process, and developmental properties of these primary, small groups as social systems could provide a theoretical link between individual ego functioning on the one hand and the larger social organizations on the other. Although much work has been done in the study of each of the various small group formations, attempts to bridge the gap between these studies and psychoanalytic ego psychology had been minimal.

This is unfortunate not only for the reasons noted by Hollingshead and Redlich but because it is almost forty years since Freud[30] approached the analysis of the ego from the vantage point of group formations and so entitled his often overlooked book, *Group Psychology and the Analysis of the Ego*. Freud focused upon the dyadic relationship within larger group formations, specifically the individual group member's emotional bond to the leader and to his fellow members. It was in this work that Freud outlined the beginning of his structural hypotheses about the ego, particularly in reference to the development of object relationships.

Similarly, in the foregoing sections I stressed the individual or dyadic relationships even though in the context of the extradyadic setting. In the reference to the work of Minuchin and his colleagues,[78,79] I did note their observations about the family as a unit and as a social system. However, apart from considerations of the structural aspects of the family group, particularly the subgroup formations, their conceptualizations were primarily in terms of the individual member's reaction *to* the system and did not include considerations of the member's reaction as *part* of the system. In other words, Minuchin and his colleagues do not refer to any characteristics or events that may reflect the unique properties of the system itself. Some writers, including myself, have postulated the existence of characteristic structures and processes as well as specific phases of development that to some extent govern the behavior of members in all primary groups.[4,8,50,52,108,118]

The point of emphasis of these two views can be demonstrated in Minuchin's studies. Minuchin and his colleagues observed the manner in which the individual member's expression of dependency needs and aggressive feelings were, to some extent, collectively expressed or channeled through the subgroup coalitions of the siblings vis-à-vis the parental subgroup. They discussed the maladaptive nature of these subgroup formations primarily in terms of its impact upon the member's ego development, in the instance of the children, and in terms of the deviance from normative expected role behavior, in the instance of the parents. However, they did not consider the nature of subgroup formations and deviance behavior as such in terms of structural and process properties of small groups.

In addition, the phases of treatment that they describe, which they feel they artificially impose upon the family, correspond to the progression of phases that Roman and I[50,52] have described as characteristic developments in small groups whose leadership follows the therapeutic or T-group model. We observed that initially, when faced by an analytic therapist or enigmatic leader with an uncertain agenda, members of a small group will interact as a unit according to the structure of their preexisting patterns of experience but that subsequently the group members will interact so as to restructure the group into subgroups and pairing formations. This process of structural rearrangements, in our observation, involved developmental phases in which the members moved from an ill-defined role differentiation to one in which a greater degree of role differentiation became tolerable and necessary.

What I am suggesting is that what Minuchin and his colleagues viewed as their therapeutic strategy, specifically designed for special problem families, is rather their own enactment with the families of predictable processes of development in small groups. While this in no way means that the results they achieved are invalid, it suggests that the reasons they give for achieving these results can be explained from another frame of reference. With this reference point new directions for study may be opened which otherwise might not be considered.

One direction that is implicit in Minuchin's study is the correlation between the lack of differentiation of the ego boundaries of the children observed and the disorganization in the families of these children. Erikson[23] has suggested that the individual's ego functioning is closely interrelated with the organization of his significant social groups. I would postulate that, in addition to the influence that a family has upon a child through internalization of parental objects and their values and attitudes, the family as a social system influences the manner in which the individual organizes his experiences in and relates to other social organizations, perhaps most particularly other primary groups. I am not suggesting an isomorphic or homologous relationship between ego organization and group organizations. However, I do believe there is a greater similarity of structure and process between the two than has been considered.

The implication of the point of view that I am suggesting is that the primary family group not only has influence upon personality and the acquisition of particular attitudes and skills but that the family as a social system "patterns" the manner in which the individual implements these skills and "executes" his relationship in primary groups other than the family. This point of view would be more significant if, as Verba[123] suggests, primary groups play an important role in the large industrial, political, and bureaucratic organizations of our society, particularly in decision making, communication, and the means by which the influence of power is transmitted.

However, the study of the interrelationship between the individual, the family, and social institutions has hardly been explored by the social scientist; the type of observations that Verba suggests are at a very early level of development. That is not to say that there is not a body of knowledge about aspects of the relationship between the individual, the family, and society. Observations about socioeconomic and cultural influences upon the family, besides those noted above, have been made in reference to the size of the nuclear family group, the nature of intrafamilial and extended family contacts, social and geographic mobility, as well as variations in individual values and attitudes.[6,7,20,57,119,124] However, there has been little exploration of mechanisms through which specific aspects of social organizations might interdigitate with and influence the structure and process of family organizations.

Moynihan[81] comments to this point following a statement that the first step in resolving the problem of the black minority is to provide "such a measure of employment that the impact of unemployment on the family structure would be removed." He adds, however, "This of course is not an inconsiderable assumption. No one knows whether it is justified or not. The relation between economic phenomena, such as employment, and social phenomena, such as family structure, has hardly begun to be traced in the United States." Until we have achieved this type of specificity about the relationship between the individual and society, we labor under difficult conditions in attempting to delineate specific treatment approaches that do justice to the uniqueness of the individual and the special circumstances within which that uniqueness is expressed.

REFERENCES

1. Ackerman, N.: *Treating the Troubled Family*. New York, Basic Books, 1966.

2. Ackerman, N., and Jahoda, M.: *Antisemitism and Emotional Disorder.* New York, Harper, 1950.
3. Alinsky, S.: The war on poverty—political pornography. *J. Soc. Issues, 21:*41, 1965.
4. Bales, R.: *Interaction Process Analysis.* Cambridge, Addison-Wesley, 1950.
5. Bauman, G., and Douthit, V.: Vocational rehabilitation and community mental health in deprived urban areas. *J. Rehab., 34:*28, 1968.
6. Bell, N., and Vogel, E.: *A Modern Introduction to the Family.* Glencoe, Free Press, 1960.
7. Bendix, R., and Lipset, S.: *Class, Status and Power: A Reader in Social Stratification.* Glencoe, Free Press, 1963.
8. Bennis, W., and Shepard, H.: A theory of group development. *Human Relations, 9:*415, 1956.
9. Bernard, V.: Psychoanalysis and the members of minority groups. *JAMA, 1:*256, 1953.
10. Black, B., and Benney, C.: *Rehabilitation: The Schizophrenic Syndrome.* New York, Grune & Stratton, 1969.
11. Brill, N., and Storrow, H.: Social class and psychiatric treatment. *Arch. Gen. Psychiat., 3:*340, 1960.
12. Caplan, G.: *Concepts of Mental Health and Consultation.* Washington, D. C., U. S. Children's Bureau, 1959.
13. Christman, J. J.: Group methods in training and practice: Non-professional mental health personnel in a deprived community. *Amer. J. Orthopsychiat., 36:*410, 1966.
14. Clark, K.: *Dark Ghetto: Dilemmas of Social Power.* New York, Harper & Row, 1965.
15. Coles, R.: Racial problems in psychotherapy. *Curr. Psychiat. Ther., 6:* 110, 1966.
16. Cooley, C., Angell, R., and Carr, L.: *Introductory Sociology.* New York, Scribner, 1933.
17. Davis, A., and Havighurst, R.: Social class and color differences in child-rearing. In Kluckhohn, C., and Murray, H. (Eds.): *Personality in Nature, Society and Culture.* New York, Knopf, 1948.
18. Deutsch, H.: The disadvantaged child and the learning process. In Passow, A. (Ed.): *Education in Depressed Areas.* New York, Bureau of Publications, Teachers College, Columbia University, 1963.
19. Dohrenwend, B.: Social status, stress, and psychological symptoms. *Amer. J. Public Health, 57:*625, 1967.
20. Dollard, J.: *Caste and Class in a Southern Town.* New Haven, Yale University Press, 1937.
21. Dunham, H.: Social structures and mental disorders: Competing hypotheses of explanation. In *Causes of Mental Disorders: A Review of*

Epidemiological Knowledge. New York, Milbank Memorial Fund, 1961.

22. Epstein, N., and Slavson, S.: Breakthrough in group treatment of hardened delinquent adolescent boys. *Int. J. Group Psychother., 12:*199, 1962.

23. Erikson, E.: *Identity and the Life Cycle.* New York, International Universities Press, 1959.

24. Fernandez-Marina, R., Maldonado-Sierra, E., and Trent, R.: Three basic themes in Mexican and Puerto Rican family values. *J. Soc. Psychol., 48:*167, 1958.

25. Fishman, J., and Solomon, F.: Youth and social action. *Amer. J. Orthopsychiat, 33:*872, 1963.

26. Foley, A., and Sanders, D.: Theoretical considerations for the development of the community health center concept. *Amer. J. Psychiat., 122:*985, 1966.

27. Foulkes, S., and Anthony, E.: *Group Psychotherapy.* London, Penguin Books, 1957.

28. Frank, J., Gliedman, L., Imber, S., Nash, E., Jr., and Stone, A.: Why patients leave psychotherapy. *AMA Arch. Neurol. Psychiat., 77:*283, 1957.

29. Freud, A.: An experiment in group upbringing. In Eissler, R. (Ed.): *The Psychoanalytic Study of the Child.* New York, International Universities Press, 1951.

30. Freud, S.: *Group Psychotherapy and the Analysis of the Ego.* London, Hogarth Press, 1921.

31. Gans, H.: *The Urban Villagers.* Glencoe, Free Press, 1962.

32. Gardner, E.: Psychological care for the poor: The need for new service patterns with a proposal for meeting this need. In Cowen, E., Gardner, E., and Zax, M. (Eds.): *Emergent Approaches to Mental Health Problems.* New York, Meredith Press, 1967.

33. Glasscote, R., Sanders, D., Forstenzer, H., and Foley, A.: *The Community Mental Health Center: An Analysis of Existing Centers.* Washington, D. C., Joint Information Service of the American Psychiatric Association and the National Association for Mental Health, 1964.

34. Glasscote, R., Sussex, J., Cumming, E., and Smith, L.: *The Community Mental Health Center: An Interim Appraisal.* Washington, D. C., Joint Information Service of the American Psychiatric Association and the National Association for Mental Health, 1969.

35. Goldberg, E., and Morrison, S.: Schizophrenia and social class. *Brit. J. Psychiat., 109:*785, 1963.

36. Greenblatt, M., and Sharaf, M.: Poverty and mental health: Implications for training. In Greenblatt, M., Emery, P., and Glucck, A., Jr.

(Eds.) : *Poverty and Mental Health.* Washington, D. C., American Psychiatric Association, 1967.

37. Greenson, R.: *The Technique and Practice of Psychoanalysis.* New York, International Universities Press, 1967.
38. Grier, H., and Cobbs, P.: *Black Rage.* New York, Basic Books, 1968.
39. Gruenberg, E.: Discussion of Frank Riessman's paper. In Greenblatt, M., Emery, P., and Glueck, A., Jr. (Eds.) : *Poverty and Mental Health.* Washington, D. C., American Psychiatric Association, 1967.
40. Hallowitz, E.: The role of the neighborhood service center in a community mental health program. *Amer. J. Orthopsychiat., 38:*705, 1967.
41. Hallowitz, E.: The use of indigenous nonprofessionals in a mental health service. *Nat. Soc. Welf. Assembly,* September, 1966.
42. Hallowitz, E., and Riessman, F.: The role of the indigenous non-professional in a community mental health neighborhood service center program. *Amer. J. Orthopsychiat., 37:*766, 1967.
43. Hollingshead, A., and Redlich, F.: *Social Class and Mental Illness.* New York, Wiley, 1958.
44. Hunt, R.: Social class and mental illness: Some implications for clinical theory and practice. *Amer. J. Psychiat., 116:*1065, 1960.
45. Jackson, D.: The study of the family. *Family Process, 4:*1, 1965.
46. Jones, M.: *The Therapeutic Community.* New York, Basic Books, 1953.
47. Kahn, R., Fink, M., and Siegel, N.: Sociopsychological aspects of psychiatric treatment. *Arch. Gen. Psychiat., 14:*20, 1966.
48. Kahn, R., Pollack, M., and Fink, M.: Sociopsychological aspects of psychiatric treatment in a voluntary mental hospital. *Arch. Gen. Psychiat., 1:*565, 1966.
49. Kaplan, B., Reed, R., and Richardson, W.: A comparison of the incidence of hospitalized and non-hospitalized cases of psychosis in two communities. *Amer. Sociol. Rev.,* August, 1956.
50. Kaplan, S.: Therapy groups and training groups: Similarities and differences. *Int. J. Group Psychother., 17:*473, 1967.
51. Kaplan, S., Boyajian, L., and Meltzer, B.: The role of the nonprofessional. In Grunebaum, H. (Ed.) : *The Practice of Community Mental Health.* Boston, Little, Brown & Co., 1969.
52. Kaplan, S., and Roman, M.: Phases of development in an adult therapy group. *Int. J. Group Psychother., 13:*10, 1963.
53. Kardiner, A., and Ovesey, L.: *The Mark of Oppression.* New York, Norton, 1951.
54. Kennedy, J.: Problems imposed in the analysis of Negro patients. *Psychiatry, 15:*313, 1952.
55. King, B., and Janis, I.: Comparison of the effectiveness of improvised versus non-improvised role-playing in producing opinion changes. *Human Relations, 9:*177, 1956.

56. Kline, L.: Some factors in the psychiatric treatment of Spanish-Americans. *Amer. J. Psychiat., 125:*88, 1969.
57. Kluckhohn, F.: *Variations in Value Orientations.* Evanston, Row, Peterson & Co., 1961.
58. Kobrin, S.: The Chicago Area Project: A 25 year assessment. *Annals of the American Academy of Political and Social Sciences, 322:*14, 1959.
59. Kohn, M.: Social class and parent-child relationships: An interpretation. *Amer. J. Sociol., 68:*11, 1963.
60. Kong-Ming New, P.: Communication: Problems of interaction between professionals and clients. *Community Mental Health J., 1:*251, 1965.
61. Kraft, A., Bennie, P., and Dickey, B.: The chronic patient. In Williams, R., and Ozarin, L. (Eds.) : *Community Mental Health.* San Francisco, Jossey-Bass, 1968.
62. Leighton, A.: Discussion of Dr. Milton Greenblatt and Dr. Myron R. Sharaf's paper. In Greenblatt, M., Emery, P., and Glueck, A., Jr. (Eds.) : *Poverty and Mental Health.* Washington, D. C., American Psychiatric Association, 1967.
63. Levine, R.: Treatment in the homes. *Social Work, 9:*19, 1964.
64. Lewis, H.: *Child-Rearing Among Low-Income Families.* Washington, D. C., Health and Welfare Council of the National Capitol Area, 1961.
65. Lewis, H.: Syndromes of contemporary urban poverty. In Greenblatt, M., Emery, P., and Glueck, A., Jr. (Eds.) : *Poverty and Mental Health.* Washington, D. C., American Psychiatric Association, 1967.
66. Lindover, S., Roman, M., and Kaplan, S.: The training of the nonprofessional. In Grunebaum, H. (Ed.) : *The Practice of Community Mental Health.* Boston, Little, Brown & Co., 1969.
67. Litwak, E.: Geographic mobility and extended family cohesion. In Stoodley, B. (Ed.) : *Society and Self.* Glencoe, Free Press, 1962.
68. MacLennan, B.: Group approaches to the problems of socially deprived youth: The classical psychotherapeutic model. *Int. J. Group Psychother., 18:*481, 1968.
69. Maldonado-Sierra, E., Trent, R., and Fernandez-Marina, R.: Neurosis and the traditional family beliefs in Puerto Rico. *Int. J. Soc. Psychiat., 6:*237, 1960.
70. Malone, C.: Some observations on children of disorganized families and problems of acting-out. *J. Child Psychiat., 2:*22, 1963.
71. Mayer, J., and Timms, N.: Clash in perspective between worker and client. *Social Casework, 49:*32, 1969.
72. McMahon, J.: The working-class psychiatric patient: A clinical view. In Fiessman, F., Cohen, J., and Pearl, A. (Eds.) : *Mental Health of the Poor.* Glencoe, Free Press, 1964

73. Mehlman, R.: The Puerto-Rican syndrome. *Amer. J. Psychiat., 118:* 328, 1961.

74. Miller, S.: The American lower-class: A topological approach. *Soc. Res., 31:*164, 1954.

75. Miller, S.: Discussion of Dr. Hyman Lewis's paper. In Greenblatt, M., Emery, P., and Glueck, A., Jr. (Eds.) : *Poverty and Mental Health.* Washington, D. C., American Psychiatric Association, 1967.

76. Miller, S., and Riessman, F.: *Social Class and Social Policy.* New York, Basic Books, 1964.

77. Mills, C., Senior, C., and Goldsen, R.: *Puerto Rican Journey.* New York, Harper, 1950.

78. Minuchin, S., Auerswald, E., King, C., and Rabinowitz, C.: The study and treatment of families who produce multiple acting-out boys. *Amer. J. Orthopsychiat., 34:*125, 1964.

79. Minuchin, S., Montalvo, B., Guerney, B., Jr., Rosman, B., and Schumer, F.: *Families of the Slums.* New York, Basic Books, 1967.

80. Mowrer, O.: *The New Group Therapy.* New York, D. Van Nostrand, 1964.

81. Moynihan, D.: Employment, income and the ordeal of the Negro family. *Daedalus, 94:*745, 1965.

82. Myers, J., and Roberts, B.: *Family and Class Dynamics in Mental Illness.* New York, Wiley, 1959.

83. Myers, J., and Schaffer, L.: Social stratification and psychiatric practice: A study of an outpatient clinic. *Amer. Sociol. Rev., 19:*307, 1954.

84. Normand, W., Fensterheim, H., Tannenbaum, G., and Sager, C.: The acceptance of the psychiatric walk-in clinic in a highly deprived community. *Amer. J. Psychiat., 120:*533, 1963.

85. Overall, M., and Aronson, H.: Expectations of psychotherapy in patients of lower socioeconomic class. *Amer. J. Orthopsychiat., 33:* 421, 1963.

86. Parsons, T.: The social structure of the family. In Ashen, R. (Ed.) : *The Family: Its Function and Destiny.* New York, Harper, 1949.

87. Parsons, T., and Bales, R.: *Family Socialization and Interaction Process.* Glencoe, Free Press, 1955.

88. Pavenstedt, E.: A comparison of the child-rearing environment of upper-lower and very low-lower class families. *Amer. J. Psychiat., 35:* 89, 1965.

89. Pearl, A., and Riessman, F.: *New Careers for the Poor.* Glencoe, Free Press, 1965.

90. Peck, H., and Bellesmith, V.: *Treatment of the Delinquent Adolescent.* New York, Family Service Association of America, 1954.

91. Peck, H., Kaplan, S., and Roman, M.: Prevention, treatment and social

action: A strategy of intervention in a disadvantaged urban area. *Amer. J. Orthopsychiat., 36:*57, 1966.

92. Peck, H., Roman, M., and Kaplan, S.: Community action programs and the comprehensive mental health center. In Greenblatt, M., Emery, P., and Glueck, A., Jr. (Eds.) : *Poverty and Mental Health.* Washington, D. C., American Psychiatric Association, 1967.

93. Peissachowitz, N., and Sarcka, A.: *Social Action Groups in a Mental Health Program.* San Francisco, Second National Professional Symposium, NASW, 1968.

94. Port, D.: Mental health consultation with a para-military youth program. *Ment. Hyg.,* 1969.

95. Rapoport, A.: *Operational Philosophy.* New York, Harper, 1954.

96. Redlich, F., Hollingshead, A., and Bellis, E.: Social class differences in attitudes toward psychiatry. *Amer. J. Orthopsychiat., 26:*60, 1955.

97. Reusch, J.: Social factors in therapy. In Wortis, S., Herman, M., and Hare, C. (Eds.) : *Association for Research in Nervous and Mental Diseases: Psychiatric Treatment, 31.* Baltimore, Williams & Wilkins, 1953.

98. Riese, H.: *Heal the Hurt Child.* Chicago, University of Chicago, 1962.

99. Roman, M., Margolin, J., and Harari, C.: Reading retardation and delinquency. *Nat. Probation and Parole Assoc. J., 1:*1, 1955.

100. Sanua, V.: *Immigration, Migration and Mental Illness: A Review of the Literature, with Special Emphasis on Schizophrenia.* San Juan, Puerto Rico, Conference on Migration and Behavioral Deviance, Nov. 4-8, 1968.

101. Schaffer, L., and Myers, J.: Psychotherapy and social stratification. *Psychiatry, 17:*83, 1954.

102. Scheidlinger, S.: Therapeutic group approaches in community mental health. *Social Work, 13:* 87, 1968.

103. Scheidlinger, S.: Three group approaches with socially deprived latency-age children. *Int. J. Group Psychother., 15:*434, 1965.

104. Scheidlinger, S., and Holden, M.: Group therapy of women with severe character disorders—The middle and final phases. *Int. J. Group Psychother., 16:*174, 1966.

105. Scheidlinger, S., and Pyrke, M.: Group therapy of women with severe dependency problems. *Amer. J. Orthopsychiat, 31:*766, 1961.

106. Scheidlinger, S., and Sarcka, A.: *A Mental Health Consultation-Education Program with Group Service Agencies in a Disadvantaged Community.* Chicago, American Orthopsychiatric Association, March, 1968.

107. Schiff, S., and Kellam, S.: A community-wide mental health program of prevention and early treatment in first grade. In Greenblatt, M., Emery, P., and Glueck, A., Jr. (Eds.) : *Poverty and Mental Health.* Washington, D. C., American Psychiatric Association, 1967.

108. Schiffer, M.: The therapeutic group in the public school. In Krugman, M. (Ed.) : *Orthopsychiatry and the School.* New York, American Orthopsychiatric Association, 1958.

109. Schutz, W.: *FIRO: A Three-Dimensional Theory of Interpersonal Behavior.* New York, Rinehart & Co., 1958.

110. Sexton, P.: *Spanish Harlem: Anatomy of Poverty.* New York, Harper & Row, 1965.

111. Slavson, S.: *An Introduction to Group Therapy.* New York, International Universities Press. 1954.

112. Spencer, C. (Ed.) : *Experiment in Culture Expansion.* Sacramento, State of California Department of Corrections, 1963.

113. Spiegel, J.: The resolution of role conflict within the family. In Bell, N., and Vogel, E. (Eds.) : *A Modern Introduction to the Family.* Glencoe, Free Press, 1960.

114. Spiegel, J.: Some cultural aspects of transference and countertransference. In Masserman, J. (Ed.) : *Individual and Familial Dynamics.* New York, Grune & Stratton, 1959.

115. Srole, L.: Poverty and mental health: Conceptual and taxonomic problems. In Greenblatt, M., Emery, P., and Glueck, A., Jr. (Eds.) : *Poverty and Mental Health.* Washington, D. C., American Psychiatric Association, 1967.

116. Srole, L., Langner, T., Michael, S., Opler, M., and Rennie, T.: *Mental Health in the Metropolis: The Midtown Manhattan Study, 1.* New York, McGraw-Hill, 1962.

117. Steiner, J., and Kaplan, S.: The use of work-for-pay activity in an outpatient group treatment program. *Amer. J. Psychother.,* 1969.

118. Stock, D., and Thelen, H.: *Emotional Dynamics and Group Culture.* New York, University Press, 1958.

119. Stoodley, B.: *Society and Self: A Reader in Social Psychology.* Glencoe, Free Press, 1962.

120. Storrow, H.: Psychiatric treatment and the lower-class neurotic patient. *Arch. Gen. Psychiat., 6:*91, 1962.

121. Stranahan, M., Schwartzman, C., and Atkin, E.: Activity group therapy with emotionally disturbed adolescents. *Int. J. Group Psychother., 7:*425, 1957.

122. Townsend, P.: Freedom and equality. *New Statesman, 61:*574, 1961.

123. Verba, S.: *Small Groups and Political Behavior.* Princeton, Princeton University Press, 1961.

124. Warner, L., and Lunt, P.: *The Social Life of a Modern Community.* New Haven, Yale University Press, 1941.

125. Wilder, J.: A case for a flexible longterm sheltered workshop for psychiatric patients. *Amer. J. Psychiat.,* 1969.

126. Wilder, J., and Coleman, M.: The walk-in psychiatric clinic: Some observations and follow-up. *Int. J. Soc. Psychiat.,* in press.

127. Williams, R., and Ozarin, L.: *Community Mental Health.* San Francisco, Jossey-Bass, 1968.
128. Willie, C.: The social class of patients that public health nurses prefer to serve. *Amer. J. Public Health, 50:*1126, 1960.
129. *Youth in the Ghetto: A Study of the Consequences of Powerlessness and a Blueprint for Change.* New York, Harlem Youth Opportunities Unlimited, Inc., 1964.
130. Zinberg, N., and Glotfeltz, J.: The power of the peer group. *Int. J. Group Psychother., 18:*155, 1968.

AUTHOR INDEX

SUBJECT INDEX

A

Adaptation and action syndromes, 26
Adlerian psychology, 7, 8, 9, 10
Adolescent boys and group therapy, 268
Agression, expression of, 44
Alcoholics Annonymous, 261
Alienation, 29, 108
  ghetto families, 61
  group therapy, 41
  life processes and crises, 22
Ambivalence, and lower social class, 257, 258, 264, 265
American Indians and mental illness, 250, 251
American Psychiatric Association, 81, 146, 159
Anger, and crisis, 23
Anomie, 108
  group therapy, 41
Anxiety, 9, 11, 50, 108, 237, 242
  reduction, 168, 169, 170, 171, 172, 173
  and therapist, 99, 100
"Ataques" and Puerto Ricans, 252
Atlanta Psychiatric Clinic, 71, 79, 89
Authority prototypes and group family therapy, 74
Autism and behavioral modification therapy, 174

B

Baltimore Psychoanalytic Institute, 216
Behavior
  Children, Kibbutz, 42, 43
  inter-relationship experiences, 95
  maladaptive and lower scocial class, 256
  models, 110, 111
  modeling and milieu therapy, 228, 229
  modification, 162-180
    "token programs," 175, 176

non-verbal and videotape playback, 199-212
techniques
  crisis therapy, 37, 38
  research, 164, 173, 174, 175, 176, 178
  RET, 146, 147, 151, 152
Behaviorism, 5, 6
Bioenergetic analysis, 118-131
Body awareness, 118, 119
Body language, 118-131
Bronx State Hospital, New York, 201

C

Character disorders, 112
Character structure and family relationships, 69
Children
  ego development, 269, 273
  family psychopathology, 62, 63
  family structure and role behavior, 42, 43
Class
  blue-collar patients and psychotherapeutic techniques, 132-145
  mental illness and therapy, 248-274
  personality, 136, 137, 138
Cognitive techniques of RET, 146, 147, 152-159
Communication, mass, proliferation of, 110, 111
Community mental health, 94
Community mental health centers, 259, 260
Confrontation, 113, 217, 218, 220
Co-therapist and analytic group therapy, 54
  and family therapy, 71, 72, 73
Co-therapy, 81-92
Counteranxiety, 9, 11
Counterresistance, 9, 11

289